My
Samsung Galaxy S6®
for Seniors

Michael Miller

que®

800 East 96th Street,
Indianapolis, Indiana 46240 USA

AARP®
Real Possibilities

My Samsung Galaxy S®6 for Seniors

Copyright © 2016 by Pearson Education, Inc.

ISBN-13: 978-0-7897-5544-5
ISBN-10: 0-7897-5544-0

Library of Congress Control Number: 2015942757

First Printing: August 2015

Trademarks

All terms mentioned in this book that are known to be trademarks or service marks have been appropriately capitalized. Que Publishing cannot attest to the accuracy of this information. Use of a term in this book should not be regarded as affecting the validity of any trademark or service mark.

Galaxy S6 images are provided by Samsung Electronics America.

Warning and Disclaimer

Every effort has been made to make this book as complete and as accurate as possible, but no warranty or fitness is implied. The information provided is on an "as is" basis. The author, AARP, and the publisher shall have neither liability nor responsibility to any person or entity with respect to any loss or damages arising from the information contained in this book or from the use of the CD or programs accompanying it.

Special Sales

For information about buying this title in bulk quantities, or for special sales opportunities (which may include electronic versions; custom cover designs; and content particular to your business, training goals, marketing focus, or branding interests), please contact our corporate sales department at corpsales@pearsoned.com or (800) 382-3419.

For government sales inquiries, please contact governmentsales@pearsoned.com.

For questions about sales outside the U.S., please contact international@pearsoned.com.

Editor-in-Chief
Greg Wiegand

Acquisitions Editor
Michelle Newcomb

Development Editor
Charlotte Kughen

Marketing Manager
Dan Powell

Director, AARP Books
Jodi Lipson

Managing Editor
Kristy Hart

Senior Project Editor
Lori Lyons

Senior Indexer
Cheryl Lenser

Proofreader
Kathy Ruiz

Technical Editor
Christian Kenyeres

Editorial Assistant
Cindy Teeters

Compositor
Bronkella Publishing

Contents at a Glance

Bonus Tasks! More than a dozen additional tasks and a Glossary are available at www. quepublishing.com/title/9780789755445. Click the Downloads tab to access the links to download the PDF files.

Table of Contents

6 Installing and Using Apps   **133**

8   Managing Your Contacts List   191

11 Browsing and Searching the Web   263

Bonus Tasks! The following additional tasks and a Glossary are available at www.quepublishing.com/title/9780789755445. (Click the Downloads tab to access the links to download the PDF files.)

Glossary

Discover Games

Download Music

Email Apps and Spam

Health Fitness Apps

Office Mobile App

Other Social Networks

Personalize Calendar

Phone and Other Apps

Phone Security

About the Author

Michael Miller is a prolific and popular writer of more than 150 nonfiction books, known for his ability to explain complex topics to everyday readers. He writes about a variety of topics, including technology, business, and music. His best-selling books for Que include *My Windows 10 Computer for Seniors, My Social Media for Seniors, My Facebook for Seniors, My Google Chromebook, Easy Computer Basics,* and *Computer Basics: Absolute Beginner's Guide.* Worldwide, his books have sold more than 1 million copies.

Find out more at the author's website: **www.millerwriter.com**

Follow the author on Twitter: **@molehillgroup**

About AARP and AARP TEK

AARP is a nonprofit, nonpartisan organization, with a membership of nearly 38 million, that helps people turn their goals and dreams into *real possibilities*™, strengthens communities, and fights for the issues that matter most to families such as healthcare, employment and income security, retirement planning, affordable utilities, and protection from financial abuse. Learn more at aarp.org.

The AARP TEK (Technology Education & Knowledge) program aims to accelerate AARP's mission of turning dreams into *real possibilities*™ by providing step-by-step lessons in a variety of formats to accommodate different learning styles, levels of experience, and interests. Expertly guided hands-on workshops delivered in communities nationwide help instill confidence and enrich lives of the 50+ by equipping them with skills for staying connected to the people and passions in their lives. Lessons are taught on touchscreen tablets and smartphones—common tools for connection, education, entertainment, and productivity. For self-paced lessons, videos, articles, and other resources, visit aarptek.org.

Dedication

To my family.

Acknowledgments

Thanks to all the folks at Que who helped turned this manuscript into a book, including Michelle Newcomb, Greg Wiegand, Charlotte Kughen, Todd Brakke, Lori Lyons, and technical editor Christian Kenyeres.

Note: Most of the individuals pictured throughout this book are of the author himself, as well as friends and relatives (and sometimes pets). Some names and personal information are fictitious.

We Want to Hear from You!

As the reader of this book, *you* are our most important critic and commentator. We value your opinion and want to know what we're doing right, what we could do better, what areas you'd like to see us publish in, and any other words of wisdom you're willing to pass our way.

We welcome your comments. You can email or write to let us know what you did or didn't like about this book—as well as what we can do to make our books better.

Please note that we cannot help you with technical problems related to the topic of this book.

When you write, please be sure to include this book's title and author as well as your name and email address. We will carefully review your comments and share them with the author and editors who worked on the book.

Email: feedback@quepublishing.com

Mail: Que Publishing
ATTN: Reader Feedback
800 East 96th Street
Indianapolis, IN 46240 USA

Reader Services

Visit our website and register this book at quepublishing.com/register for convenient access to any updates, downloads, or errata that might be available for this book.

In this chapter, you learn how to set up and start using your new Samsung Galaxy S6 or S6 Edge. Topics include the following:

→ Unboxing and Charging Your New Phone
→ Getting to Know the Galaxy S6
→ Turning Your Phone On and Off
→ Using the Galaxy S6
→ Performing Basic Operations
→ Managing Your Phone's Power

1

Getting Started with Your Samsung Galaxy S6

The Galaxy S6 and S6 Edge are the latest models in Samsung's popular line of smartphones. There's a lot of functionality built into these phones, which means there's a bit to learn before you start using them. Just what do you find when you open the box—and how do you move around from screen to screen? That's what this chapter tells you, so start reading!

Unboxing and Charging Your New Phone

So you've taken the plunge and purchased a new Samsung Galaxy S6 or S6 Edge. What do you need to do to get it up and running?

Take Your New Phone Out of the Box

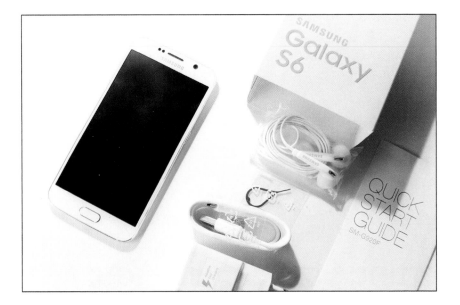

If you purchased your new phone at a retail store, or from your mobile carrier, the store personnel probably configured the phone with your new or existing phone number. Thus configured, your phone is usable right out of the box—assuming it's charged up, of course!

Here's what you'll find in the box:

- Samsung Galaxy S6 or S6 Edge phone
- Samsung quick charger (also known as an Adaptive Fast Charging charger)
- microUSB v2.0 cable
- Headphones + alternate ear buds
- SIM removal pin
- *Quick Start Guide*
- Product Safety & Warranty Information booklet
- Various informational booklets from your mobile carrier

Obviously, you should read the Quick Start Guide before you do anything else. The other items you immediately need from the box are the quick charger, microUSB cable, and, of course, the phone itself.

Fast Charging

The Galaxy S6 features fast charging that enables you to add up to 4 hours of battery life with just 10 minutes of charging. To take advantage of this feature, you need to use the quick charger (also known as the Adaptive Fast Charging charger) included with your phone. If you use a third-party charger, your phone might not charge as fast.

Connect and Recharge Your Phone

It's possible that your phone arrived fully charged. It's also possible that it didn't—in which case, you need to connect it to a power source and charge it up before you use it. You can get about four hours' worth of charge by leaving the phone connected for about ten minutes. Keep the phone connected longer to get a full charge.

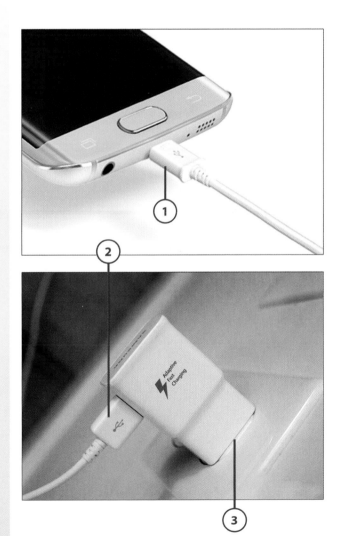

(1) Insert the small end of the microUSB cable into the multi-function jack on the bottom of the phone.

(2) Insert the larger end of the microUSB cable into the quick charger.

(3) Plug the quick charger into a powered wall outlet.

How Do I Know When It's Fully Charged?

The charging light on the front of the phone will flash red while the phone is charging, and go green when fully charged.

>>>Go Further
WIRELESS CHARGING

The Galaxy S6 also features built-in wireless charging. This means you can charge the phone without plugging it in; all you have to do is set it on a compatible wireless charging unit.

The Galaxy S6 supports both the Qi and PMA wireless charging standards, so you can use wireless chargers of either technology. As an example, there's Samsung's Wireless Charging Pad Mini, a small round pad that uses the Qi standard. Simply plug in the charging pad and then place your phone on top of it; the phone charges automatically—no cables to connect!

Getting to Know the Galaxy S6

After your phone is charged, it's time to start using it! Of course, it helps to know which keys do what—and where you can find various features and functions on the device itself.

Volume up key ——————

Volume down key ——————

The Galaxy S6 has two keys on the left edge of the unit. Use these keys to control the volume level up and down—and, in some apps, change the size of the onscreen font.

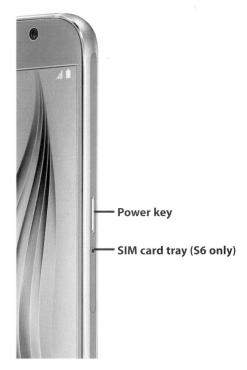

—— **Power key**

—— **SIM card tray (S6 only)**

On the right edge of the unit you find the Power key. Use this key to power the phone on and off, as well as lock and unlock the phone when not in use. If you have a Galaxy S6 (not the S6 Edge), the right edge also hosts the SIM card tray.

SIM Card

Information about your mobile phone account, including your mobile phone number, is stored on a subscriber identification module (SIM) card—actually, on the Galaxy S6, it's a smaller card called a nano-SIM. This card resides in the SIM card slot on the right or top edge of the phone. You need a special SIM removal pin, included with your phone, to access this slot and remove the SIM card.

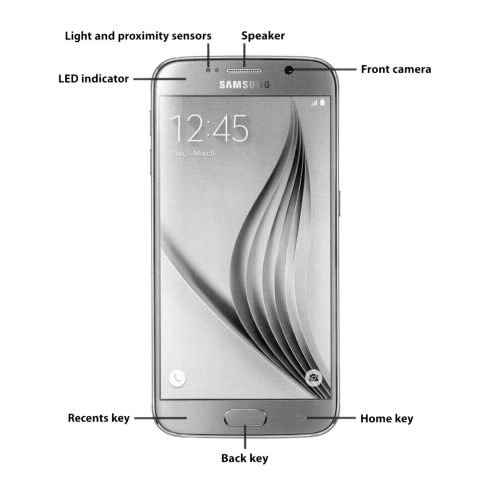

Moving to the front of the unit, there are three important keys on the bottom. In the middle is the Home key, which is a traditional push key you use to both activate the screen when off and navigate to the phone's Home screen. (It has other functions, as well, which come up throughout this book.)

To the left and right of the Home key are flat areas that host touch keys. These areas light up and become active when you touch them with your finger. The touch key on the left is the Recents key; tap this key to display all open apps on your phone. The touch key on the right is the Back key, which you tap to go back one screen in most apps.

At the top of the front is the front-facing camera, which you use for taking selfies. Next to the camera are ambient light and proximity sensors, and a speaker. There's also a small LED indicator light on the left top. This light glows three colors: red when the phone is charging, green when it's plugged in and fully charged, and blinking blue when you have waiting messages.

On the back of the phone is the main rear-facing camera, along with the LED flash and a heart rate monitor you use with your finger. The back of the Galaxy S6 is Gorilla Glass, same as the front; only the edges of the phone are metal.

Gorilla Glass

Gorilla Glass is a special toughened glass, manufactured by Corning, designed to be thin, light, and damage resistant. As such, it's widely used in smartphones and other mobile devices.

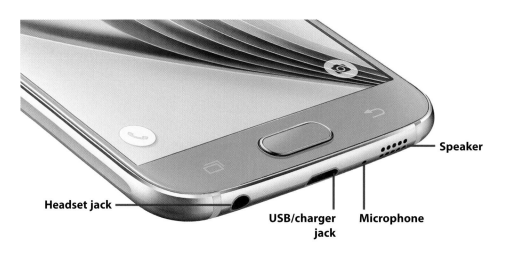

Headset jack — USB/charger jack — Microphone — Speaker

On the bottom edge of the phone is the USB/charger port, dubbed the multi-function jack, where you connect the microUSB charging cable. Next to that is the headphone jack, to which you can connect external headphones or earbuds, as well as a microphone and another speaker.

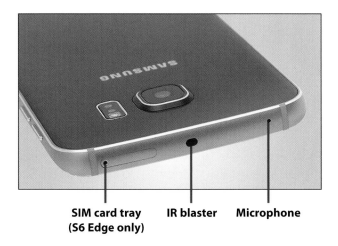

SIM card tray (S6 Edge only)　IR blaster　Microphone

The top edge of the phone hosts an infrared (IR) blaster, which is used with certain apps to turn your phone into a remote control for your living room TV. If you have an S6 Edge, the SIM card tray is also on the top edge. There's a microphone on top, as well.

Turning Your Phone On and Off

It's easy to power your new Galaxy S6 on and off. You can also lock the phone without powering it off, to turn off the screen and conserve power.

Power On Your Phone

Out of the box, your phone is turned completely off. To power it on, you use the Power key on the right side of the unit.

① Press and hold the Power key.

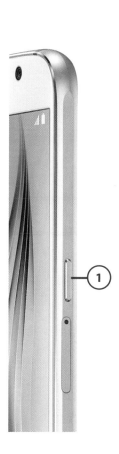

2 The screen lights up, briefly flashes the Samsung logo, then displays the Lock screen. (You also hear the Samsung "start" sound.) Swipe right to move to the Home screen.

Setup Wizard

The very first time you power up your phone you see the Setup Wizard, which enables you to quickly set up email accounts, sync contacts that were previously backed up from another phone, turn on location services, and more. Follow the onscreen instructions to complete this initial setup process.

Lock Your Phone

When you're not using your phone, you should lock it. This turns off the display and pauses all running apps, but the phone is still activated to receive calls and texts.

 Press the Power key.

2 The screen goes blank.

Automatic Locking

Your new phone locks itself if it isn't used for a brief period of time (30 seconds, by default—although you can change this on the Settings screen, as discussed in Chapter 3, "Personalizing the Way Your Galaxy S6 Looks and Works"). In practice this means that if you haven't interacted with your phone for that period of time, the screen dims and goes blank, and all running programs are paused. To resume whatever it is you were doing, you must unlock the phone—as discussed next.

Unlock Your Phone

Unlocking the Galaxy S6 is similar to powering on, although it's a much quicker process. That's because the phone itself is still powered on when locked, even if the screen is turned off.

1 Press the Power key *or…*

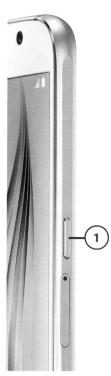

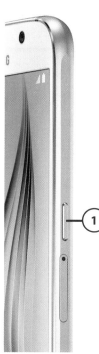

(2) Press the Home key.

(3) The screen lights up and displays the Lock screen. Swipe right to display the Home screen.

PINs and Fingerprints

To ensure that unauthorized users can't unlock and access your phone, you can configure your Galaxy S6 to unlock only after you've entered a PIN or password, or touched your fingerprint to the Home key. Both of these options are discussed in Chapter 24, "Making Your Phone More Secure."

Turn Off Your Phone

If you are not using your phone at all and don't want to receive calls or texts, you can turn it completely off. When you power the phone off, everything is powered off.

(1) Press and hold the Power key to display the options panel.

(2) Tap Power Off.

(3) Tap Power Off again. The screen goes blank and the unit completely powers down.

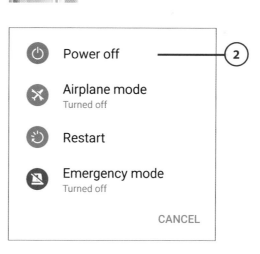

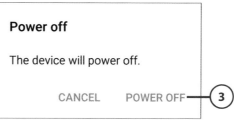

Restart Your Phone

On occasion you might want to power down your phone and then immediately power it back up. You do this by selecting the restart option.

1. Press and hold the Power key to display the options panel.

2. Tap Restart.

3. Tap Restart again. The phone powers down and then immediately powers back up, displaying the Lock screen.

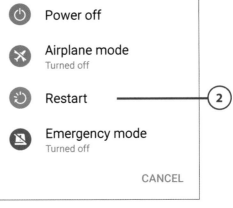

	Power off
	Airplane mode Turned off
	Restart
	Emergency mode Turned off

CANCEL

Restart

The device will restart.

CANCEL   RESTART

Using the Galaxy S6

The Galaxy S6 functions much like any other modern smartphone, including its predecessor the S5 and the competing Apple iPhone. Most operations are accomplished by tapping or swiping the screen, using a series of touch gestures.

Learn Essential Touch Gestures

To effectively operate your new Galaxy S6, you need to learn a variety of motions and gestures that you perform with your fingers on the device's touchscreen. The most common gestures are listed in the following table.

Gesture	Name	Operation	Description
	Tap	Tap an onscreen object once with your finger	Opens apps, selects menu items, pushes onscreen keys, etc.
	Drag	Touch your finger to an onscreen object, then drag your finger across without lifting	Moves an item from one location to another, activates onscreen toggle switches, etc.
	Swipe	Touch your finger anywhere on the screen, then drag your finger across without lifting	Swipe right from the Lock screen to unlock your phone; swipe left or right from the Home screen to view other panels; swipe up or down to scroll through a page or list
	Tap and hold	Tap the screen and leave your finger on the screen	Accesses available options of the selected onscreen object
	Double-tap	Tap an onscreen object twice quickly with your finger	Zooms into or out of a selected picture or web page

Gesture	Name	Operation	Description
	Spread	Place two fingers together on the screen and then spread them apart	Zooms into the screen
	Pinch	Place two fingers apart on the screen and then pinch them together	Zooms out of the screen

There are also several gestures specific to the S6 Edge. Learn more in Chapter 2, "Using the Galaxy S6 Edge."

>>>Go Further

ADDITIONAL MOTIONS AND GESTURES

There are additional gesture shortcuts you can activate on the Galaxy S6 for specific applications. You activate these gestures by swiping down from the top of the screen and tapping Settings. From the Settings page, scroll to the Motions and Gestures sections and switch on or off the following:

- **Direct Call:** Automatically calls the contact whose details are currently onscreen when you bring the phone to your ear.

- **Smart Alert:** Your phone vibrates when you pick it up if you have any missed calls or messages.

- **Mute:** Mutes incoming calls and alarms when you place your hand on the screen or turn the phone over.

- **Screen capture:** Takes a screenshot when you swipe the edge of your hand from left to right across the screen.

I find the last three options useful, and Direct Call less so—which may be why it's the only one of these options not activated by default.

Navigate the Lock Screen

Status bar

Time

Date

Phone Quick Launch

Camera Quick Launch

The screen you see when you power on or unlock your Galaxy S6 is the Lock screen. By default, this screen displays the current date and time. The status bar shows any notifications or messages you've received since you last used the phone.

To answer or initiate a phone call from the Lock screen, drag the Phone icon upward. This displays the phone dialpad.

To take a photograph from the Lock screen, drag the Camera icon upward. This displays the camera screen.

Quick Launching the Camera

To "quick launch" the camera from any screen on your phone, double press the Home key; this opens the camera app. You can even double press the Home key to access the camera when your phone is locked.

To unlock your phone for full usage, swipe right on the Lock screen. This displays the Home screen.

Navigate the Home Screen

The Home screen is just one of several panels that display your apps. Swipe the screen left or right to view additional panels. The dots, or screen indicators, above the Favorite Apps area indicate which of the panels you're currently viewing.

The icons on the Home screen panels represent some of the individual apps installed on the phone. (Not all apps are displayed on the Home screens, only those you manually add.) Tap the icon for any app you want to launch.

Managing Apps

Learn more about managing the apps displayed on the Home screens in Chapter 6, "Installing and Using Apps."

Some apps are grouped into folders. Tap a folder to view its contents in a separate panel. Tap the Back key to return to the standard Home screen view.

At the bottom of the Home screen is the Favorite Apps area. By default this area displays icons for the Phone, Contacts, Messages, and Chrome apps, but you can customize this area to display any apps you use frequently. There is a fifth icon, as well, for Apps; tap this icon to display the Apps screen, where all your apps are listed.

To return to the Home screen at any time, press the Home key.

Understand the Status Bar

At the top of the Home screen is the status bar. This area contains icons that indicate the status of various phone functions. The following table details the indicator icons you may see in the status bar.

Status Bar Indicator Icons

Icon	Description
⊘	No signal
◢	Signal strength (more bars = stronger signal)
4G	Connected to 4G/LTE network
📶	Connected to Wi-Fi network
Ⓝ	NFC (Near-Field Communication) enabled
✳	Bluetooth enabled
🔇	Mute mode enabled
🔇	Vibrate mode enabled

Icon	Description
	GPS location sensing activated
	Call in progress
	Missed call
	Call on hold
	Call using speakerphone
	New voicemail message
	New text message
	Battery power level (percent of charge remaining indicated)
	Battery is charging
	New email message
	New Gmail message
	Download in process
	File being uploaded
	App updates available
	App updates complete
	Keyboard is in use
	Alarm set

Navigate the Apps Screen

As noted, when you tap the Apps icon on the Home screen, you see the Apps screen—actually, a series of panels. These panels display all the apps installed on your phone. Use the Apps screen to access apps not displayed on the Home screen, select which apps to display on the Home screen, and uninstall unwanted apps.

To return to the Home screen, press the Home button.

View the Notification Panel

The notification panel pulls down from any screen to display any active notifications, as well as links to key system settings.

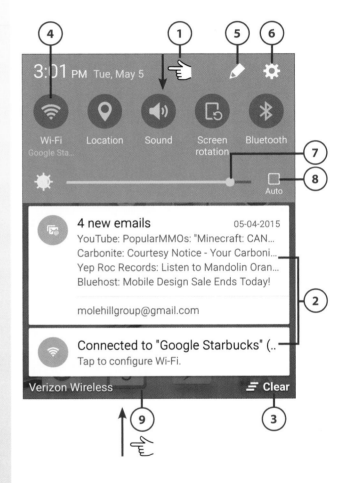

1. Swipe down from the top of any screen to display the notifications panel.

2. Any notifications are displayed beneath this panel. Tap a notification to read messages and perform related actions. Drag a notification to the left or right to clear it from the screen.

3. Tap Clear to clear all notifications from the notification panel.

4. Tap any of the Quick Settings icons to turn on or off Wi-Fi, GPS (Location), Sound, Screen Rotation, or Bluetooth.

5. Tap the Edit (pencil) icon to rearrange the Quick Settings icons.

6. Tap Settings to display the Settings screen.

7. Tap and drag the brightness slider to adjust screen brightness.

8. Tap to select the Auto option to activate automatic screen brightness.

9. Swipe up from the bottom of the notification panel to close the panel.

It's Not All Good

Auto Brightness

The automatic brightness function attempts to set the proper brightness level for the ambient light in your current location. This sounds good in theory, but may not be the best in practice.

The first issue is that some people find that auto brightness results in screens that are too dark. This is especially a problem for people with vision issues, where you need increased brightness to read text clearly.

The second issue is that auto brightness doesn't always work well. The ambient light sensor sometimes doesn't accurately track the outside light level, resulting in a screen that is too dark or too light for the current conditions. In addition, the light sensor might significantly lag behind any changes in lighting as you move from location to location.

For these reasons, you might want to disable the auto brightness option on your phone— or at least experiment with it before committing one way or the other.

Move from Screen to Screen

Moving from screen to screen on the Galaxy S6 is a simple matter of tapping and swiping.

1. From the Lock screen, swipe to the right to unlock the phone and display the Home screen.

(2) From the Home screen, swipe left or right to display additional panels.

(3) Tap the Apps button to display the Apps screen.

4. From the Apps screen, swipe left or right to display additional panels.

5. Tap the Back key to return to the previous screen.

6. Press the Home key to return to the Home screen.

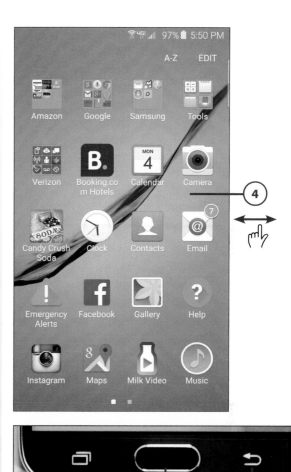

View and Close Open Apps

The apps you open on your phone stay open, but paused, until you manually close them. Use the Recents key to display your open apps, navigate to those you want to reuse, and close those you no longer need open.

1. Tap the Recents key to display all open apps in a stack.

(**2**) Swipe up or down to view all the apps in the stack.

(**3**) Tap an app to reopen it fullscreen.

(**4**) Tap the X on a given app to close it, or just drag the app left or right off the screen.

Close Your Apps

In general, you want to close your apps when you're done with them. Leaving apps running in the background—even if they're theoretically paused—can use enough power to unnecessarily drain your battery.

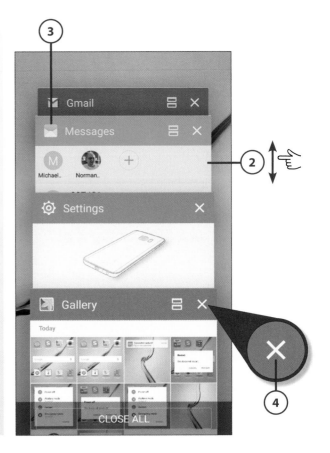

Performing Basic Operations

Your new Galaxy S6 or S6 Edge can do a lot of things—run apps, send and receive text messages and email, play music and videos, and more. But there are some basic operations, such as controlling the volume and screen brightness, that apply to all operations.

Change the Volume Level

Many applications on the Galaxy S6 generate sound, whether it's the ringing of the phone, the click of the onscreen keyboard, or music that you're playing. The Galaxy S6 features volume up and down keys on the left side of the device—but there's more you can adjust than just that.

(**1**) Press and hold the up volume key to raise the volume level of the current application. If no application is running, this adjusts the volume level of the phone's ringtone.

(**2**) Press and hold the down volume key to lower the volume level of the current application. If no application is running, this adjusts the volume level of the phone's ringtone.

(**3**) When you press either of the volume keys, the phone displays a volume panel onscreen. You can drag the slider in this panel to adjust the volume level of the ringtone.

(**4**) To adjust the volume level of other functions, tap the Settings (gear) icon in the volume panel. This displays an extended volume panel. You can make individual adjustments to the volume levels for these functions—Ringtone, Media, Notifications, and System.

5 Drag the slider in the Media section to adjust the volume level of music and video playback.

6 Drag the slider in the Notifications section to adjust the volume level of notifications and alerts.

7 Drag the slider in the System section to adjust the volume level of system sounds.

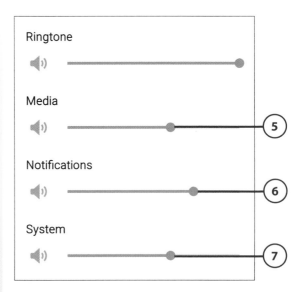

Put the Phone on Vibrate or Mute

By default, when someone calls or texts you on your Galaxy S6, the phone rings. If you're in a quiet area, however, you might want incoming calls or texts to be less obtrusive. In this instance, you can turn off the ringtone and instead have your phone vibrate or be totally silent.

1 Swipe down from the top of the screen to display the notification panel.

2 Tap the third Quick Settings icon to switch between Sound (default ringtone and the phone vibrates), Vibrate (no sound, but phone vibrates), and Mute (phone neither rings or vibrates) modes.

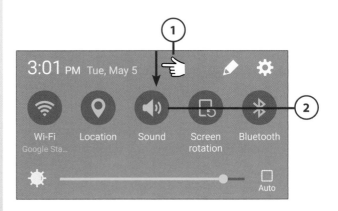

Adjust the Brightness Level

Some users find the Galaxy S6's default screen brightness to be a little too dim to comfortably read, especially in direct light. You can, however, easily make the screen brighter or dimmer.

(1) Swipe down from the top of the screen to display the notification panel.

(2) Tap and drag the brightness slider to the right to make the screen brighter, or drag to the left to make it less bright.

3:01 PM Tue, May 5

Wi-Fi   Location   Sound   Screen   Bluetooth
Google Sta...   rotation

Auto

Rotate the Phone

You can hold your new Samsung smartphone so that the longest edge is vertical (portrait mode) or horizontal (landscape mode). Although portrait mode is the normal mode for most uses, you might find that some onscreen content is easier to read or manage when you rotate the phone 90 degrees.

The Home screen itself doesn't rotate, but many apps do. Many users find that the onscreen keyboard (discussed next) is easier to type on when the phone is held horizontally; the keys get bigger to fill the wider width. You might also find that some web pages and documents are easier to read with the phone rotated, for the same reason; the onscreen text gets bigger when the screen's width is larger.

(1) To switch to landscape mode, turn the phone 90 degrees in either direction. (It doesn't matter whether you have the Home key on the left or the right.)

(2) Most (but not all) apps now rotate to match the new screen orientation. Move back to portrait mode by rotating the phone so that the Home key is back on the bottom.

Disable Rotation

By default, the Galaxy S6's screen rotates when you rotate the phone. If you want to lock the screen into portrait view, even when the phone is rotated, select Settings, Display and Wallpaper, Screen Rotation and then tap Stay in Portrait View.

Enter Text with the Onscreen Keyboard

When you need to enter text on your phone—to send text messages, create emails, post to Facebook, enter website URLs, work in word processing documents, and the like—an onscreen keyboard automatically appears at the bottom of the screen. Use this keyboard to enter text, numbers, and other characters.

(1) The onscreen keyboard automatically appears whenever text entry is required.

(2) Tap a letter or number key to enter that character.

3 Tap the spacebar to enter a space.

4 Tap the up arrow once to enter a single uppercase character.

5 Tap the up arrow twice to enter all-cap mode.

6 Tap the up arrow three times to return to normal lowercase entry.

First Word Capitalization

The onscreen keyboard automatically capitalizes the first word of a sentence. It knows that a new sentence starts when you enter a period (.) or if you have entered two spaces in a row.

7 Tap the Delete (x) key to remove the previous character.

8 Tap the Sym button to display the symbol keyboard when you need to enter punctuation marks and symbols.

9 There are two screens of symbols available. Tap the 1/2 or 2/2 buttons to switch between symbol screens.

10 Tap the ABC button to return to the alphanumeric keyboard.

11 To enter Emoji instead of text, tap the Emoji button.

Emoji

The word *emoji* means "picture letter" in Japanese. An emoji is a small picture or icon used to express an emotion or idea.

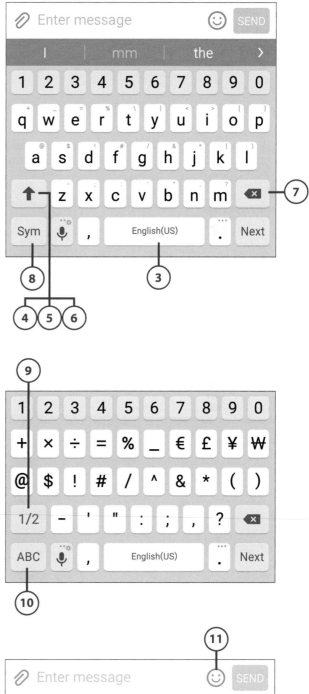

12 This displays the first of several screens of emoji. Scroll right and left to view additional emoji.

13 Tap an emoji to enter it in your message or document.

14 Tap the emoji button to return to the alphanumeric keyboard.

15 Tap the Back button to hide the onscreen keyboard.

>>>Go Further
PREDICTIVE KEYBOARD

Your Samsung Galaxy S6 uses a *predictive keyboard*. This means that the keyboard looks at what you're typing and predicts what you'll type next, suggesting possible words. As you type, suggestions for the next word appear in the row space above the top row of number keys. To accept a suggestion, all you have to do is tap it.

The predictive keyboard also includes auto-correct functionality. This means if you mistype a word, the keyboard automatically inserts what it thinks is the correct word. Although this auto-correct often does a good job of catching spelling mistakes, it can also change perfectly acceptable words into something else entirely. For this reason, you still need to look at the screen when typing; you can't rely on the predictive keyboard to always make the right choices.

Copy and Paste Text

When you're entering text, you may find it more convenient to copy and paste text from one location or document to another. For example, you might want to copy an address from a web page and paste it into a text message or maps application.

1. Tap and hold the text you want to copy. This selects the current word.

2. Select more than one word by tapping and dragging the blue selection bars to enlarge the selection.

3. Tap Copy to copy the text to your phone's clipboard.

4. Move to and tap where you want to insert the selected text.

5. Tap Paste.

>>>Go Further

HOW TO TAKE A SCREENSHOT

To take a digital picture (screenshot) of the visible screen on your Galaxy S6, hold down the Power and Home keys simultaneously until the screen flashes. The screenshot is stored in the Screenshots album in your photo gallery.

You can also use a palm swipe to capture a screenshot. To do this, place the edge of your hand on the left side of the screen, then swipe it to the right.

Set an Alarm

Your Samsung smartphone can also serve as your mobile alarm clock. The Galaxy S6 and S6 Edge includes a Clock app that you can use to set your morning wake-up alarm—or any other alarms throughout the day.

1. From your phone's Home screen, tap the Apps icon to open the Apps screen.

2. Tap the Clock icon to open the Clock app.

3. Tap to select the Alarm tab.

4. Tap the time controls to set the alarm time.

5. Tap AM or PM to set morning or afternoon.

6. Tap Repeat to set the option to repeat the alarm on a schedule (such as Monday through Friday).

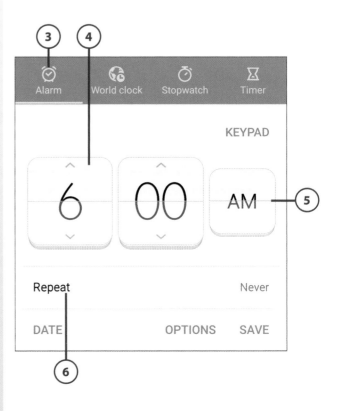

7 Tap to select how often and when you want this alarm to repeat.

8 Tap the back arrow to return to the main Clock screen.

9 Tap Date to set the day this alarm will sound.

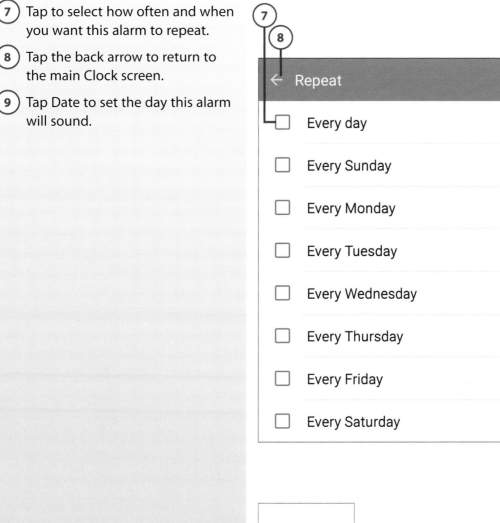

← Repeat

☐ Every day

☐ Every Sunday

☐ Every Monday

☐ Every Tuesday

☐ Every Wednesday

☐ Every Thursday

☐ Every Friday

☐ Every Saturday

Repeat

DATE

(10) Tap the date you want on the calendar.

(11) Tap Done.

(12) Tap Options to adjust the sound and snooze options.

(13) By default, the alarm sounds at the selected time. To have your phone vibrate instead, or vibrate along with the sound, tap Alarm Type and make a selection.

(14) Tap and drag the sound slider to adjust the volume level of the alarm sound.

(15) Tap Alarm Tone to select a specific alarm sound.

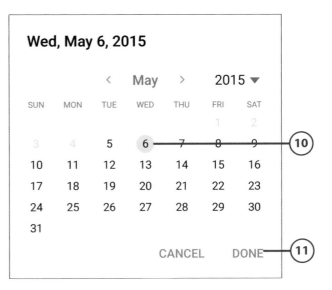

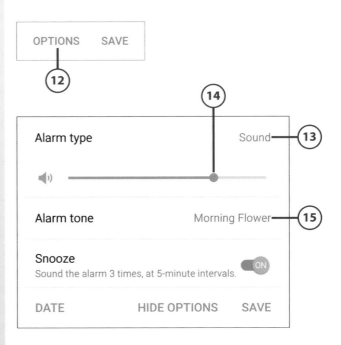

16 Tap to select the alarm tone you want. When you tap a tone, you hear a preview of that sound.

17 Tap the back arrow to return to the previous screen.

18 By default, the alarm sounds until you tap the snooze button, then repeats two more times at five minute intervals. If you'd rather not utilize this snooze function, tap "Off" the Snooze switch.

19 Set the alarm sound to start soft and then increase in volume by tapping "On" the Increasing Volume switch.

20 Tap Alarm Name to give the alarm a name.

21 Tap Save to save this alarm.

17

← Alarm tone

○   Fresh Morning

○   Hangouts Call

○   Hangouts Message

◉   Morning Flower

○   Mystic Tone

○   Ocean Voyage

16

Snooze
Sound the alarm 3 times, at 5-minute intervals.   ON — **18**

Increasing volume
Increase the alarm volume for the 1st 60 sec.   OFF — **19**

Alarm name   None — **20**

DATE   HIDE OPTIONS   SAVE — **21**

Set a Timer

In addition to being an alarm, the Clock app also functions as a clock (of course), stopwatch, and timer. The timer function is particularly useful when you need to keep track of something cooking or otherwise in progress.

1. From within the Clock app, tap to select the Timer tab.

2. Tap the Hours, Minutes, and Seconds controls to set the length of the timer.

3. Tap Start to begin the countdown.

Managing Your Phone's Power

Your Galaxy S6 is a mobile device, running on power from its internal battery. This battery is rechargeable, of course; most people charge their phones overnight, so they have a full charge when they get up in the morning.

Monitor Battery Usage

The amount of charge left in your phone's battery is indicated in the status bar at the top of the screen, as a percentage. For example, if the indicator reads 40%, that means that you have 40% of a full charge left. More detailed battery usage is available, however.

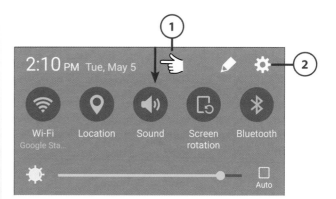

1. Swipe down from the top of the screen to display the notification panel.

2. Tap Settings to display the Settings screen.

3. Scroll to the Device section and tap Battery.

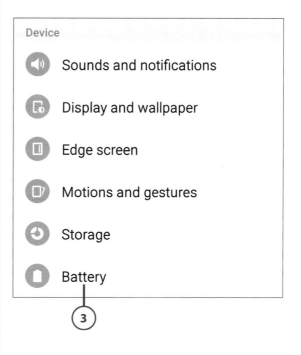

4 The Battery screen displays various configuration options for your phone's battery usage, including a detailed graph that estimates how much time the phone has left on the current charge.

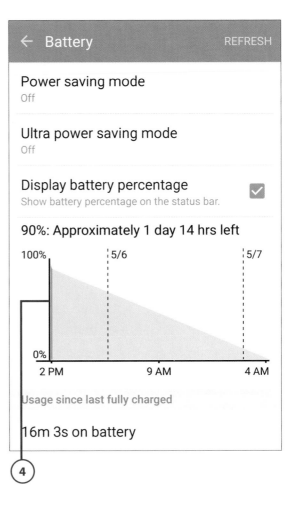

Deal with a Low Battery

Your phone notifies you when the battery is running low. At this point, the best thing to do is connect your phone to the quick charger and plug it into a power outlet to recharge. If you do not have a power outlet handy, you need to start conserving power until you can recharge.

There are many ways to conserve power on your phone. You can manually turn off power-hungry functions, such as Wi-Fi and Bluetooth. You can also enter one of two power-saving modes:

- **Power Saving Mode**. Limits maximum CPU performance, reduces screen brightness, turns off touch key lights, and turns off vibration feedback.

- **Ultra Power Saving Mode**. Switches to a grayscale display, limits the number of usable apps to only essential applications, and turns off Wi-Fi, Bluetooth, and location services.

In most instances, the normal Power Saving Mode will be enough to get you through until you can recharge your phone. Switch to Ultra Power Saving Mode when it's unlikely you'll be able to recharge within the next hour or so.

Cables

Your new Samsung phone came with one microUSB cable, which you use to charge your phone. Many users like to purchase additional microUSB cables; they leave one at home (for charging), but carry a second in their purse or briefcase for charging when they're on the go—and maybe even a third in the car, for charging (and connecting) when driving.

Turn On Power Saving Modes

1. Swipe down from the top of the screen to display the notification panel.

2. Tap Settings to display the Settings screen.

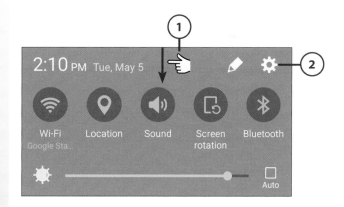

3 Scroll to the Device section and tap Battery.

4 Start Power Saving Mode by tapping Power Saving Mode and then tapping On to activate.

5 Start Ultra Power Saving Mode by tapping Ultra Power Saving Mode and then tapping On to activate.

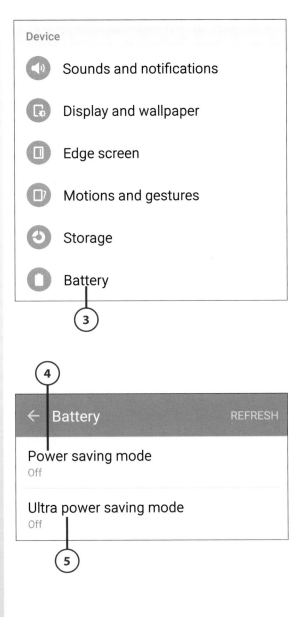

>>>*Go Further*

EMERGENCY MODE

Your Samsung Galaxy S6 offers a special Emergency Mode for use in an emergency. This mode extends the life of your phone's battery by turning off all but essential functions. It also enables you to use your phone to dial 911, send your location to a designated contact, and even sound an alarm.

To enter Emergency Mode, press and hold the Power key and then tap Emergency Mode. Agree to the various terms and conditions and then tap Turn On.

You now see the grayscale Emergency Mode screen. To use your phone as a flashlight, tap Flashlight. To make a regular phone call, tap Phone. To dial 911, tap Emergency Call. To sound an emergency alarm, tap Emergency Alarm. To message your current location to a designated contact, tap Message Location.

When the emergency has passed, you exit Emergency Mode by tapping More, Turn Off Emergency Mode.

In this chapter, you learn how to use those features exclusive to the Samsung Galaxy S6 Edge. Topics include the following:

→ Getting to Know the Galaxy S6 Edge
→ Using Edge Lighting and People Edge
→ Using the Information Stream
→ Using the Night Clock

Using the Galaxy S6 Edge

The Galaxy S6 and the S6 Edge share many of the same features and functionality. But the curved screen edge on the S6 Edge provides for a handful of additional features, all of which use the extra screen space.

Getting to Know the Galaxy S6 Edge

There are actually two versions of the Galaxy S6. There's the standard S6 and there's the S6 Edge. The difference is… well, in the edge.

The screen of the S6 Edge has curved edges on the left and right. This makes for a rather striking design (and a slightly different feel in your hand), and also provides for added functionality.

Specifically, the Edge screen on the S6 Edge provides additional screen space for information and alerts. Here's what you can choose to display on the Edge screen:

- **Edge Lighting:** The Edge screen lights up when you receive a call or notification when your phone is facing downward. (The Edge screen lights in an assigned color if you receive a call from one of your priority contacts.)

- **People Edge:** The Edge screen displays a tab in an assigned color if you have a message from one of your priority contacts.

- **Information Stream:** Displays news and other real-time information you select, in a scrolling ticker.

- **Night Clock:** Displays the date and time on the Edge screen.

S6 Edge Only

These features are all exclusive to the Samsung Galaxy S6 Edge. They are not available on the plain Galaxy S6.

Configure Edge Screen Position

You can configure the S6 Edge to use either the left or right edge to display various Edge-related messages and alerts. Make sure you position the phone so that you can see the side you've designated as the Edge.

1. Swipe down from the top of the screen to display the notification panel.

2. Tap Settings to display the settings screen.

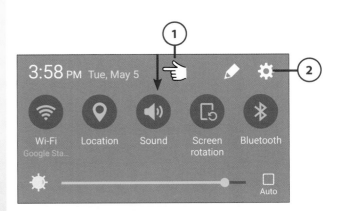

3 Scroll to the Device section and tap Edge Screen.

4 Scroll to the bottom of the page and tap Edge Screen Position.

5 Tap either Right Side (default) or Left Side.

Device

🔊 Sounds and notifications

📱 Display and wallpaper

📱 Edge screen ————————— **3**

More features

Information stream
On

Night clock
10:00 PM ~ 6:00 AM

Edge screen position ————————— **4**
Right side

← Edge screen position

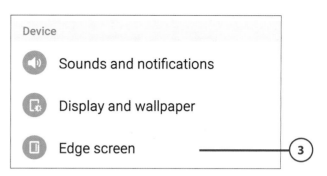

⦿ Right side ————————— **5**

○ Left side

It's Not All Good

Difficult to Read

The Edge screen is very thin, less than a half inch tall, which limits the information that can be displayed on it. You're basically looking at a single line of information, no more than that.

The thinness also makes the information on the Edge difficult to read, especially for those with any degree of vision problems. So while the Information Stream or Night Clock might sound interesting, you'll probably have to put on your glasses to read them—which might reduce their usefulness.

Using Edge Lighting and People Edge

The S6 Edge's Edge Lighting feature lights up the Edge screen when you receive a call or notification—but only when the phone is sitting facedown. If you activate the People Edge feature, the Edge screen lights in the color you've assigned to that contact, so you can see at a glance who's calling.

Configure Edge Lighting and People Edge

Before you use the Edge Lighting feature, you have to turn it on and then configure which notifications will light up when it's in use. If want to use the People Edge feature, you also have to tell your phone which people are assigned which colors—what Samsung calls your My People list.

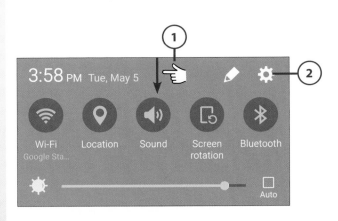

(1) Swipe down from the top of the screen to display the notification panel.

(2) Tap Settings to display the settings screen.

(3) Scroll to the Device section and tap Edge Screen.

(4) Tap Edge Lighting to display the Edge Lighting screen.

(5) Tap On the switch at the top of the screen to enable Edge Lighting.

(6) You can also opt to reject any incoming call and send a pre-selected message to the caller by placing your finger on the heartrate sensor on the back of the Galaxy S6 Edge. This is called Quick Reply; to activate this feature, tap Quick Reply and then tap On the switch at the top of the next screen.

(7) Tap the back arrow at the top of the screen to return to the Edge Screen screen.

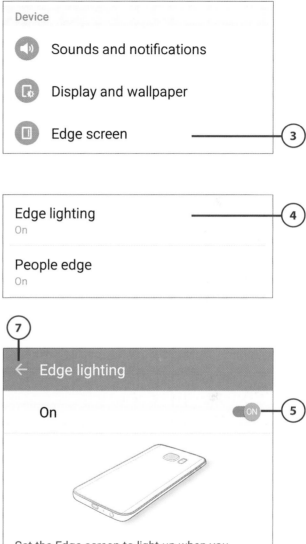

Device

🔊 Sounds and notifications

📷 Display and wallpaper

▯ Edge screen ———————— (3)

Edge lighting ———————— (4)
On

People edge
On

(7)

← Edge lighting

On ⬤ ON — (5)

Set the Edge screen to light up when you receive calls or notifications while the phone is turned over. If People edge is also on, the color of the indicator will depend on your My people settings.

Quick reply
On

(6)

8 Tap People Edge to display the People Edge screen.

9 Tap On the switch at the top of the screen to enable the People Edge feature.

10 Tap My People to set which contacts will display color Edge alerts.

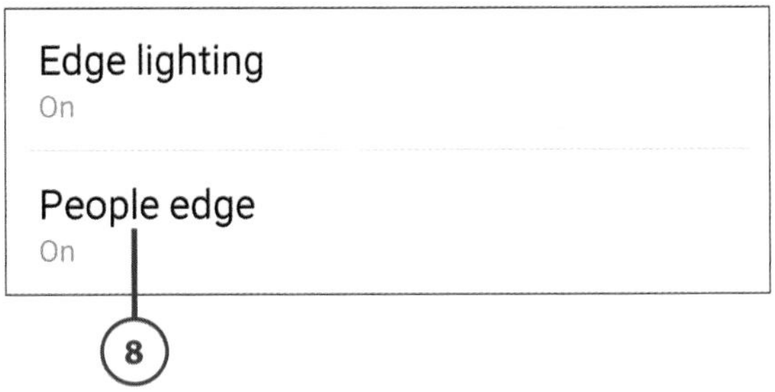

Edge lighting
On

People edge
On

8

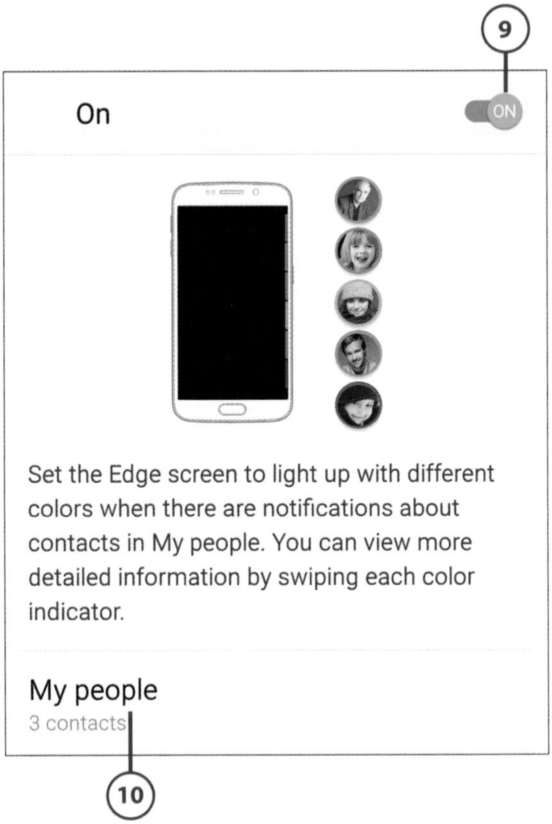

9

On
ON

Set the Edge screen to light up with different colors when there are notifications about contacts in My people. You can view more detailed information by swiping each color indicator.

My people
3 contacts

10

11 Tap the + icon for the color you want to assign to a contact; your contacts list displays. (If a color is already assigned, you still see the contacts list to reassign this color.)

12 Tap the contact you want to assign to this color.

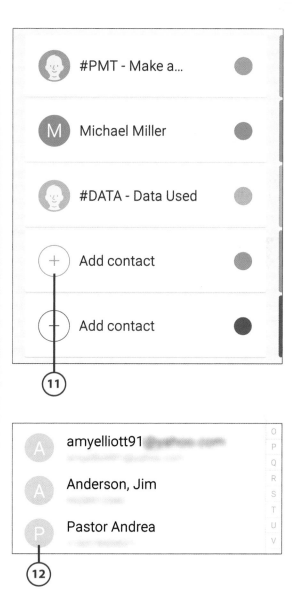

13 Tap the back arrow at the top of the screen to return to the People Edge screen.

14 To display an alert if there are notifications from people on your My People list when you pick up your phone, go to the Alert When Picking Up section and click "On" the switch.

15 Tap the back arrow at the top of the screen to return to the Edge Screen screen.

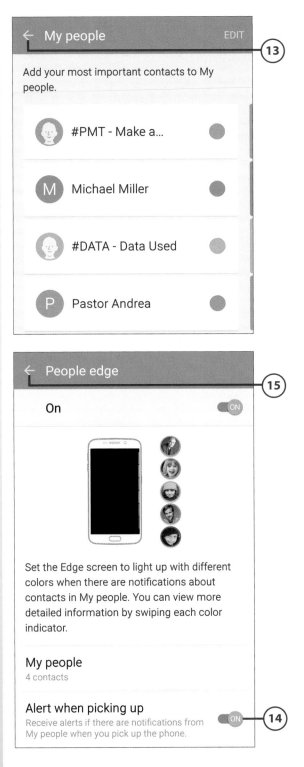

16 Tap Select Notifications to display the Select Notifications screen.

17 You can opt to have the Edge screen light when you have a missed call or receive messages or emails. Tap On those notifications of which you want to be alerted in this fashion.

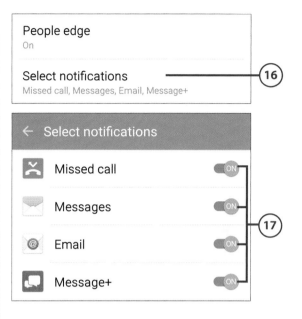

People edge
On

Select notifications — **16**
Missed call, Messages, Email, Message+

← Select notifications

Missed call   ON

Messages   ON   **17**

@ Email   ON

Message+   ON

Use Edge Lighting and People Edge

After you've activated the Edge Lighting, People Edge, and Notifications features, all you have to do is set your phone facedown when you're not using it. This is particularly useful at night, with your phone on the nightstand beside your bed.

1 When you receive a call, message, or notification, the entire designated Edge screen on your phone lights with a pulsing light. If you receive a call or message from someone on your My People list, the pulsing light is in the color assigned to that person. For example, if you assign your friend Joe to the color green, if Joe texts or calls you, the Edge screen lights up green.

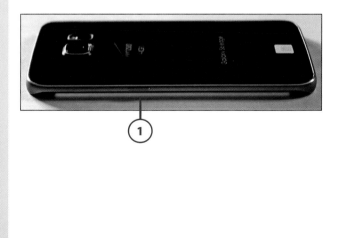

1

(2) The light displays for only a few seconds and then your screen goes dark and your phone relocks. When you pick up and unlock your phone, the Edge screen displays a colored bar, which lets you know you received a message from your friend. Tap and drag the colored bar to the left to display information about the messages you've received.

(3) Tap your friend's name to read messages you've received.

(4) Tap the Phone icon to call this person.

(5) Tap the Message icon to read all messages from this person.

(6) Tap the X to remove the message area from the screen.

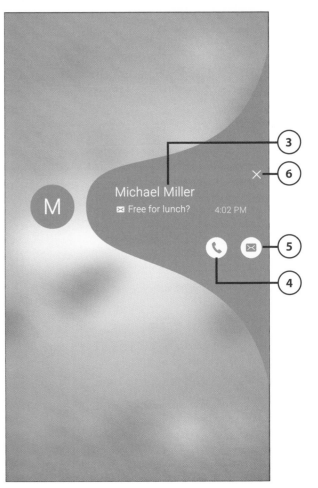

Using the Information Stream

The Information Stream is a type of news feed that scrolls across the Edge screen. It can display any or all of the following:

- **Briefing Feed:** Your phone's notifications
- **Twitter Trends:** Trending Twitter hashtags and topics
- **Yahoo! News:** Top news headlines
- **Yahoo! Finance:** Stock updates on the stocks you choose
- **Yahoo! Sports:** Scores from your favorite teams

Activate and Configure the Information Stream

To display the Information Stream on your Edge screen, you have to both activate and configure it for the types of information you want to receive.

1. Swipe down from the top of the screen to display the notification panel.

2. Tap Settings to display the settings screen.

3. Scroll to the Device section and tap Edge Screen.

4. Tap Information Stream to display the Information Stream screen.

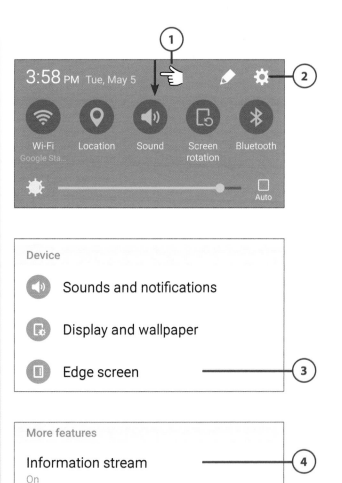

(5) To activate the Information Stream, tap On the switch at the top of the page.

(6) Tap Manage Feeds to display the Manage Feeds screen.

(7) Check those feeds you want to display. Uncheck those you don't want to read.

(8) To change the order of the feeds, tap Reorder; then tap and drag the feeds into a different position.

(9) Some feeds have settings to customize what information you see. For example, you can configure which stocks to follow in the Yahoo! Finance feed, or what sports teams to follow in the Yahoo! Sports feed. Tap the gear icon for a given feed to customize its settings.

(10) Tap the back arrow at the top of the screen to return to the Information Stream screen.

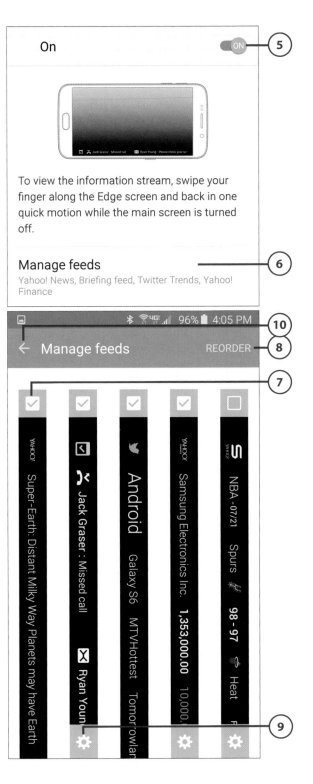

On

To view the information stream, swipe your finger along the Edge screen and back in one quick motion while the main screen is turned off.

Manage feeds
Yahoo! News, Briefing feed, Twitter Trends, Yahoo! Finance

96% 4:05 PM

← **Manage feeds**   REORDER

Super-Earth: Distant Milky Way Planets may have Earth

Jack Graser : Missed call

Ryan Youn

Android   Galaxy S6   MTVHottest   Tomorrowlan

Samsung Electronics Inc.   **1,353,000.00**   10,000.

NBA-07/21   Spurs   **98 - 97**   Heat

(11) By default the Information Stream displays for 15 seconds and then turns off. To change the time the Information Stream is visible, tap Edge Screen Timeout.

(12) Tap the amount of time you want, from 15 seconds to 10 minutes.

(13) To configure the weather settings for the Information Stream, tap Weather.

Location Services

The first time you configure the Weather settings, you're asked to enable your phone's location services. This is necessary to display the correct weather information for your current location. (Learn more about location services in Chapter 25, "Configuring Your Phone's Settings.")

(11)

Edge screen timeout
15 seconds

Weather

(12)

← Edge screen timeout

◉ 15 seconds

○ 30 seconds

○ 1 minute

○ 2 minutes

○ 5 minutes

○ 10 minutes

Edge screen timeout
30 seconds

Weather

(13)

14 The Weather Settings screen contains various options for the weather function on the Edge screen, Lock screen, and calendar. Make sure the Edge Screen option is switched On.

15 Confirm or edit the other settings on this screen, including Unit (for degrees, Fahrenheit by default), Auto Refresh (every 6 hours by default), and Use Current Location (on by default).

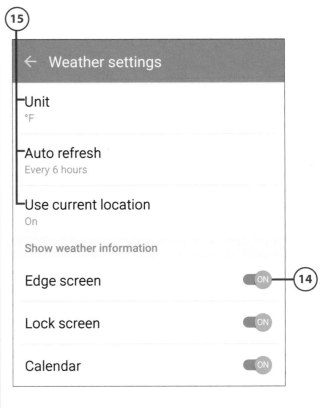

15

← Weather settings

Unit
°F

Auto refresh
Every 6 hours

Use current location
On

Show weather information

Edge screen   ON **14**

Lock screen   ON

Calendar   ON

View the Information Stream

The Information Stream does not appear automatically; you have to toggle it on when you want to read it.

1 Press the Power key to turn off your phone's screen.

1

(2) With the phone locked, quickly slide your finger up and then down the Edge screen.

(3) The Information Stream now displays on the Edge screen. Swipe left or right (up or down on the Information Stream) to cycle through different feeds.

(4) Tap a headline or item to view that item on your phone's main screen.

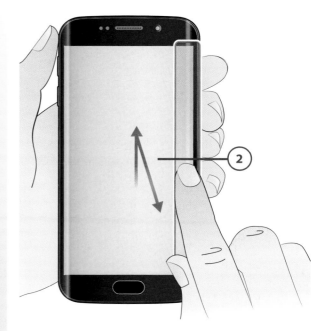

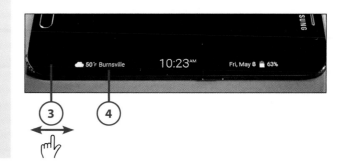

Using the Night Clock

The S6 Edge's Night Clock feature turns your phone into a nighttime alarm clock and night light. With Night Clock activated, the Edge screen displays the current date and time, along with the time of the next alarm. The Edge screen itself is slightly dimmed, so it won't keep you awake all night.

Activate the Night Clock

When you activate the Night Clock, you tell your phone during what hours you want to see it. You can specify a maximum 12-hour period.

① Swipe down from the top of the screen to display the notification panel.

② Tap Settings to display the settings screen.

③ Scroll to the Device section and tap Edge Screen.

④ Tap Night Clock to display the Night Clock screen.

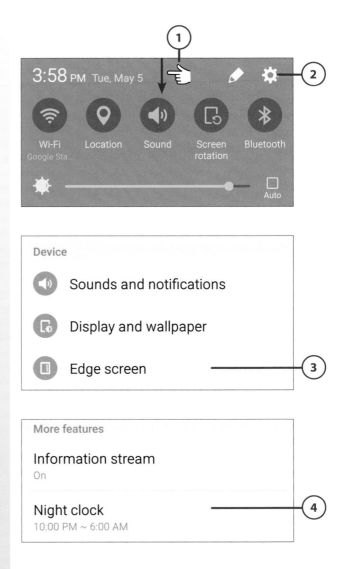

5 Tap On the switch at the top of the screen to turn on the Night Clock.

6 Tap the up and down arrows to set the Start Time. Tap the AM/PM button to switch between AM and PM.

7 Tap the up and down arrows to set the End Time. Tap the AM/PM button to switch between AM and PM.

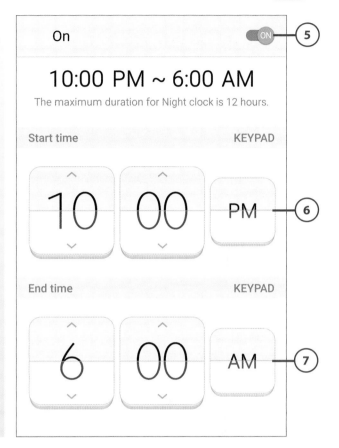

On ON **5**

10:00 PM ~ 6:00 AM

The maximum duration for Night clock is 12 hours.

Start time KEYPAD

10 00 PM **6**

End time KEYPAD

6 00 AM **7**

View the Night Clock

10:02 AM Mon, May 11

When activated, the Night Clock appears on the Edge screen at the start time you set, and stays on until the specified end. Note that the Night Clock light is very low, so that it won't disturb your sleep; you might have trouble viewing it in daylight.

Low Battery

The Night Clock turns off when battery power reaches the 15% level.

In this chapter, you discover various ways you can personalize your new Samsung smartphone. Topics include the following:

→ Personalizing the Screen Background
→ Personalizing Screen Settings
→ Personalizing Sounds and Notifications

3

Personalizing the Way Your S6 Looks and Works

Out of the box, Samsung's Galaxy S6/S6 Edge is a nice looking phone. It's easy enough to learn how to use, the screens look good, and the operations feel natural.

That doesn't mean that there isn't anything about that you might want to change. Maybe you want a different screen background. Maybe you don't like the sounds of the notifications. Maybe you don't like notifications at all.

Well, you're in good luck. There are lots of ways you can personalize your new Galaxy S6 or S6 Edge to make the phone better fit the way you like to use it.

Personalizing the Screen Background

One of the first things that many people personalize about their phones is the screen background. On the Galaxy S6, you can set different backgrounds for the Lock screen and the Home screens. You can choose from preselected wallpaper images, or use one of your own photos as the background.

Readability

When choosing background images and colors, make sure that there's enough contrast between the background and the foreground icons and text. Don't sacrifice readability for a cool looking background.

Change the Lock Screen Wallpaper

The Lock screen is the screen that appears when you power on or unlock your phone. You can set the Lock screen to have its own background wallpaper, or to share the background of the Home screen.

1. Swipe down from the top of the screen to display the notification panel.

2. Tap Settings to display the Settings screen.

3. Scroll to the Device section and tap Display and Wallpaper.

4. Tap Wallpaper.

5. Tap the down arrow at the top of the screen and select Lock Screen.

Home and Lock

To use the same image for the Lock and Home screens, tap the down arrow and select Home and Lock Screens.

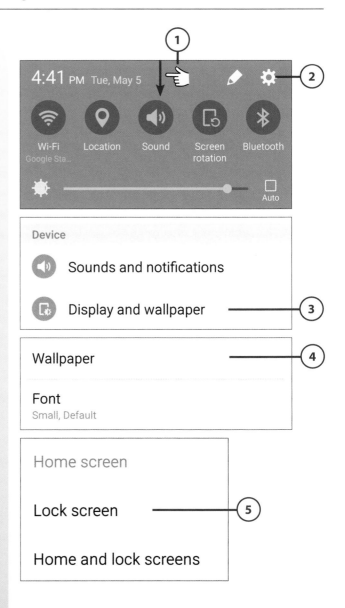

6 Scroll through the available images and tap the one you want to use.

7 Tap Set as Wallpaper *or…*

8 To use a photograph as a background image, tap From Gallery. Your photo gallery opens.

9 Tap the photo you want to use.

10 Tap Done.

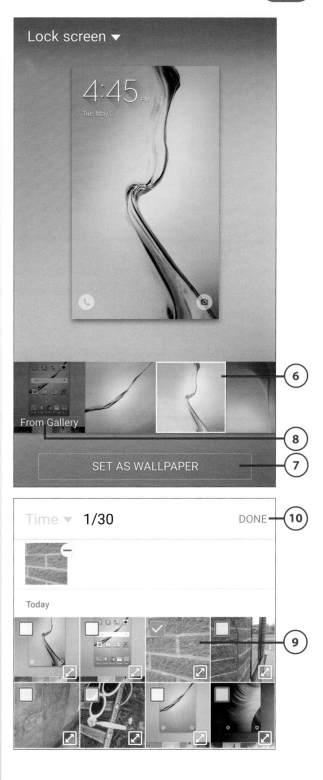

(11) Tap Done to approve the image you've chosen.

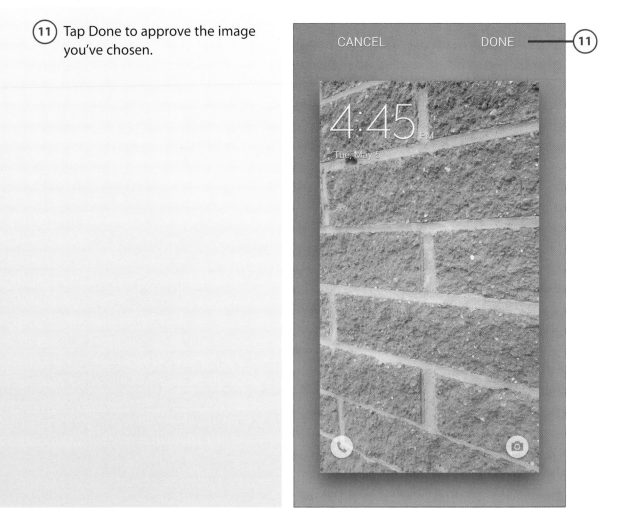

>>>Go Further

PICTURES FOR WALLPAPER

Many of us like to use personal pictures—of our partners, children, or grandchildren—as background wallpaper on our phones. As you've just learned, it's easy enough to choose a photo for your background, as long as that photo is already stored on your phone, in the Gallery. So if you have a picture you'd like to use, just make sure you save it to the Gallery first.

What about pictures you might receive via email or text message? Well, you can save these to the Gallery, also, just by using the "save" function within the appropriate app. For example, to save a picture you receive in the Messages app, tap the picture to display it fullscreen, then tap the Save icon at the top of the screen. When prompted to save the attachment, tap OK.

You can also set a picture as your wallpaper directly from most apps. Using the Messages app as an example, tap to display the picture fullscreen, then tap the Menu button at the top right, then tap Set As. When prompted, select to save this picture as either the Home screen, Lock screen, or both Home and Lock screens.

You have similar options with your email apps, and with other messaging apps. When you receive a picture that you'd like to set as your Home or Lock screen background, just select the "set as" option and go from there.

Change the Home Screen Wallpaper

You can similarly change the background image on your phone's Home screens. (Actually, on both the Home and Apps screens.)

1. Swipe down from the top of the screen to display the notification panel.

2. Tap Settings to display the Settings screen.

3. Scroll to the Device section and tap Display and Wallpaper.

4. Tap Wallpaper.

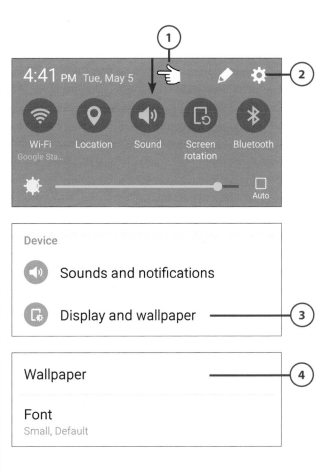

(5) Tap the down arrow at the top of the screen and select Home Screen.

(6) Scroll through the available images and tap the one you want to use.

(7) Tap Set as Wallpaper *or...*

(8) To use a photograph as a background image, tap From Gallery. Your photo gallery opens.

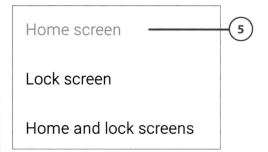

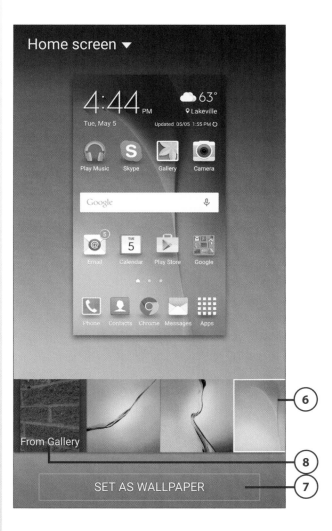

9 Tap the photo you want to use.

10 Tap Done to approve the image you've chosen.

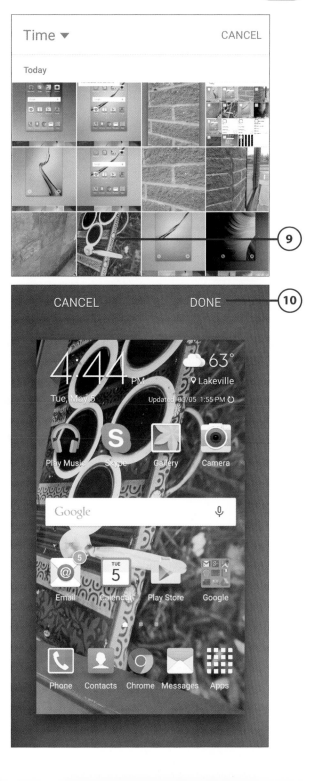

Change Your Phone's Theme

If you want a more radical change to the way your phone looks, you can change the phone's entire visual theme. A theme is a preset combination of background images, fonts, and icons that affect the look and feel of every system screen.

1. Swipe down from the top of the screen to display the notification panel.

2. Tap Settings to display the Settings screen.

3. Scroll to the Personal section and tap Themes.

4. A handful of themes are preselected on your phone. Tap to select one of these themes. You are taken to the theme on the Samsung Theme Store.

5. Tap Download.

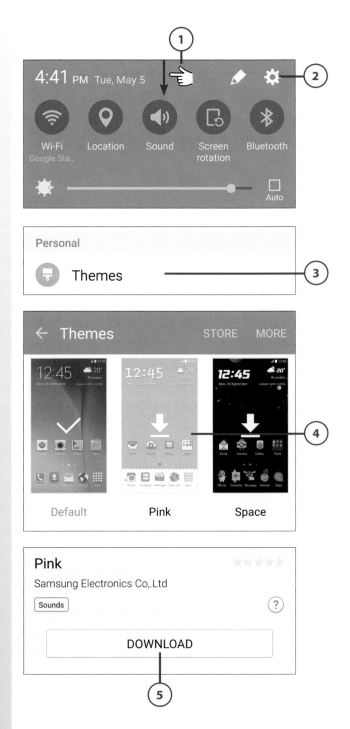

(6) When prompted, tap Accept and Download.

(7) Samsung now downloads them. Tap Apply.

(8) When prompted, tap Apply to close all open apps and apply the new theme *or…*

(9) Additional themes are available in the Samsung Theme Store. To view these themes, tap Store on the Themes screen.

Pink

Pink does not require any special access permissions.

CANCEL

ACCEPT AND DOWNLOAD——(6)

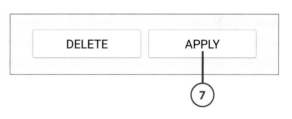

DELETE   APPLY

(7)

Pink

Applying this theme will close all apps and unsaved data will be lost.

CANCEL   APPLY——(8)

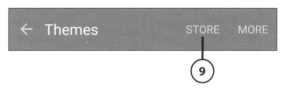

← Themes   STORE   MORE

(9)

10 Scroll through to find the theme you want and then tap it.

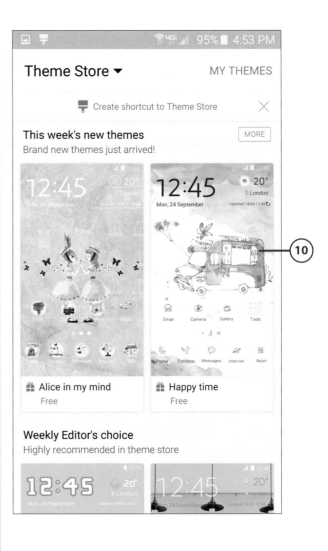

(11) Repeat steps 5 through 8 to download and install the theme.

(12) To return to your phone's default theme, return to the Themes screen and tap Default.

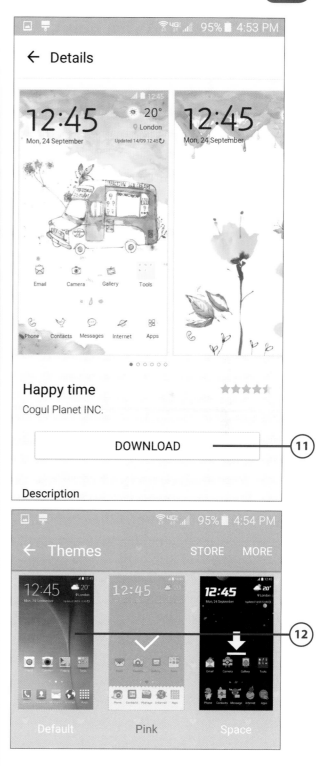

(13) Tap Apply. This closes all open apps and reinstalls the original theme.

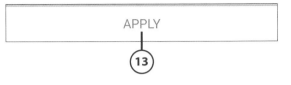

Personalizing Screen Settings

There are a number of other screen settings you can configure that help to personalize your user experience.

Screen Mode Options

There are ways to fine tune the way colors appear on your phone's screen. The Samsung S6 offers four different screen modes, each of which optimizes the color range, saturation, and sharpness of your screen in different ways, as explained in the following table:

Screen Mode	Description
Adaptive Display	Dynamically adjusts images and videos depending on content. Provides higher color saturation than other modes. (This is the default mode.)
AMOLED Cinema	Optimizes display for movie playback.
AMOLED Photo	Optimizes display for photographic images. Provides calibration to the Adobe RGB standard, used in Photoshop and similar photo-editing applications.
Basic	Provides the most technically accurate color rendition—although colors may look less vivid than in other modes.

Which mode should you use? For the most accurate color rendition, Basic mode is best. If you prefer more vivid colors, however, you may like the Adaptive Display mode. For viewing movies on your phone, the AMOLED Cinema mode provides good results. And if you use your phone for editing digital photos, you'll get the best results from the AMOLED Photo mode. It all depends on what you want.

Set the Screen Mode

You set your desired screen mode from the Display and Wallpaper section of the Settings screen.

1. Swipe down from the top of the screen to display the notification panel.

2. Tap Settings to display the Settings screen

3. Scroll to the Device section and tap Display and Wallpaper.

4. Tap Screen Mode to display the Screen Mode screen.

5. Tap the desired screen mode. The preview picture at the top of the page changes to reflect the selected mode.

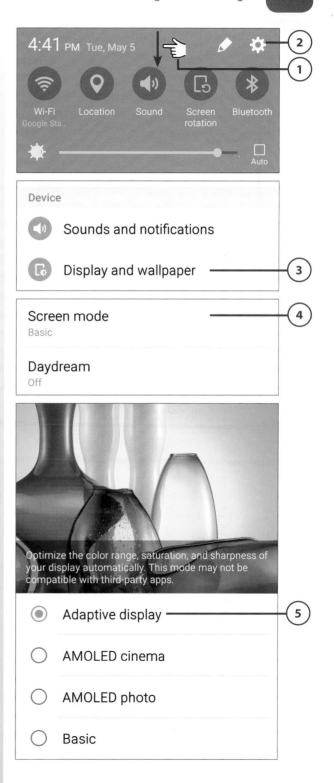

Set Screen Timeout

By default, the screen on your new smartphone turns itself off (and the phone goes into lock mode) if you haven't done anything in 30 seconds. Some people find this 30-second time-out too limiting, and want to extend the amount of time the screen stays lit.

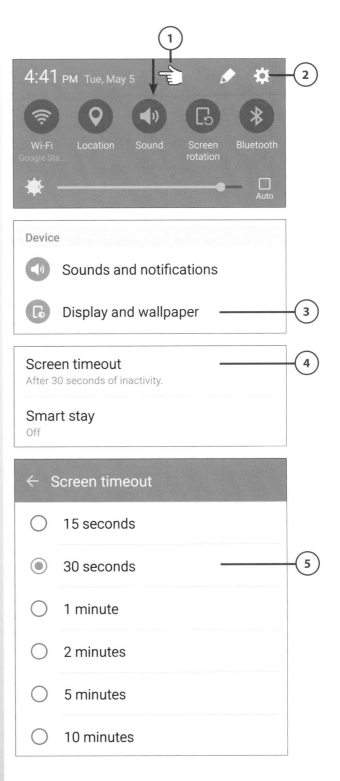

(1) Swipe down from the top of the screen to display the notification panel.

(2) Tap Settings to display the Settings screen.

(3) Scroll to the Device section and tap Display and Wallpaper.

(4) Tap Screen Timeout to display the Screen Timeout screen.

(5) Select a new timeout value, from 15 seconds to 10 minutes.

Timeout and Battery Life

Leaving the screen lit for extended periods of time when you're not using the phone drains your phone's battery. Choose a shorter timeout value to con-serve battery life.

Configure Smart Stay

Another way to keep the screen lit when you're using the phone is to enable the Smart Stay feature. Smart Stay prevents your phone from turning off the display as long as you're still looking at it. (It's a great feature if you use your phone to read eBooks or other onscreen content that might not require you to interact with the phone otherwise; it works by using the phone's front camera to detect your face.)

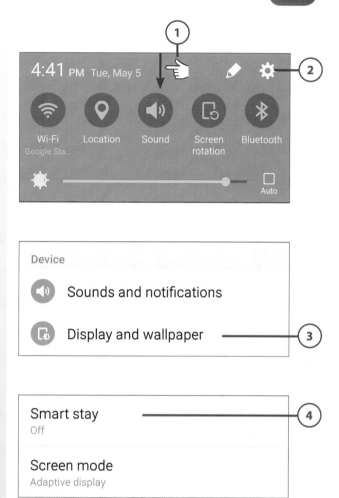

(1) Swipe down from the top of the screen to display the notification panel.

(2) Tap Settings to display the Settings screen.

(3) Scroll to the Device section and tap Display and Wallpaper.

(4) Tap Smart Stay to display the Smart Stay screen.

(5) Tap On the switch at the top of the screen.

Stay Smart?

Many people find the Smart Stay function to be less than useful, as it also tends to shut off the display when you glance away from the phone. It also has problems when the phone is placed on a flat surface. For that reason, experiment with Smart Stay before you decide to use it full time.

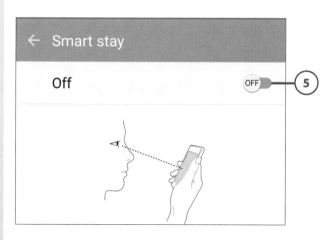

Display a Screen Saver While Charging

By default, your phone's screen turns off when you're not using it—even if the phone is plugged in and charging. If you'd rather the phone display a screensaver when charging, activate Daydream mode.

1. Swipe down from the top of the screen to display the notification panel.

2. Tap Settings to display the Settings screen.

3. Scroll to the Device section and tap Display and Wallpaper.

4. Tap Daydream to display the Daydream screen.

5. Tap On the switch at the top of the screen.

6. Tap the screensaver you want to display—Colors, Google Photos, Photo Frame, or Photo Table.

Photo Screensavers

For the three photo screensavers, you can select from where the phone picks the photos to display. Just tap the Settings (gear) icon for that screensaver, and make a selection.

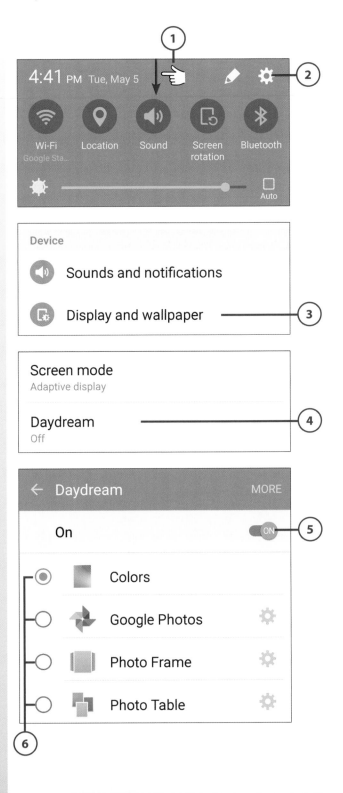

Personalizing Sounds and Notifications

Your Galaxy S6 phone can tell you a lot about what's going on. You can opt to be notified when you receive a new message or voice mail, when the phone requires some interaction from you, or when something interesting happens in a particular app.

How you choose to be notified is up to you. You can have the phone make a sound, vibrate, or display notifications on the Lock screen.

Configure Sounds and Ringtones

You can personalize your phone by choosing which sounds play for specific events:

(1) Swipe down from the top of the screen to display the notification panel.

(2) Tap Settings to display the Settings screen.

(3) Scroll to the Device section and tap Sounds and Notifications.

(4) Tap Ringtones and Sounds.

(5) To select a ringtone for when you receive incoming phone calls, tap Ringtone.

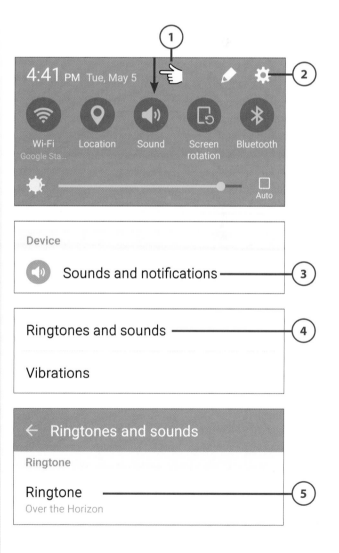

6 Tap to select the ringtone you want. When you tap a ringtone, you hear a preview of that sound.

7 Tap the back arrow at the top of the screen to return to the Ringtones and Sounds screen.

8 To change the sound that plays when you receive a notification, tap Default Notification Sound.

9 Tap to select the sound you want.

10 Tap the back arrow at the top of the screen to return to the Ringtones and Sounds screen.

11 Tap Messages to turn on or off message notifications.

7

← Ringtone

○ Ocean Voyage

○ On the Stage

○ One Step Forward

◉ Over the Horizon ——— **6**

Default notification sound ——— **8**
Verizon Alert

Messages

10

← Default notification sound

○ Peanut

○ Postman

○ Pure Bell ——— **9**

○ Run

Messages ——— **11**

Calendar

(12) By default, you receive notification of messages on your phone. To turn off message notifications, tap Off the switch at the top of the screen.

(13) Tap Notification Sound and make a selection to change the sound you hear when you receive a message notification.

(14) By default, your phone also vibrates when you receive a message. To turn off this vibration, tap "Off" the Vibrate switch.

(15) Tap the back arrow at the top of the screen to return to the Ringtones and Sounds screen.

(16) Tap Calendar to configure notifications about events on your calendar.

(17) By default, you receive notification about upcoming calendar events. To turn off these notifications, tap "Off" the switch at the top of the screen.

(18) Tap Notification Sound and make a selection to change the sound you hear when you receive a calendar notification.

(19) By default, your phone also vibrates when it displays a calendar notification. To turn off this vibration, tap "Off" the Vibration switch.

(20) Tap the back arrow at the top of the screen to return to the Ringtones and Sounds screen.

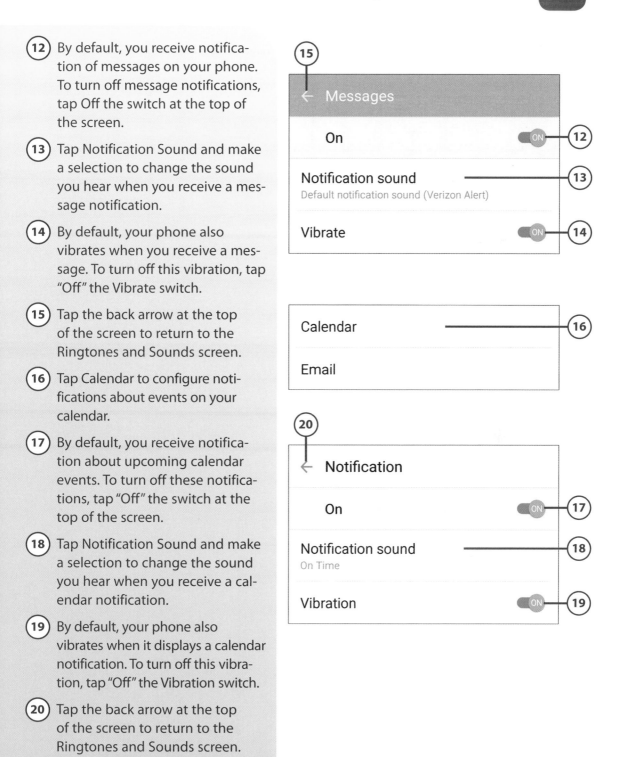

(15)

← Messages

On   ON   (12)

Notification sound   (13)
Default notification sound (Verizon Alert)

Vibrate   ON   (14)

Calendar   (16)

Email

(20)

← Notification

On   ON   (17)

Notification sound   (18)
On Time

Vibration   ON   (19)

(21) Tap Email to configure the notifications displayed when you receive email messages.

(22) If you've set up one or more email accounts on your phone, you have the option of receiving notifications from those accounts. By default, you receive notifications when you receive email from designated priority senders. To turn off these notifications, tap Priority Senders then tap Off. (You can also turn on or off notification vibrations and change the notification sound.)

(23) You also, by default, receive notifications about messages from entire email accounts. Configure notifications for these accounts by tapping the name of the account and then proceeding from there.

(24) Tap the back arrow at the top of the screen to return to the Ringtones and Sounds screen.

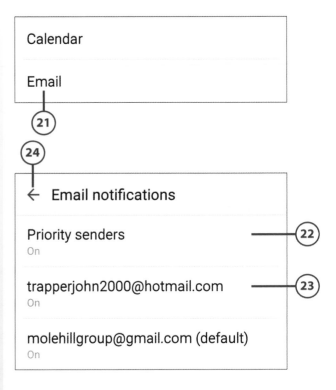

Email Accounts

Learn more about setting up email accounts in Chapter 10, "Sending and Receiving Email."

25 Tap Off the switch in the Touch Sounds section to turn off the sounds your phone makes when you tap the touchscreen.

26 Tap Off the switch in the Dialing Keyboard Tone section to turn off the sounds your phone makes when you tap the keypad in the Phone app.

27 Tap Off the switch in the Screen Lock Sounds section to turn off the sounds your phone makes when you lock and unlock the screen.

28 Tap Emergency Tone and select from Alert, Vibrate, or Silent to change the sound your phone makes in emergency situations.

29 Tap Off the switch in the Keyboard Sound section to turn off the sounds your phone makes when you tap the onscreen keyboard.

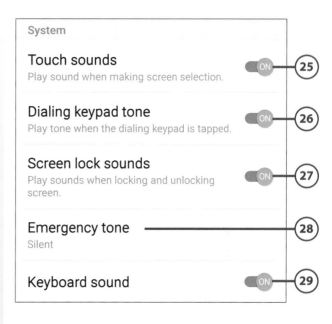

Configure Vibrations

You can also configure when and how your phone vibrates.

1 Swipe down from the top of the screen to display the notification panel.

2 Tap Settings to display the Settings screen.

3 Scroll to the Device section and tap Sounds and Notifications.

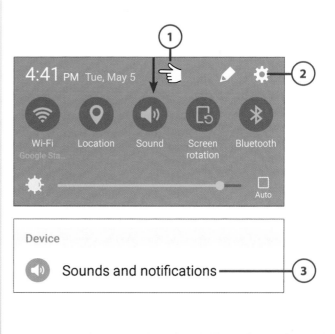

4 Tap Vibrations to display the Vibrations screen.

5 Tap Vibration Intensity to change the intensity of the phone's vibrations.

6 Adjust the sliders to the right (stronger vibration) or left (weaker vibration) for incoming calls, notifications, or overall vibration feedback.

7 Tap the back arrow at the top of the screen to return to the Vibrations screen.

8 Tap Vibration Pattern to change the pattern of the vibration.

Vibrations ——— **4**

Sound quality and effects
Turn on sound effects and set Adapt sound settings.

← Vibrations

Vibration intensity ——— **5**

7

← Vibration intensity

Incoming call

Notifications ——— **6**

Vibration feedback

Vibration pattern ——— **8**
Basic call

Vibrate when ringing OFF

9 Tap the vibration pattern you want—Heartbeat, Ticktock, and so forth. When you select a pattern, you feel a preview of that vibration.

10 Tap the back arrow at the top of the screen to return to the Vibrations screen.

11 Tap On the Vibrate When Ringing switch to feel vibrations when the phone rings.

12 By default, the phone vibrates slightly when you tap certain onscreen "soft keys." To turn off these vibrations, tap Off the Vibration Feedback switch.

13 Tap On the Keyboard Vibration switch to feel vibrations when you tap the onscreen keyboard.

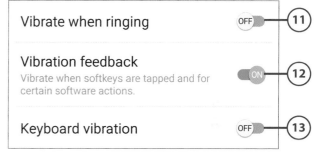

Configure Notifications

Your Galaxy S6 displays a lot of notifications. Fortunately, you have some control over the notifications you receive.

1 Swipe down from the top of the screen to display the notification panel.

2 Tap Settings to display the Settings screen.

3 Scroll to the Device section and tap Sounds and Notifications.

4 Tap Do Not Disturb to activate your phone's Do Not Disturb mode, which silences all calls and alerts.

5 Tap On the switch at the top of the Do Not Disturb screen.

6 Tap Allow Exceptions to set exceptions to the rule by selecting what things you want to be disturbed by.

7 Tap On the Set Schedule switch and then configure when you want your quiet period to start and stop if you want to activate Do Not Disturb mode according to a preset schedule.

8 Tap the back arrow at the top of the screen to return to the Sounds and Notifications screen.

9 By default, notifications are displayed on the Lock screen. To hide these notifications, tap Notifications On Lock Screen and then tap Do Not Show Notifications.

10 Tap App Notifications to allow or block notifications from individual apps. You see a list of all the apps installed on your phone.

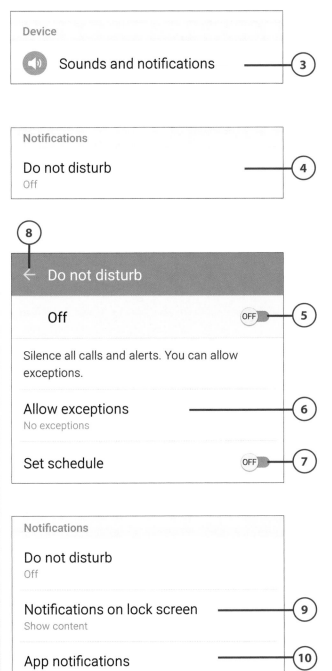

Device

Sounds and notifications — **3**

Notifications

Do not disturb — **4**
Off

8

← Do not disturb

Off   OFF — **5**

Silence all calls and alerts. You can allow exceptions.

Allow exceptions — **6**
No exceptions

Set schedule   OFF — **7**

Notifications

Do not disturb
Off

Notifications on lock screen — **9**
Show content

App notifications — **10**
Allow or block notifications from individual apps.

11 Tap the app you want to configure.

12 Tap On the Block Notifications switch to block all notifications from this app. Tap this switch Off to receive notifications.

13 For some apps, you can opt to show notifications at the top of the notification panel and while Do Not Disturb mode is on. To make notifications from this app a priority, tap On the Set as Priority switch.

14 Tap the back arrow at the top of the screen to return to the App Notifications screen, then again to return to the Sounds and Notifications screen.

15 By default, the LED indicator on the front of your phone lights when charging or when you've received incoming messages or notifications. To turn off this LED light, tap Off the LED Indicator switch.

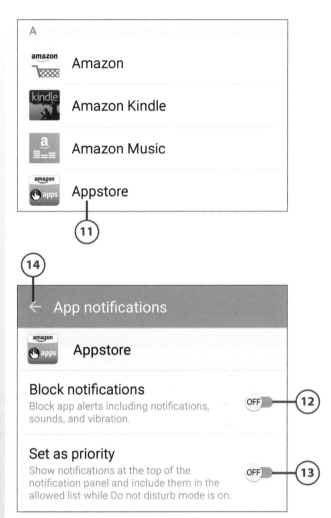

In this chapter, you explore how to configure your phone's accessibility options—and make it easier to use. Topics include the following:

→ Working with Easy Mode
→ Changing Screen Fonts and Sizes
→ Using Voice Feedback
→ Configuring Visibility Options
→ Configuring Hearing Options
→ Configuring Dexterity and Interaction Options
→ Working with the Assistant Menu

Making the Galaxy S6 More Accessible

Let's face it. As we get older, it often becomes more difficult to read fine print and sometimes to perform fine motor functions. And your phone packs a lot of things into its relatively small package. The result is that we sometimes have trouble seeing what's onscreen, or tapping where we need to tap.

Fortunately, there are several settings on the Galaxy S6/S6 Edge that can make life easier for us. These include accessibility options as well as a special Easy Mode that simplifies the phone's operation.

Working with Easy Mode

Today's smartphones can do so many things that it's easy to get confused. With so many options available, just what things should you tap—and which should you ignore?

If you have difficulty operating your phone, or if you find that the default screen icons are just too small to see or use comfortably, consider switching to Easy Mode. This mode presents a different screen layout and experience than the default mode.

Switch to Easy Mode

You can easily switch back and forth between Easy Mode and your phone's default mode.

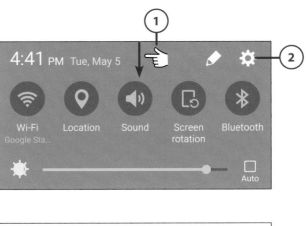

1. Swipe down from the top of the screen to display the notification panel.

2. Tap Settings to display the Settings screen.

3. Scroll to the Personal section and tap Easy Mode.

4. Tap to select Easy Mode.

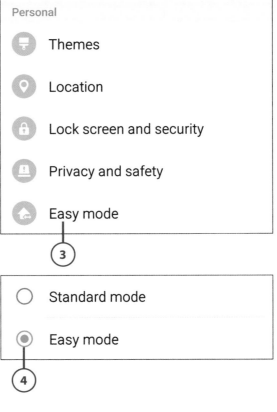

(5) Scroll to the Easy Applications section and tap On each of the apps you want to display in Easy Mode. You can choose to display the Camera, Email, Gallery, Messages, Music, My Files, Phone, Calendar, and Video apps. Select only those you think you'll use regularly.

(6) Tap Done. Your phone resets itself in Easy Mode.

Back to Normal

To switch back to standard mode, select Settings, Easy Mode and then tap to select Standard Mode.

CANCEL   DONE

Easy applications

Camera   ON

Email   ON

Gallery   ON

Messages   ON

Music   ON

My Files   ON

Phone   ON

Calendar   ON

Video   ON

Use Easy Mode

Easy Mode displays fewer icons per screen, but the icons are larger. You see icons only for those apps you selected during the configuration process. In addition, all the onscreen text is larger, which makes it easier to see for anyone with vision difficulties.

(1) Swipe left or right to view additional screens.

(2) Tap any icon to launch that application.

(3) To remove an application from the screen, tap Edit.

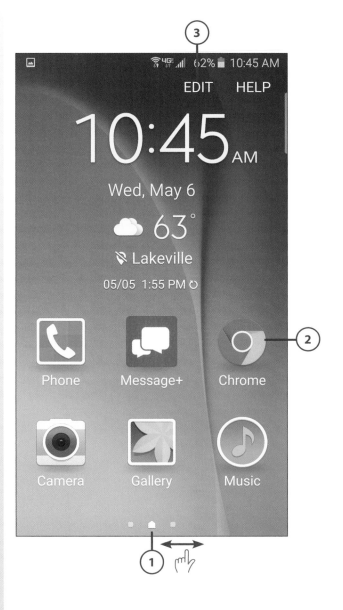

4 Tap the minus sign to hide that app from the Easy Mode screen.

5 Tap Done when you're done hiding icons.

6 To view all the apps installed on your phone, even if they're hidden in Easy Mode, tap More Apps.

7 To add the icon for another app to the Easy Mode screen, tap one of the + icons.

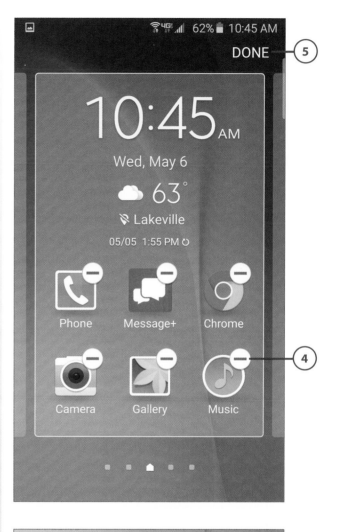

(8) Tap the app you want to add and an icon for that app is added to the Easy Mode screen.

Changing Screen Fonts and Sizes

If you find the onscreen text on your Galaxy S6 or S6 Edge difficult to read, you can change it. Samsung enables you to change both the font and the font size displayed for icon labels, screen headings, and the like.

Select Screen Fonts and Sizes

(1) Swipe down from the top of the screen to display the notification panel.

(2) Tap Settings to display the Settings screen.

(3) Scroll to the Device section and tap Display and Wallpaper.

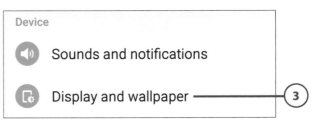

(**4**) Tap Font.

(**5**) Drag the Font Size slider to the left (smaller) or right (larger) to change the font size.

(**6**) Tap the name of a font to switch to that font.

(**7**) Tap Default to return to Samsung's default font.

(**8**) Tap Done.

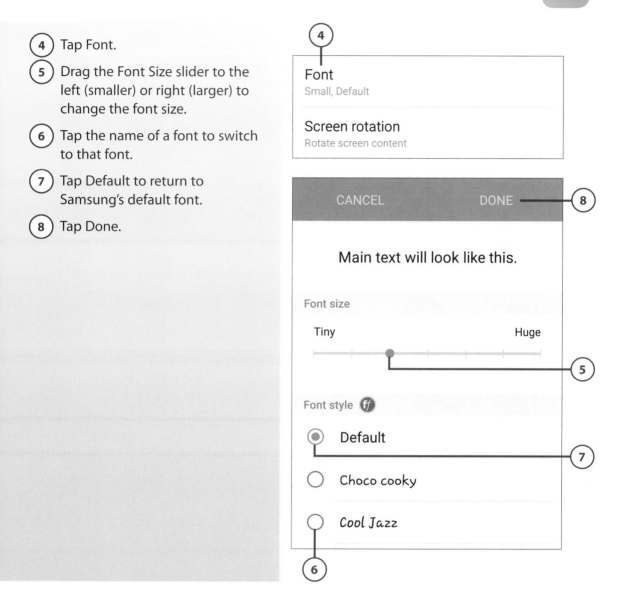

Using Voice Feedback

If you have trouble seeing what's on the screen, you can enable Galaxy TalkBack, which provides voice feedback when you're using your phone.

Enable Galaxy TalkBack

The Galaxy TalkBack feature reads aloud whatever is selected on the Galaxy S6 screen. When activated, your phone reads whatever is under your finger when you tap.

1. Swipe down from the top of the screen to display the notification panel.

2. Tap Settings to display the Settings screen.

3. Scroll to the System section and tap Accessibility.

4. Tap Vision to display the Vision screen.

5. Tap Galaxy TalkBack.

6. Tap On the switch at the top of the screen.

7. Tap Turn On when you're prompted to use Galaxy TalkBack.

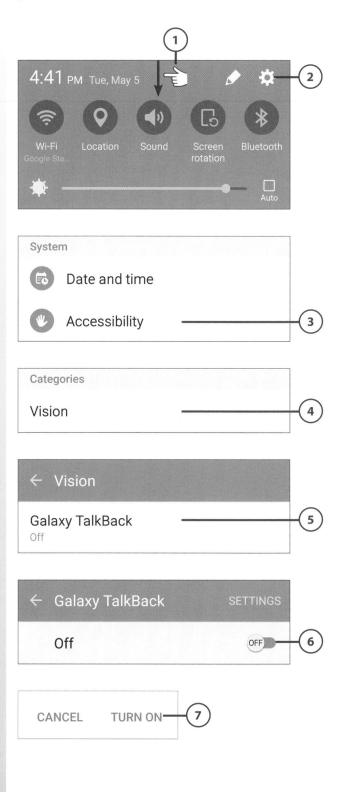

Use Galaxy TalkBack

With TalkBack activated, any item you tap onscreen generates a voice telling you what that item is—and, in some instances, information about that item. For example, if you tap the Email icon when you have new messages waiting, TalkBack tells you how many new messages you have. You can also tap an open item to have TalkBack read the content of a message or document.

Because tapping an item tells you about it, with TalkBack activated you have to double-tap apps to open them or perform specific operations. In fact, most touch gestures change when you're using TalkBack, as indicated in the following table.

Gesture	Action
Tap	Reads aloud the item under your finger.
Double-tap	Opens the selected item.
Double-tap and hold	Moves an item across the screen or accesses an available option.
Swipe left	Moves to previous item.
Swipe right	Moves to next item.
Swipe up or down	Uses the most recent menu item or changes its settings. In text selection mode, moves the cursor backward or forward to select text.
Swipe left then right (in one motion)	Scrolls up the screen.
Swipe right then left (in one motion)	Scrolls down the screen.
Swipe up then down (in one motion)	Move to the first item on the screen.
Swipe down then up (in one motion)	Move to the last item on the screen.

Explore the Screen

To explore the items on the screen in TalkBack mode, simply place your finger on the screen and then move it around.

Configuring Visibility Options

In addition to Galaxy TalkBack, there are several other options you can configure to make it easier to operate your phone if you have vision problems. These are detailed in the following table.

Option	Description
Voice Label	Record voice labels you can place on various items around your house, and have your phone read them back to you.
Font Size	Changes the size of onscreen fonts from Tiny to Huge.
Magnification Gestures	Zooms into or out of areas of the screen when you triple-tap the screen.
Magnifier Window	Displays a small window that magnifies the selected area of the screen. (Tap and drag to move the magnification window around the screen.)
Grayscale	Changes the phone's display from color to grayscale.
Negative Colors	Reverses the onscreen colors. (White background changes to black; black text changes to white.)
Color Adjustment	Enables adjustment of onscreen colors for better viewing.
Accessibility Shortcut	Displays accessibility options when you hold down the Power key or tap and hold the screen with two fingers.
Text-to-Speech Options	Adjusts the speed of Samsung's text-to-speech engine.

Voice Label

The Voice Label feature works in conjunction with special labels you can purchase from Samsung. You use your phone to record your voice saying what the label is affixed to; then you place the label on that item. Later, you can hover your phone over the item and its label to use your phone's NFC technology to "read" the label to you. It's a great way for people with vision impairment to better get around—and locate items in—their homes.

Enable Visibility Options

All visibility options are accessed via the Visibility screen.

(**1**) Swipe down from the top of the screen to display the notification panel.

(**2**) Tap Settings to display the Settings screen.

(**3**) Scroll to the System section and tap Accessibility.

(**4**) Tap Vision to display the Vision screen.

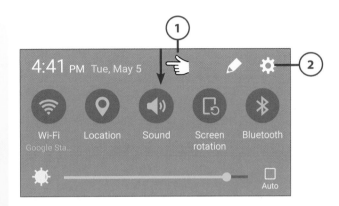

System

Date and time

Accessibility

Categories

Vision

⑤ Enable those options you want to use.

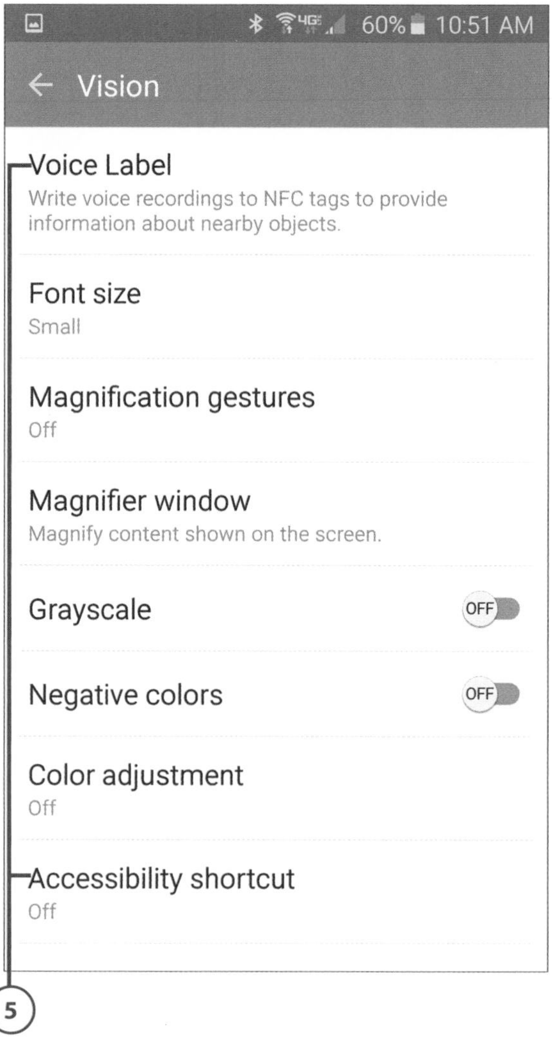

⑤

> | ▣ | ✳ 📶 4G 📶 60% 🔋 10:51 AM |
> |---|---|

← **Vision**

Voice Label
Write voice recordings to NFC tags to provide information about nearby objects.

Font size
Small

Magnification gestures
Off

Magnifier window
Magnify content shown on the screen.

Grayscale `OFF`

Negative colors `OFF`

Color adjustment
Off

Accessibility shortcut
Off

Configuring Hearing Options

Your Samsung S6 or S6 Edge offers several options of use if you have impaired hearing. These are detailed in the following table.

Option	Description
Sound Detectors	Vibrates the phone when a baby cries or the doorbell rings.
Flash Notification	Flashes the camera's LED flash when you receive notifications or alarms.
Turn Off All Sounds	Turns off all of the phone's sounds.
Hearing Aids	Adjusts the phone's sound quality to work better with hearing aids.
Samsung Subtitles	Enables and configures Samsung's subtitle function.
Google Subtitles	Enables and configures Google's subtitle function, built into the Android operating system.
Left and Right Sound Balance	Adjusts the left and right audio balance.
Mono Audio	Switch from stereo to mono audio for when you are using a single earphone.
Auto Haptic	Vibrates the phone in time when you're listening to music, watching videos, or playing games.

Enable Hearing Options

All hearing options are configured on the Hearing screen.

1. Swipe down from the top of the screen to display the notification panel.

2. Tap Settings to display the Settings screen.

3. Scroll to the System section and tap Accessibility.

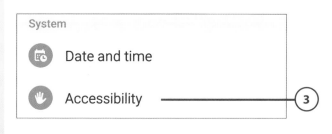

(4) Tap Hearing to display the Hearing screen.

(5) Tap to enable or configure the options you want.

Categories

Vision

Hearing ——————————— (4)

⊡   ✳ 📶 4G 📶 60% ▪ 10:52 AM

← Hearing

Sound detectors
Receive alerts when the phone detects a baby crying or the doorbell.

Flash notification
Set your phone to flash the camera light when you receive notifications or when alarms sound. Turn the phone over to stop the flashing.   `OFF`

Turn off all sounds   `OFF`

Hearing aids
Improve the sound quality of your phone for use with hearing aids.   `OFF`

Samsung subtitles (CC)
Off

Google subtitles (CC)
Off

Left and right sound balance
Adjust the left and right sound balance for listening to media players via earphones.

(5)

Configuring Dexterity and Interaction Options

Your phone also contains a number of options that make it easier to use if you have any physical impairments. These are detailed in the following table.

Option	Description
Universal Switch	Create custom switches to interact with your phone and select onscreen items.
Assistant Menu	Display an Assistant icon that provides one-handed access to important system operations. (Discussed later in this chapter.)
Gesture Wake Up	Enables you to wake up your phone by moving your hand above the screen.
Touch and Hold Delay	Adjusts the delay for when you touch and hold the screen.
Interaction Control	Customizes the way you interact with apps and settings, by blocking or unblocking areas of the screen, turning off auto rotate, and only showing app notifications on the notification panel and status bar.

Enable Dexterity and Interaction Options

All of these options are enabled on the Dexterity and Interaction screen.

1. Swipe down from the top of the screen to display the notification panel.

2. Tap Settings to display the Settings screen.

3. Scroll to the System section and tap Accessibility.

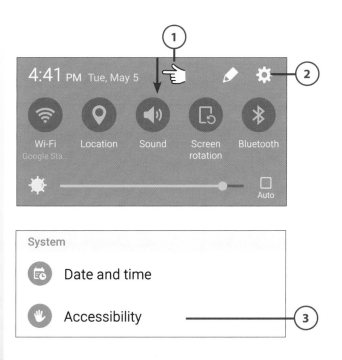

(**4**) Tap Dexterity and Interaction to display the Dexterity and Interaction screen.

(**5**) Tap to enable or configure the options you want.

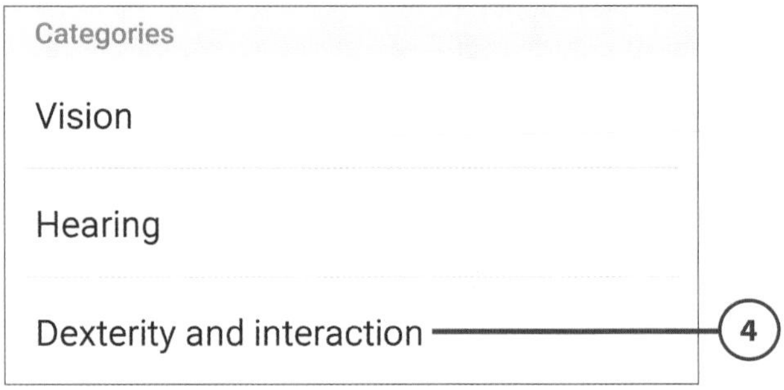

Categories

Vision

Hearing

Dexterity and interaction —————————(**4**)

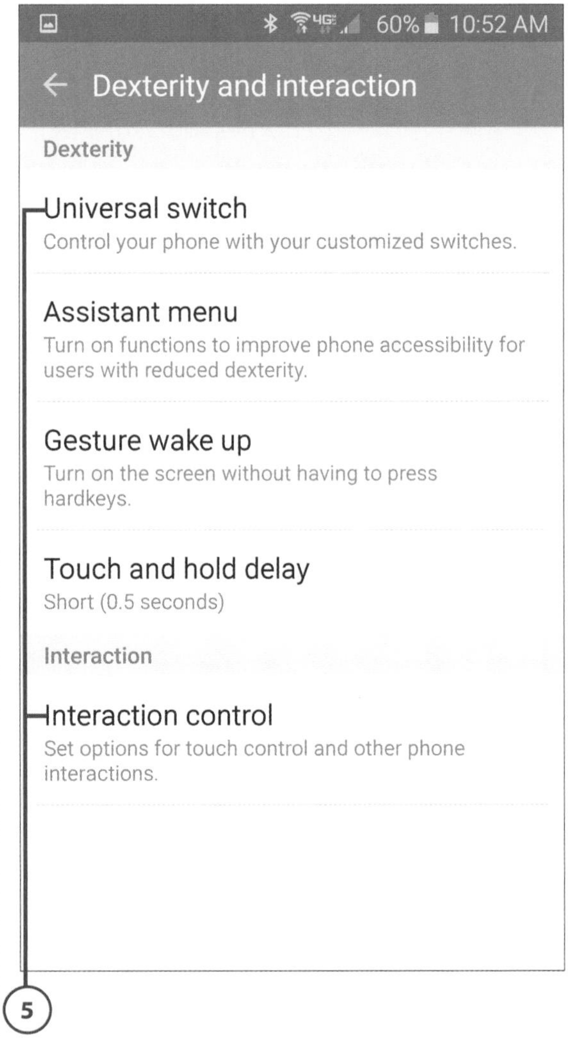

★ 📶 4G 🔋 60% 📶 10:52 AM

← Dexterity and interaction

Dexterity

Universal switch
Control your phone with your customized switches.

Assistant menu
Turn on functions to improve phone accessibility for users with reduced dexterity.

Gesture wake up
Turn on the screen without having to press hardkeys.

Touch and hold delay
Short (0.5 seconds)

Interaction

Interaction control
Set options for touch control and other phone interactions.

(**5**)

Working with the Assistant Menu

Your Samsung S6 or S6 Edge can be configured to display an Assistant menu, in the form of a round button that floats at the bottom right of every screen. When tapped, this button displays large icon shortcuts to key phone operations. The Assistant menu enables you to operate your phone with one hand.

Enable the Assistant Menu

The Assistant menu is disabled by default. When you enable the menu, there are several settings you can configure.

(1) Swipe down from the top of the screen to display the notification panel.

(2) Tap Settings to display the Settings screen.

(3) Scroll to the System section and tap Accessibility.

(4) Tap Dexterity and Interaction to display the Dexterity and Interaction screen.

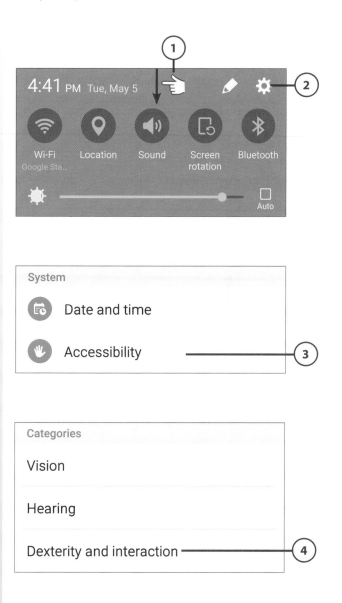

5 Tap Assistant Menu to display the Assistant Menu screen.

6 Tap On the switch at the top of the screen.

7 By default, the Assistant icon appears at the bottom right of the screen. To switch it to the left side, tap Dominant Hand and then select Left.

8 To change or rearrange the items on the Assistant menu, tap Edit and then make your changes.

9 To include contextual menu options for selected applications in the Assistant menu, tap Assistant Plus and then toggle on those apps you want.

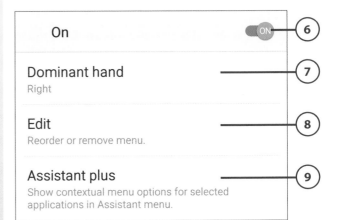

Dexterity

Universal switch
Control your phone with your customized switches.

Assistant menu ——————— **5**
Turn on functions to improve phone accessibility for users with reduced dexterity.

On   ON **6**

Dominant hand ——————— **7**
Right

Edit ——————— **8**
Reorder or remove menu.

Assistant plus ——————— **9**
Show contextual menu options for selected applications in Assistant menu.

Use the Assistant Menu

When activated, the Assistant icon appears at one side at the bottom of your phone's screen.

1 Tap the Assistant icon to display the Assistant panel.

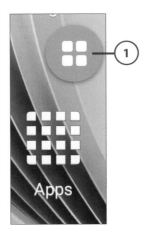

Apps

2 Scroll up or down to see more items.

3 Tap to launch an item.

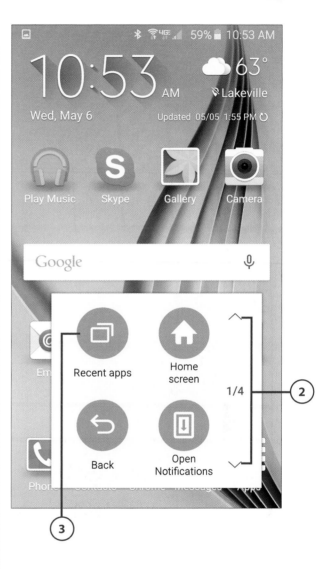

This chapter shows you how to connect your Samsung smartphone to the Internet. Topics include the following:

→ How Your Galaxy S6 Connects
→ Connecting to the Internet via Wi-Fi
→ Connecting to the Internet via Cellular
→ Monitoring and Managing Your Data Usage
→ Turning Your Phone Into a Mobile Hotspot

5

Connecting to the Internet (and Other Networks)

Without an Internet connection, your smartphone is just an expensive phone. You need to connect to the Internet to play streaming music and videos, browse Facebook and other social networks, send and receive email, participate in video chats, and use many apps and games.

How Your Galaxy S6 Connects

Your Samsung S6 or S6 Edge can connect to the Internet in two different ways. If there's a Wi-Fi network or hotspot handy, it can connect via Wi-Fi. If there's no Wi-Fi network nearby (such as when you're driving down the interstate), it can connect to the Internet via the same cellular network you use for voice calls and text messages.

By default, your phone attempts to connect via Wi-Fi if a Wi-Fi network or hotspot is available; that's because you incur no data charges when using Wi-Fi. If there's no Wi-Fi connection, your phone uses your cellular network to connect to the Internet—but it switches back to Wi-Fi when a network becomes available.

Cellular Networks

Your phone is always connected to your carrier's cellular network, which handles all your voice calls and text messages—the one you pay AT&T, Sprint, T-Mobile, Verizon, or other carrier each month to use.

Chances are that your carrier charges you in two or more stages. First, you pay for the basic voice service, typically a flat dollar amount per month. Some carriers include text messaging in this fee; others charge separately for a limited or unlimited number of texts.

Then there's what your carrier calls the data plan. This refers to digital data downloaded from the Internet to your phone via the cellular network. (It also includes data you upload to the Internet, in the form of email messages and files you send.)

Most U.S. carriers sell you a certain amount of data (measured in gigabytes, or GB) per month, for a set fee. If you use more than the set amount of data, you're charged extra—sometimes a lot extra. For this reason, you want to limit the amount of Internet usage over your cellular network. When given the choice, you should always opt to connect to the Internet over Wi-Fi instead of cellular, because your phone carrier doesn't have anything to do with what you do when you're connected to Wi-Fi.

Wi-Fi Networks

A Wi-Fi network is much different from a cellular network. Wi-Fi is a type of wireless protocol designed to carry digital data only, not voice calls, and most Wi-Fi networks operate over a limited distance. Thus you might have a Wi-Fi network that covers all the rooms in your house, but doesn't stretch to your neighbor's house. In a larger building, such as a hotel or office building, the network size is bigger thanks to the use of multiple wireless routers that are linked together.

Wi-Fi

Wi-Fi (short for *Wireless Fidelity*) is the consumer-friendly name for the IEEE 802.11 wireless networking standard. Most of today's wireless networks are Wi-Fi networks and use Wi-Fi-certified products.

Wi-Fi networks use a hub-and-spoke configuration where each Wi-Fi-enabled device connects to a central hub or router. Devices do not connect directly to each other; the signal from a given device goes to the router first, and is then routed to other connected devices.

The Wi-Fi router is also connected to the Internet, and routes the Internet signal to all devices connected to the network. So when your smartphone connects to the Internet over your home network, it's actually connecting to your Wi-Fi router first, which in turn connects to the Internet.

(Public Wi-Fi hotspots work the same way. Your phone connects to the hotspot's router and the router connects to the Internet.)

The nice thing about connecting to the Internet via Wi-Fi (instead of cellular) is you don't pay for the data transmitted. Many public Wi-Fi hotspots, like you find at Starbucks and McDonald's, are free. Those that do charge (like you find at some hotels) only charge you a flat rate, no matter how much data you use. And, of course, it doesn't cost anything to connect to your home Wi-Fi network—save for the monthly bill you pay to your Internet service provider.

Connecting to the Internet via Wi-Fi

If you have a Wi-Fi network or hotspot available, this is how you want to connect to the Internet. This could be the Wi-Fi network in your home or office, or a Wi-Fi hotspot at a local retailer, hotel, or restaurant.

Disable and Re-Enable Wi-Fi

Your phone's Wi-Fi functionality is turned on by default. You can manually turn off Wi-Fi (to conserve battery power) and turn it back on.

(1) Swipe down from the top of the screen to display the Notification panel.

(2) Tap off the Wi-Fi icon. This disables your phone's Wi-Fi functionality. (The icon dims when off, and lights up green when on.)

(3) To re-enable it, tap the Wi-Fi icon.

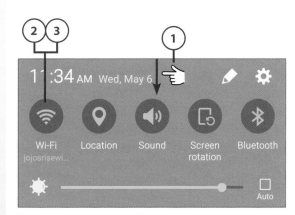

Connect to a New Wi-Fi Network

When your phone is near an active Wi-Fi network or hotspot, you see a "not connected" icon in the status bar. (And if you're on the Lock screen, you see a notification about "Wi-Fi networks available.") You choose which Wi-Fi network to connect to, and then you connect to it.

1. Swipe down from the top of the screen to display the notification panel.

2. Tap the Wi-Fi Networks Available notification *or…*

3. Tap and hold the Wi-Fi icon.

4. You now see the Wi-Fi screen, with available Wi-Fi networks listed in descending order of signal strength. Open networks (those that don't require a password) have a basic icon, whereas private networks that do require a password have a lock on the icon. Tap the network to which you want to connect.

5. If you're connecting to a public network, you may see a panel for that network warning that information sent over this network may be available to others. This is normal with most public hotspots, and nothing to be concerned about. Tap Connect to connect to the network.

Private network

Open (public) network

xfinitywifi

You are connecting to the unsecure network "xfinitywifi". Information sent is not encrypted and may be visible to others. Do you still want to connect?

☐ Show advanced options

CANCEL   CONNECT

6 If you're connecting to a private network, you see a panel for that network and the onscreen keyboard appears. Use the onscreen keyboard to enter the network's password into the Password box. (Tap Show Password if you want to see the actual characters as you type; otherwise, you just see dots.)

7 Tap Connect. You're now connected to the network and can start using the Internet.

jojosrisewine

Password
Enter password ————————————— **6**

☐ Show password

☐ Show advanced options

CANCEL   CONNECT —— **7**

Switching Networks

If multiple Wi-Fi networks are nearby, you may accidentally connect to the wrong one. To switch from one wireless network to another, open the Wi-Fi screen and then tap a different network to connect.

>>>*Go Further*

SIGNING IN

Private Wi-Fi networks are like the one you have in your home. Private networks require you to enter a password (sometimes called an SSID, for Service Set Identifier) to access the network. This password is typically created when you first set up your wireless router, or provided by the network host if you're connecting to an office network.

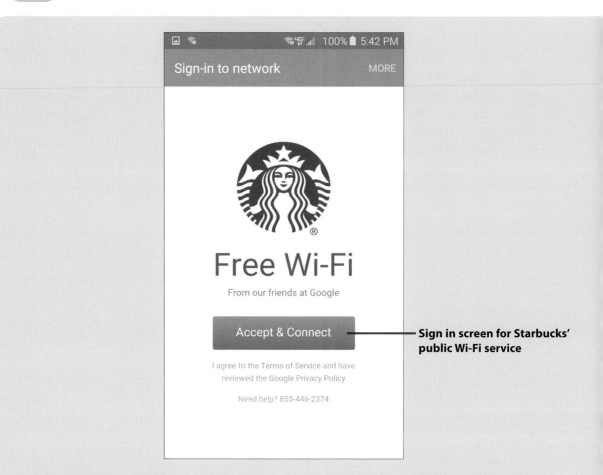

Sign in screen for Starbucks' public Wi-Fi service

Public Wi-Fi networks do not require a password to connect. However, some public hotspots do require you to manually sign in. In some instances, your phone automatically launches the Chrome web browser after you connect to the network, with the host's sign in page displayed. In other cases you have to manually launch the Chrome browser and try to open any web page; the host's sign in page is then displayed instead of the normal web page, and you can sign in from there.

Some sign-in pages ask you to agree to the host's terms of service as to how you'll use the connection. Others just want you to click the "sign in" button. Whatever the case, do what's asked of you so you can sign in and get started on the Internet.

Connect to a Wi-Fi Network You've Used Before

When you're in range of a Wi-Fi network that you've connected to before, there's nothing you have to do. Because your phone remembers the networks you've connected to, your phone automatically connects to this familiar network.

It's Not All Good

Connection Problems

Not all Internet connections are always good. Sometimes the Wi-Fi network or hotspot you connect to has problems, which can keep you from connecting to the Internet.

For example, the Wi-Fi hotspot I use at one of my local coffeehouses has a tendency to go missing every few hours. That is, I'll be connected one minute and the next minute find that I'm not connected—and that the hotspot itself is no longer visible on my phone. Normally I wait a minute or two, the hotspot reappears, and my phone reconnects. The best I can figure is that the coffeehouse's Wi-Fi router has rebooted, for some reason, which kicks everyone using it off until it powers back on.

You can also run into connection problems at home. My editor tells me that her mother's Wi-Fi gateway will sometimes lose its connection to the Internet. Her phone and computer and other devices stay connected to her wireless network, but the network itself is no longer connected to the Internet. In this instance, she has to reboot her gateway/router to re-establish the Internet connection.

If you run into Internet connection problems, and it doesn't fix itself after a few minutes, try turning off your phone's Wi-Fi and then turning it back on. This forces your phone to establish a new connection to the wireless network or hotspot, which often fixes the problem.

Connect Directly to Other Devices with Wi-Fi Direct

Some devices, such as set-top boxes and smart TVs, let you connect to them without first connecting to a central Wi-Fi network. This feature is called Wi-Fi Direct.

1. Swipe down from the top of the screen to display the notification panel.

2. Tap and hold the Wi-Fi icon to display the Wi-Fi page.

3. Tap Wi-Fi Direct. Your phone automatically scans for nearby devices.

4. Tap a device to connect and then follow the onscreen instructions.

>>>Go Further

ACTIVATING AIRPLANE MODE

If you fly, you know the drill about turning off all your devices during takeoff and landing. After you're in the air, most airlines let you (pay to) connect to their in-flight Wi-Fi service. But you can also use your phone during flight with all connectivity turned off. This way you can still listen to downloaded music, watch downloaded videos, or read downloaded eBooks while you're in-flight.

The best and easiest way to do this is to enable your phone's Airplane mode. To switch to Airplane mode, swipe down from the top of the screen and tap Settings. From the Settings screen, tap Airplane Mode, then tap On the switch. This turns off all connectivity for voice calls, texts, and data/Internet. You can turn off Airplane mode when you land to resume normal operation.

Connecting to the Internet via Cellular

Your Samsung smartphone automatically connects to the cellular network of your mobile phone carrier. (When you have a network connection available, of course.) AT&T has its own cellular network, as do Sprint, T-Mobile, Verizon, and other carriers. The networks are not interchangeable; if you're a Verizon user, for example, you can't connect your phone to AT&T's network. (Verizon users can, of course, make phone calls to AT&T subscribers; you just can't connect to their network.)

When you purchased your new Galaxy S6 or S6 Edge, your mobile carrier or retailer programmed your phone to connect to your carrier's network. This involved registering your phone number and other technical stuff. The end result is that you were handed a working phone, capable of making and receiving phone calls right out of the box.

As part of the purchase process, you had to sign up for your mobile service, and probably for some sort of data plan. It's the data plan that lets you connect to the Internet through your mobile carrier. If you didn't sign up for a data plan, you can't connect to the Internet via AT&T or T-Mobile or whomever; instead, you can only connect via Wi-Fi.

While connecting to the Internet via your mobile carrier can be costly (you only pay for a certain amount of data use; anything beyond that costs extra), it's necessary if you want to access the Internet when there are no Wi-Fi networks or hotspots nearby. If you're driving down the interstate in your car, for example, you need to connect to the Internet via your mobile carrier. If you're out in a park or field or in the middle of a lake, far away from any big buildings, you need to connect to the Internet via your mobile carrier. If you're visiting a friend and don't want to or can't connect to their home wireless network, you need to connect to the Internet via your mobile carrier.

The speed of your Internet connection depends on the type of data service offered by your mobile carrier. Older second generation (2G) networks, sometimes called EDGE networks, are extremely slow, much like old-fashioned dial-up phone connections—not nearly fast enough to transmit streaming video or audio. Third-generation (3G) networks are considerably faster, fast enough for streaming audio and video, but they still feel sluggish at times. Newer fourth-generation (4G) networks, sometimes dubbed LTE networks, are much, much faster—ideal for anything you need to stream or send over the Internet. (The following table details typical connection speeds for each type of mobile network.)

Type of Network	Typical Download Speed (in megabits per second)
1G (AMPS)	Up to 14.4 kbps
2G (EDGE)	Up to 0.2 Mbps
3G (HSPA)	Up to 14.4 Mbps
4G (LTE)	100 Mbps to 300 Mbps

Different mobile carriers offer different data networks in different parts of the country. If you live in a big city, chances are your carrier offers 4G coverage. If you're in a smaller town or in the suburbs, you might have 4G coverage or you may be in a 3G zone. If you're out in the sticks, it's possible your carrier only offers 2G networking. Check your carrier's coverage maps to see where you stand.

The type of network you're connected to is displayed in the S6's status bar at the top of the screen. If you see you're connected to a slower 2G network, you might want to refrain from doing any data-intensive tasks, such as watching movies or listening to Pandora. (Personally, I find 2G networks too slow to even download radar weather maps!)

Mobile network type

Mobile network signal strength

You don't have to do anything to connect your phone to your carrier's mobile network; it connects automatically whenever you're in range of a signal. However, your Galaxy S6 is designed by default to use Wi-Fi to connect to the Internet. So if there's a Wi-Fi network nearby your phone attempts to connect to it for Internet usage, even if it's already connect to your mobile carrier for voice calls.

Manually Connect to a Data Network

If, for whatever reason, you want to use your mobile carrier for Internet even when there are Wi-Fi networks available, you have to manually turn off your phone's Wi-Fi.

1. Swipe down from the top of the screen to display the notification panel.

2. Tap off the Wi-Fi icon. Your phone now turns off its Wi-Fi (and thus disconnects from any Wi-Fi networks) and switches to your carrier's mobile data network.

3. To re-enable Wi-Fi, tap on the Wi-Fi icon.

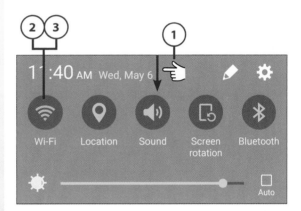

Enable Smart Network Switching

Sometimes you can be connected to a Wi-Fi network that has a poor or unstable connection to the Internet. In this instance, you're better off disconnecting from that Wi-Fi network and using your mobile carrier's data network until the connection improves. You can do this automatically by enabling your phone's smart network switching.

1. Swipe down from the top of the screen to display the notification panel.

2. Tap and hold the Wi-Fi icon. This displays the Wi-Fi screen.

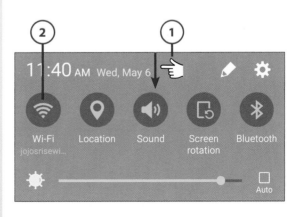

(3) Tap More at the top of the screen.

(4) Tap Smart Network Switch to display the Smart Network Switch panel.

(5) Tap On. Your phone automatically switches to your carrier's data network when it senses a poor Internet connection via Wi-Fi.

← Wi-Fi   Wi-Fi Direct   MORE —(3)

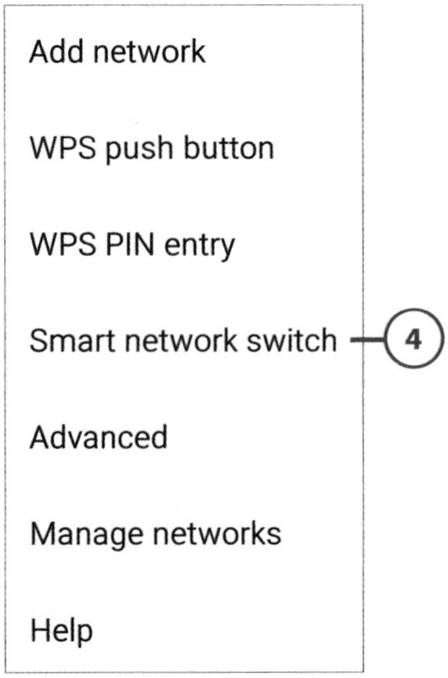

Add network

WPS push button

WPS PIN entry

Smart network switch —(4)

Advanced

Manage networks

Help

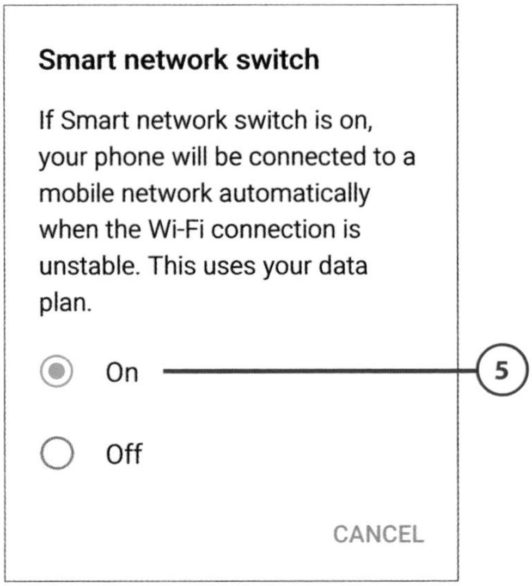

Smart network switch

If Smart network switch is on, your phone will be connected to a mobile network automatically when the Wi-Fi connection is unstable. This uses your data plan.

◉   On —————————(5)

○   Off

CANCEL

Monitoring and Managing Your Data Usage

Given the restrictions most carriers place on their mobile data plans, it pays to keep track of just how much data you're using each month. This way you'll know when you're nearing your plan limits, and can adjust your usage accordingly.

Monitor How Much Data You've Used

Your phone keeps track of how much data you upload and download via your mobile carrier.

(1) Swipe down from the top of the screen to display the notification panel.

(2) Tap Settings to display the Settings page.

(3) Go to the Wireless and Networks section and tap Data Usage.

(4) The graph on this page displays data usage by day. Your total data usage for this month's plan is displayed above the graph.

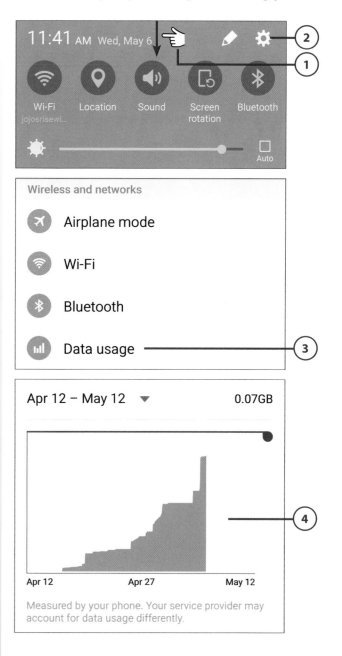

5 Scroll down the screen to see data usage by application. This shows you which apps are using the most data bandwidth.

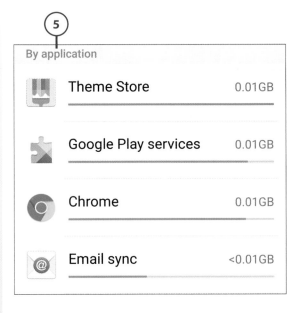

Set Data Usage Alerts

To avoid going over your data plan limits, you might want to set an alert that notifies you when your usage reaches a level you select.

1 Swipe down from the top of the screen to display the notification panel.

2 Tap Settings to display the Settings page.

3 Go to the Wireless and Networks section and tap Data Usage.

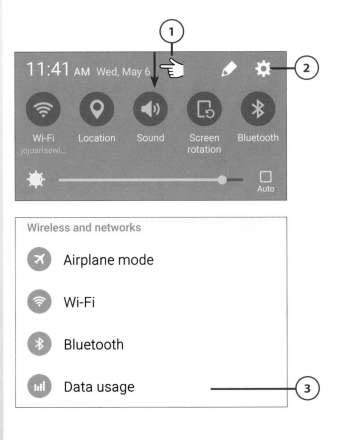

4 Tap On the Alert Me About Data Usage switch.

5 When you see the Data Usage Alert panel, tap OK.

6 Back on the Data Usage screen, tap to drag the usage level line to a specific level. You will now receive an alert when your data usage reaches this level.

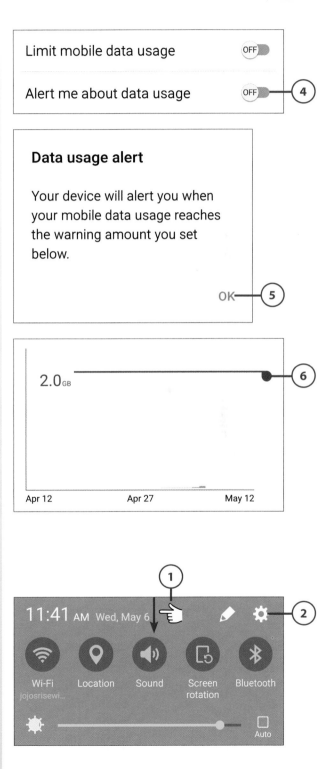

| Limit mobile data usage | OFF |
| Alert me about data usage | OFF — **4** |

Data usage alert

Your device will alert you when your mobile data usage reaches the warning amount you set below.

OK — **5**

2.0 GB — **6**

Apr 12   Apr 27   May 12

Limit Data Usage

If warning you about your usage level isn't enough, you can configure your Galaxy S6 to turn off data usage when you reach your plan's limit. With the Limit Data Usage option turned on, your phone disables mobile data functionality when a preset level (typically the top end of your data usage plan) is reached.

1 Swipe down from the top of the screen to display the notification panel.

2 Tap Settings to display the Settings page.

11:41 AM Wed, May 6 — **1**

2

Wi-Fi   Location   Sound   Screen rotation   Bluetooth

jojosrisewi...

Auto

3 Go to the Wireless and Networks section and tap Data Usage.

4 Tap On the Limit Mobile Data Usage switch.

5 When you see the Data Usage Limit panel, tap OK.

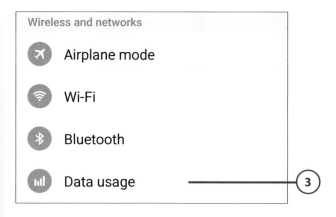

Data usage limit

Your mobile data connection will be turned off when your data usage reaches the limit you selected.

Data usage is measured by your phone. Your carrier may account for usage differently, so consider setting a limit that's a little lower than your data plan.

OK —— **5**

(6) Back on the Data Usage screen, tap to drag the red limit line to a specific level. Your phone's data functionality is disabled when your usage reaches this level.

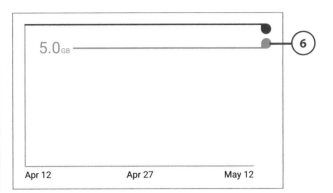

Turning Your Phone into a Mobile Hotspot

Sometimes you're in a location where there is no Wi-Fi available, but you want to connect your computer or tablet to the Internet. Well, if you have your Samsung S6 or S6 Edge with you, and you have a strong connection to your mobile data network, you can connect your computer or tablet to your phone, wirelessly, to share that data connection.

In effect, this turns your phone into a mobile Wi-Fi hotspot. Your phone connects to the Internet via your mobile data network, then your other devices connect to your phone via Wi-Fi.

It's Not All Good

Data Tethering Concerns

To share your phone's data connection, your carrier's data plan needs to include what they call *data tethering*. Some carriers let you do this at no charge, as part of the basic plan; others charge extra for tethering functionality. Make sure you can use tethering on your phone before you try to use this feature.

Also, know that when you use your smartphone as a mobile Wi-Fi hotspot for other devices, you typically end up using a lot of data bandwidth. All that data counts against the limits on your data plan. You should avoid heavy-duty operations with your computer or tablet, such as watching movies or downloading big files, when you're using your phone in this fashion.

Enable a Mobile Hotspot

Before you turn your phone into a mobile hotspot, make sure you have a strong mobile signal. (A 4G connection is preferable to 3G; 2G is probably not usable in this situation.) You can then enable the mobile hotspot function.

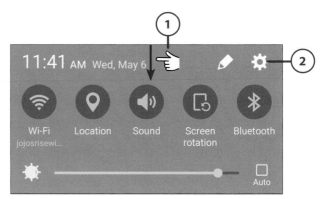

(1) Swipe down from the top of the screen to display the notification panel.

(2) Tap Settings to display the Settings screen.

(3) Go to the Wireless and Networks section and tap More.

(4) Tap Mobile Hotspot to display the Mobile Hotspot screen.

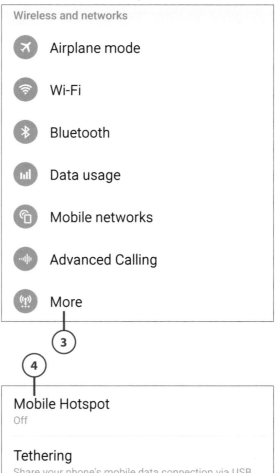

5 Tap On the switch at the top of the screen.

6 You see a notification that enabling mobile hotspot functionality turns off your phone's Wi-Fi. Tap OK.

7 The Mobile Hotspot screen displays the name of and password for the new network. Keep this screen open or write down the name and password; you'll need them to log onto the mobile hotspot from another device.

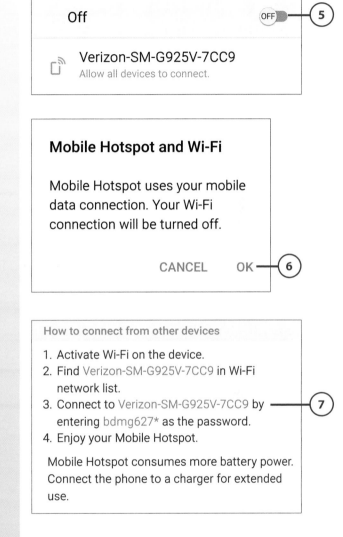

Off   (OFF) **5**

Verizon-SM-G925V-7CC9
Allow all devices to connect.

Mobile Hotspot and Wi-Fi

Mobile Hotspot uses your mobile data connection. Your Wi-Fi connection will be turned off.

CANCEL   OK **6**

How to connect from other devices

1. Activate Wi-Fi on the device.
2. Find Verizon-SM-G925V-7CC9 in Wi-Fi network list.
3. Connect to Verizon-SM-G925V-7CC9 by entering bdmg627* as the password. **7**
4. Enjoy your Mobile Hotspot.

Mobile Hotspot consumes more battery power. Connect the phone to a charger for extended use.

Connect Another Device to Your Phone via Wi-Fi

You can connect your computer or tablet to your phone via Wi-Fi.

1. On your other device, make sure that Wi-Fi is enabled and then display the list of available networks.

2. Select your smartphone from the list of devices. (The device name for your phone was displayed on the Mobile Hotspot screen.)

3. When prompted to enter the network security key or password, enter the password displayed on your phone's Mobile Hotspot screen. You should now be connected and using your phone's data connection.

Tether Another Device to Your Phone

You can also connect your computer or tablet to your phone via USB or Bluetooth to share your phone's Internet connection. Samsung calls this data tethering. (Yes, that's the same phrase your carrier uses for any sharing of mobile data.)

1. Swipe down from the top of the screen to display the notification panel.

2. Tap Settings to display the Settings screen.

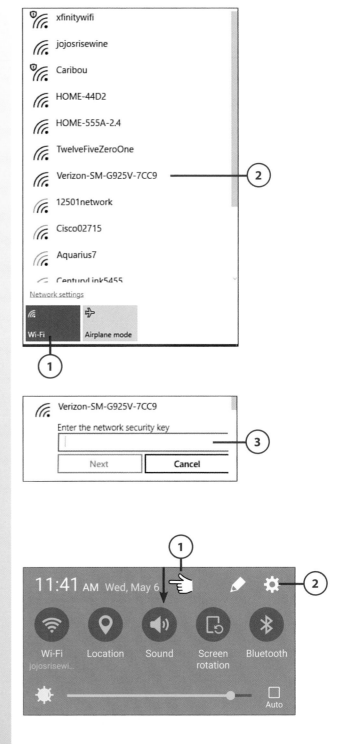

(**3**) Go to the Wireless and Networks section and tap More.

(**4**) Tap Tethering to display the Tethering screen.

(**5**) To tether via USB, connect the other device to your phone via USB cable, then tap On the USB Tethering switch.

(**6**) To tether via Bluetooth wireless, make sure the device is paired with your phone, then tap On the Bluetooth Tethering switch.

Bluetooth Pairing

You must pair the other device with your phone via Bluetooth before using Bluetooth pairing. Learn more in Chapter 7, "Making Phone Calls."

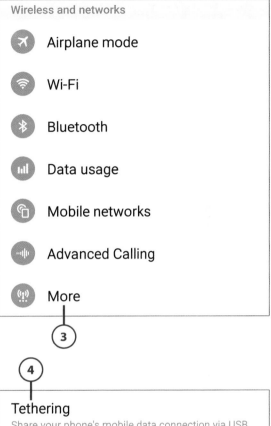

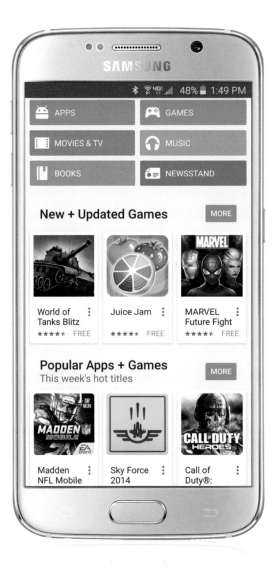

In this chapter, you learn how to find, install, use, and manage apps on your Galaxy S6 or S6 Edge. Topics include the following:

→ Using Apps
→ Managing Installed Apps
→ Downloading New Apps from the Google Play Store

6

Installing and Using Apps

Most of what you do on your Galaxy S6 or S6 Edge you do via applications, or apps. An app is a self-contained program designed to perform a particular task or serve a specific purpose. There are apps for news and weather, apps for email and text messaging, apps for Facebook and Pinterest, even apps for listening to music and watching videos. The camera function on your phone is actually an app, as is the phone dialer. Whatever you want to do on your Galaxy S6 or S6 Edge, there's probably an app for it.

Your new phone came with more than a dozen apps preinstalled, but these aren't the only apps you can use. There are tens of thousands of additional apps available, most for free or low cost, in the Google Play Store. It's easy to find new apps and install them on your phone—and then use them every day.

Installed Apps

For a list of apps that come already installed on your phone, download the bonus task "Phone And Other Apps" from the book's website at www.informit.com/title/9780789755445.

Using Apps

Your apps are displayed in two different places on your phone. All of your apps are listed on the Apps screen, which you access by tapping the Apps icon at the bottom of any Home screen. Shortcuts to your favorite apps are displayed on the Home screens; you have to manually add these shortcuts from the complete list of apps on the Apps screen.

View All Your Apps on the Apps Screen

Shortcuts to the apps you use most often are displayed on the Home screen, which you access by pressing the Home key on the front of your phone. When you want to view or access all the apps installed on your phone, you need to display the Apps screen. The Apps screen is also where you create shortcuts to place on your Home screen, as well as uninstall apps you no longer use.

1. From any Home screen, tap the Apps icon.

2. Swipe left or right to view additional Apps screens.

3. To view your apps in alphabetical order, tap A-Z at the top of the screen.

(4) Press the Home key to return to the Home screen.

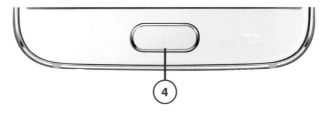

Open an App

You can open an app from the Apps screen or from the Home screen. The process is identical.

(1) Navigate to the screen that displays the icon for the app you want to open.

(2) Tap the icon to open the app.

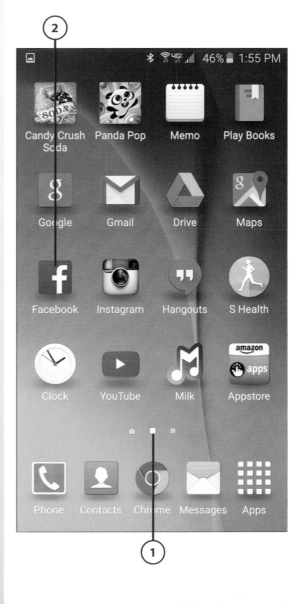

Close an App

Apps remain open until you manually close them. When you're not using an app, it remains paused in the background, but it doesn't consume system resources. Because of this, you don't have to close an app when you're done with it—although you can if you want.

1. Tap the Recents key to display a stack of recently opened apps.

2. Tap the X for the app you want to close, or just tap and drag the app off to one side until it disappears.

3. Tap Close All to close all open apps.

Switch Between Open Apps

When you have more than one app open, how do you switch from one app to another? By using the same app-switcher functionality you use to close apps.

1. Tap the Recents key to display a stack of recently opened apps.

2. Swipe up or down to scroll through all the apps.

3. Tap the app you want to switch to.

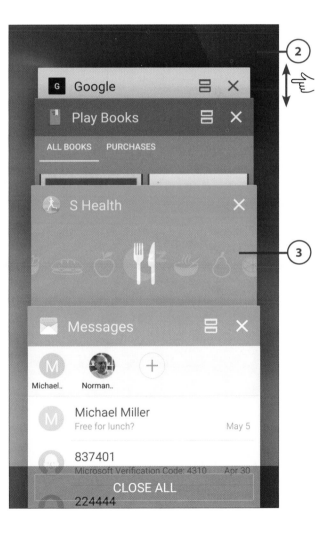

Use Multi Window

The Galaxy S6 and S6 Edge each has a fairly large 5.1-inch display. By default, apps run full-screen on this display. You can, however, display two apps in a split-screen display that Samsung calls Multi Window.

Compatibility

Not all apps support Multi Window display. If an app cannot be displayed in the split screen, you'll see an onscreen notification to that effect.

1. Display the first app you want to view.

2. Tap and hold the Recents key.

Recent Apps View

You can also launch Multi Window from the recent apps view. Tap the Recents key to display the stack of recent apps; those apps that support Multi Window have a special icon in their title bars. Tap this Multi Window icon to launch the app in split-screen view.

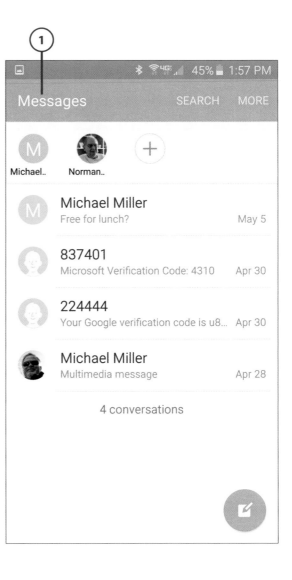

3 The first app is now displayed at the top of the split screen, with other app icons displayed at the bottom. Tap the icon for the other app you want to display.

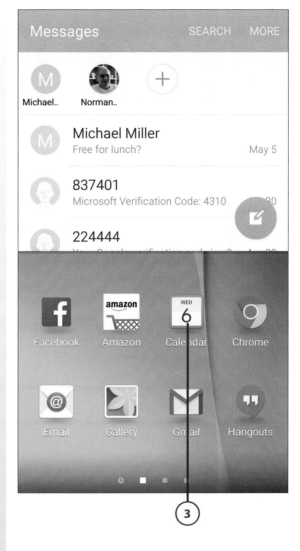

(4) Both apps are now displayed onscreen together; the active app is the one with the blue border. To resize the windows, select one of the application windows to display the border button in the middle of the window border; then tap and drag the border up or down, accordingly.

(5) Tap the border button to display window controls.

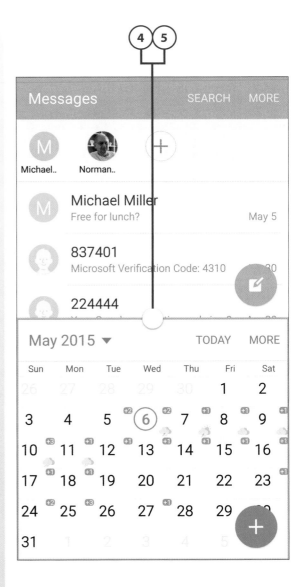

6 Tap the Switch Windows button to switch the top and bottom app positions.

7 Tap the Drag and Drop button to move content from one app to the other.

8 Tap the Minimize Window button to minimize the selected app window.

9 Tap the Maximize Window button to view the selected app in full-screen view.

10 Tap the Close App (X) button to close the selected app.

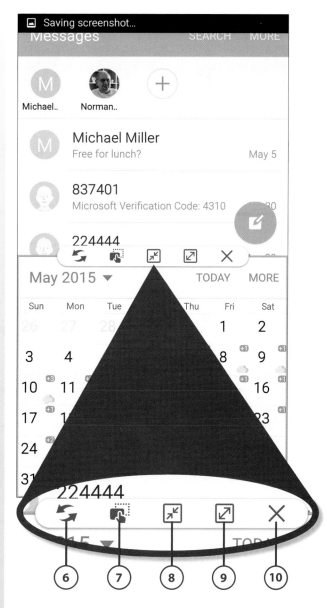

Managing Installed Apps

You can easily personalize which apps appear on your phone's Home screens, and where they appear. You can also organize apps into folder, and uninstall those apps you don't use.

Add App Shortcuts to the Home Screen

You add app shortcuts to the Home screen from the Apps screen.

1. Tap the Apps icon to display the Apps screen.

2. Tap and hold the icon for the app you want to add. The display changes to show the Home screens on your device.

3. Drag the icon to the desired Home screen and then release. The shortcut icon is now displayed on that screen.

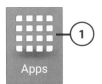

Rearrange Apps on the Home Screens

One of the easiest ways to personalize your Galaxy S6 or S6 Edge is to rearrange app shortcuts on the Home screens.

(1) Tap and drag the app icon to a new position on the current screen or…

(2) Tap and drag the icon to a different Home screen.

Remove an App Shortcut from the Home Screen

If you find that you're not using a specific app all that much, you may want to free up space by removing that app's shortcut from the Home screen.

(1) From a Home screen, tap and hold the icon for the app you want to remove.

(2) Drag the app's icon up and then drop it onto the Remove (trash can) icon above the screen.

Remove, Not Uninstall

Removing a shortcut from the Home screen does not remove that app from your phone. The app remains and is still accessible from the Apps screen. To remove the app from your phone, you have to uninstall the app, as discussed next.

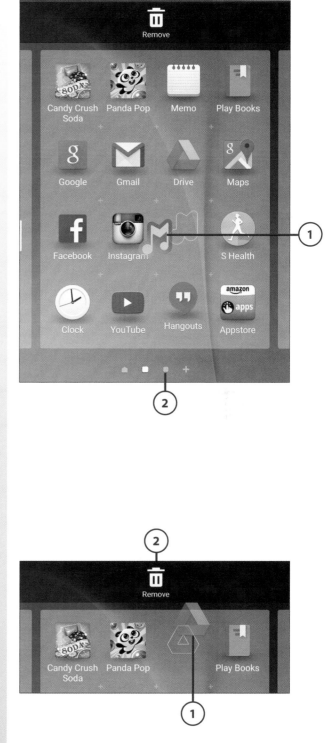

Uninstall an App

You can uninstall or disable and hide from view apps that you have downloaded onto your phone. However, some apps that were preloaded onto your phone cannot be uninstalled or disabled.

1. Tap the Apps icon to display the Apps screen.

2. Tap Edit. Apps that can be uninstalled or disabled display with a minus (–) icon.

3. Tap the minus (–) icon for the app you want to remove and then follow the onscreen instructions to either uninstall or disable the app.

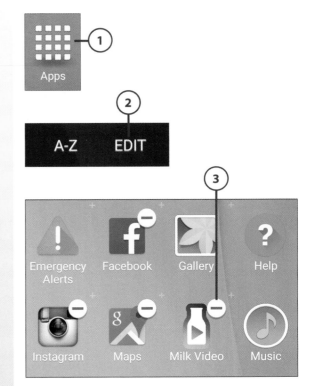

Manage the Screens on the Home Screen

The Home screen is actually a series of screens, each holding 16 shortcut icons plus the favorites row at the bottom of the screen. If you have more shortcut icons than you presently have Home screens to hold them, you can add new screens to the Home screen—and rearrange the Home screens in any order.

1. Pinch any Home screen to display the Home screens in editing mode.

(2) To remove a screen, tap and drag it to the Remove (trash can) icon at the top of the screen.

(3) To make a given screen the main Home screen that displays when you tap the Home key, tap the Home icon at the top of that screen.

(4) To change the order of the screens, tap and drag a screen left or right to a new position.

5 To add an new screen, scroll to the last Home screen and tap +.

6 To exit screen editing mode, press the Home key.

Add a Widget to the Home Screen

In addition to app shortcut icons, you can also place widgets on the Home screens. A widget is a self-contained application that runs on the screen itself. Out of the box, your Galaxy S6 came with two such widgets, both on the first Home screen—the Weather widget and the Google Search widget. (Many widgets, like the weather widget, have transparent backgrounds so they appear seamlessly against the screen background.)

Weather widget —

Google search widget —

Your Galaxy S6 comes with a number of preinstalled widgets that are ready to be added to your Home screens. You can find other widgets in the Google Play Store, as described later in this chapter. Many apps have their own widgets that display specific information on the Home screen. Other apps, like the Music app, let you operate them via widgets. Other widgets display news headlines, messages, and the like.

Space

Most widgets are a specific size, and can only fit on screens that have that same-sized space available. For example, a 4 × 1 widget takes up 4 icons wide by 1 icon tall; a 4 × 2 widget is 4 icons wide by 2 icons tall. Make sure you have adequate empty space for the widgets you want.

1. Pinch any Home screen to display the Home screens in editing mode.

2. Tap Widgets at the bottom of the screen. This displays all the widgets installed on your phone.

3. Touch and drag the widget you want to the desired Home screen.

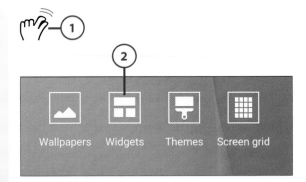

Wallpapers   Widgets   Themes   Screen grid

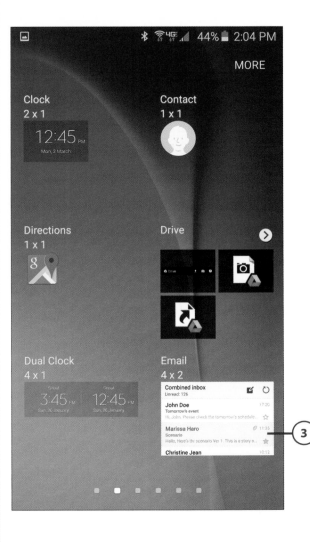

* 4G 44% 2:04 PM

MORE

Clock
2 x 1

12:45 PM
Mon, 2 March

Contact
1 x 1

Directions
1 x 1

Drive

Dual Clock
4 x 1

3:45 PM
Sun, 26 January

12:45 PM
Sun, 26 January

Email
4 x 2

Combined inbox
Unread: 126

John Doe   17:20
Tomorrow's event
Hi, John. Please check the tomorrow's schedule...

Marissa Haro   11:35
Scenario
Hello, Here's the scenario Ver 1. This is a story a...

Christine Jean   10:12

Remove a Widget from the Home Screen

You remove a widget from the Home screen much as you remove shortcut icons.

(1) From a Home screen, tap and hold the widget you want to remove.

(2) Drag the widget up and then drop it onto the Remove (trash can) icon above the screen.

Organize Apps into Folders

If you have a lot of similar apps on your phone, you might want to organize those app shortcuts into folders on your Home screen. A folder can contain several screens worth of apps and help you minimize the screen real estate devoted to app shortcuts.

(1) From any screen, tap and drag the icon for the first app onto the icon for the second app you want in the folder.

(2) This creates the folder, with the first two apps inside.

(3) Tap Enter Folder Name and enter the name for this folder.

(4) Tap outside the folder to return to the Home screen.

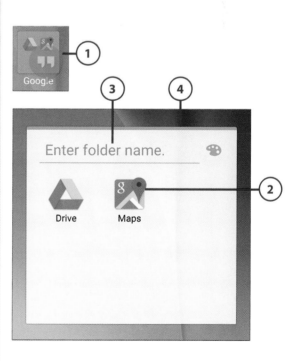

(5) To add another app shortcut to the folder, tap and drag the icon onto the folder icon.

Open and Close a Folder

After you've organized your apps into folders, it's easy to access those apps.

(1) Tap the folder you want to open.

(2) The folder opens, displaying the apps inside. Tap an app to open it.

(3) Tap outside the folder to close it and return to the Home screen.

Remove a Folder from the Home Screen

It's easy to remove a folder from the Home screen. When you delete a folder, the apps themselves are not deleted, and remain available on the Apps screen.

(1) Tap and hold the icon for the folder you want to remove.

(2) Drag the folder's icon up and then drop it onto the Remove (trash can) icon above the screen.

Set Default Applications

There are a lot of applications out there, many of which perform similar operations. For example, there are tons of music player apps for playing music on your phone, and most manufacturers preinstall at least two text messaging apps (the default Android one and one from your mobile carrier) on the Galaxy S6. If you have multiple applications of the same type, you need to tell your phone which one to use by default.

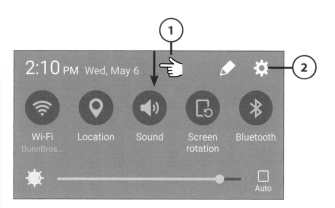

1. Swipe down from the top of the screen to display the notification panel.

2. Tap Settings to display the Settings screen.

3. Scroll to the Device section and tap Applications to display the Applications screen.

4. Tap Default Applications to display the Default Applications screen.

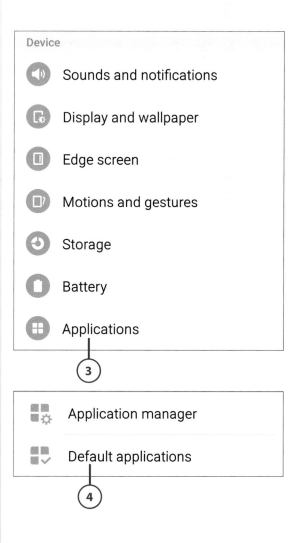

5. Tap the type of operation you want to set.

6. Tap the app you want to use for this operation.

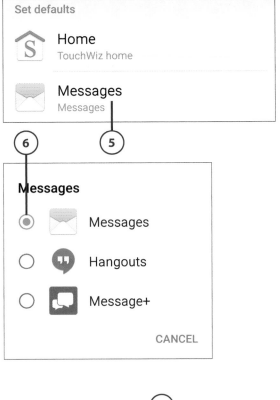

Use the Application Manager

Your Samsung smartphone includes an Application Manager you can use to see which apps you've downloaded, which are currently running, and how many resources each app is using. You can also use Application Manager to stop an app that may be taking up too many resources or causing other problems.

1. Swipe down from the top of the screen to display the notification panel.

2. Tap Settings to display the Settings screen.

3. Scroll to the Device section and tap Applications to display the Applications screen.

4. Tap Application Manager to open the Application Manager.

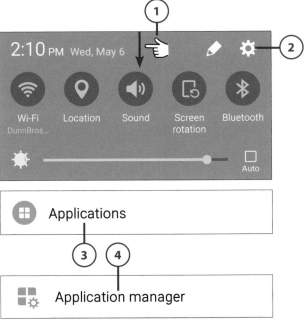

5 The Downloaded section displays your most recently downloaded apps.

6 Scroll right to view the Running section, that displays all currently running apps along with information about each app—how much memory that app is using, and how long that app has been running.

7 Tap an app you want to stop.

5

DOWNLOADED	RUNNING

Amazon Kindle
88.41MB

Amazon Music
33.95MB

Android System WebView
120MB

ANT Radio Service
1.23MB

ANT+ Plugins Service
14.00MB

Booking.com Hotels
45.64MB

6

OWNLOADED	RUNNING	ALL

RAM status

System	1.2GB
Apps	742MB
Free	778MB

RAM usage by applications

Settings   247MB
1 process and 0 services

IPsec Service   447KB
1 process and 1 service   28:52

7

(8) Tap the Stop button.

It's Not All Good

Stop with Caution

It's safe enough to stop most apps from running. Be cautious, however, about stopping any system processes, such as the Android System itself. Stopping a key process can cause your phone to freeze up or otherwise behave badly. (If this happens, power off your phone and then restart it.)

>>>Go Further
UPDATING APPS

Apps are software programs, and like any software program, are occasionally updated to include new features, bug fixes and the like. Most apps update automatically when updates are available, and you'll see a notification of this on the Lock screen and notification panel.

Some app updates need your approval to proceed. If you receive a notification to this effect, tap the notification and you'll be transferred to the Google Play Store. Tap the Update or Update All (if there are multiple apps that need updating) button to proceed.

By the way, if you'd rather manually approve every single app update, you can turn off the auto update feature. Launch the Google Play Store app, then tap the Options (three-line) button and select Settings. Go the General section and tap Auto-Update Apps. On the next panel, tap Do Not Auto-Update Apps.

The other options are to update only when you're connected via Wi-Fi and to auto-update apps at any time, over any type of network. That last option isn't recommended, as updating large apps can eat up a ton of your mobile data usage—and cost you money in data charges.

Downloading New Apps from the Goo Play Store

Where do you find new apps to use on your smartphone? There's one central source that offers apps from multiple developers—the Google Play Store.

Browse and Search the Google Play Store

The Google Play Store is an online store that offers apps, music, videos, and eBooks for Android phones. Most apps in the Google Play Store are free or relatively low cost. It's easy to find new apps by either browsing or searching.

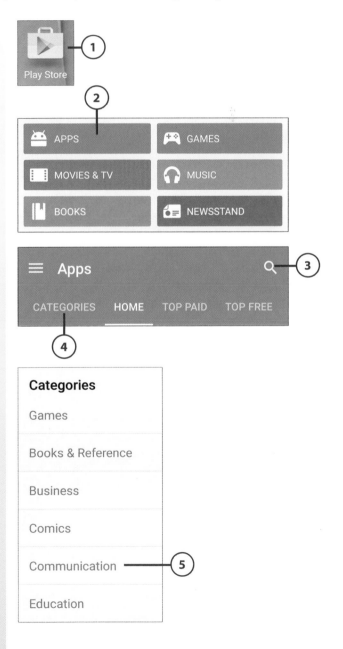

1. Tap the Play Store icon to open the Google Play Store.

2. Tap Apps to display available apps.

3. Tap in the Search box and enter the name or type of app you're looking for *or…*

4. Tap the Categories tab to browse for apps by category.

5. Tap the category you're interested in to display apps of that type.

6. Tap a tab at the top of the screen to narrow your results—Top Paid, Top Free, Top Grossing, Top New Paid, Top New Free, or Trending.

7. Tap the app you're interested in.

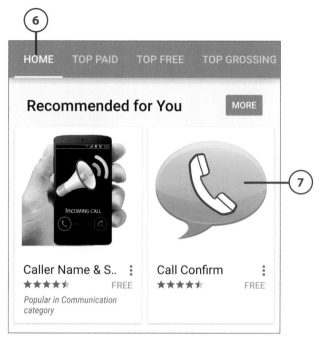

Purchase and Download Apps

Many apps in the Google Play Store are free. Others you have to pay for.

1. Download a free app by tapping the Install button.

2. Tap Accept on the permissions panel. The app is downloaded to and installed on your phone.

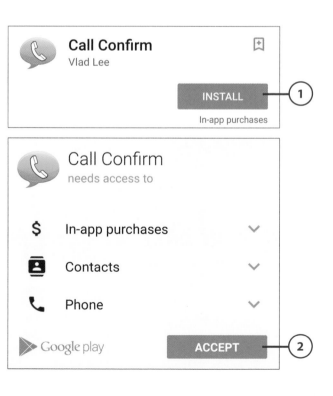

(3) Purchase a paid app by tapping the price button.

(4) Tap Accept on the permissions panel. The purchase panel displays.

(5) Tap the payment area to enlarge the panel, then tap Payment Methods.

Call Recorder Pro
Clever Mobile

$5.99 — 3

Call Recorder Pro
needs access to

👤 Identity ⌄

📇 Contacts ⌄

📞 Phone ⌄

🖼 Photos/Media/Files ⌄

🎤 Microphone ⌄

ℹ Device ID & call information ⌄

Google play   ACCEPT — 4

Call Recorder Pro $5.99 ︿
PayPal:

Payment methods — 5

Redeem

molehillgroup@gmail.com

By tapping "Buy", you agree to the Google Wallet Terms of Service.

Google play   BUY

6 Select a payment option.

7 If you have not yet set up a payment method, tap either Add Credit or Debit Card or Add PayPal and then follow the onscreen instructions to add your payment information.

8 Tap the Buy button to complete the transaction and download the app.

Fun and Useful Apps

For a list of other apps you might like to install, download the bonus task "PhoneAndOtherApps" from the book's website at www.informit.com/title/9780789755445.

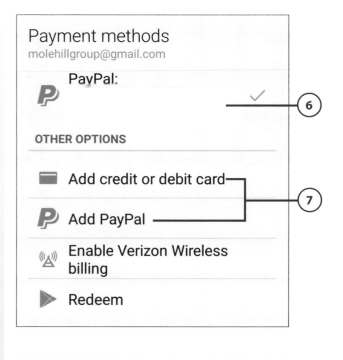

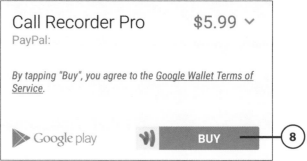

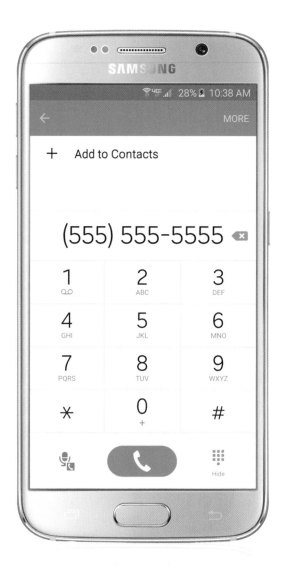

In this chapter, you learn how to make and receive mobile phone calls on your Samsung Galaxy S6 or S6 Edge. Topics include the following:

→ Calling on Your Galaxy S6
→ Using Speed Dial
→ Handling Multiple Calls and Activities
→ Managing Your Call Log
→ Using Voice Mail
→ Configuring Call Settings
→ Connecting via Headset or Car Speaker

Making Phone Calls

Despite all the web connectivity, app downloads, and other bells and whistles, your new Galaxy S6 or S6 Edge smartphone is, first and foremost, a mobile telephone. This chapter shows you how to use the phone features of your new smartphone, as well as how to manage your voice mail and call logs.

Calling on Your Galaxy S6

Of all the things that your new Samsung smartphone can do, the one that it does first and best is send and receive mobile phone calls. Making a call is as simple as dialing a number—as long as you have a strong signal from your carrier, of course!

When you talk on your Galaxy S6 or S6 Edge, hold it to the side of your face as you would an old-school telephone handset. Your new smartphone may look like a high-tech, shiny, glass-and-metal rectangle, but it works just like a traditional phone. You'll hear the other person from a tiny speaker at the top of the phone, and speak into a tiny microphone at the bottom. Speak loud enough for the other person to hear you, and you should hear her just fine, as well.

Dial a Number

There are many ways to make a call from your Samsung Galaxy S6. The simplest is to just dial the number.

(1) From the Home screen, tap the Phone icon to open the Phone app.

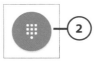

(2) If the keypad is not visible, tap the green Keypad icon.

(3) Tap the number you want to dial into the onscreen keypad.

(4) Tap the green Dial (phone) icon to dial the number. When the other party answers, hold the phone to the side of your head to listen to and speak with that person.

Area Codes

When dialing from a mobile phone, you always need to enter the area code in front of the standard seven-digit number, like this: 555-555-5555. You do not need to enter a "1" before the area code.

From the Lock Screen

If you don't have your lock screen protected by a PIN or password, you can dial directly from the Lock screen without first unlocking your phone. Just drag the Phone icon up to display the call screen, and proceed from there.

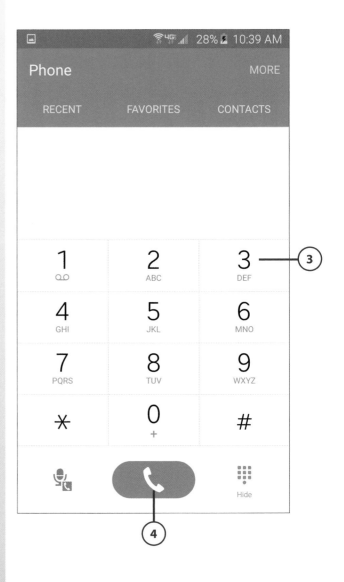

Quick-Dial from Your Contacts List

Your Samsung phone includes a Contacts app that lets you store information about the people you know—including their phone numbers. After you've entered a contact's information, it's a lot easier to dial that person from within your contacts list than try to remember the person's full phone number.

(1) From the Home screen, tap the Contacts icon to open the Contacts app or...

(2) From within the Phone app, tap the Contacts tab.

(3) Scroll to and tap the name of the contact you want to call.

(4) Tap the green phone icon next to this person's phone number. If a contact has more than one phone number listed (home, mobile, and work, for example), tap the appropriate phone number. The person is now called.

Contacts

Learn more about your contacts and contacts list in Chapter 8, "Managing Your Contacts List."

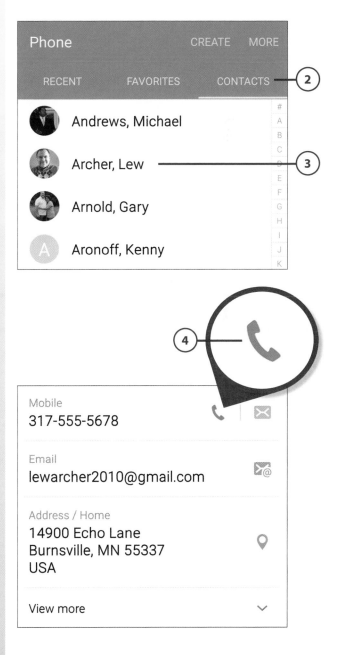

Dial a Favorite Contact

In the Contacts app, you can specify any number of people as favorites. This makes it easier for you to find and dial these contacts' numbers.

 From within the Phone app, tap the Favorites tab.

② Tap the name of the favorite you want to call.

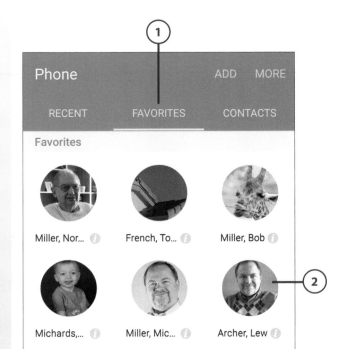

Dial a Recent Number

Your phone keeps track of calls you've made and received. If you want to redial someone you've recently talked to, you can easily do so.

① From within the Phone app, tap the Recent tab.

② Tap the name or number of the recent call you want to revisit. You see a list of recent calls to/ from this person.

3 Tap the green Dial (phone) icon to redial this person.

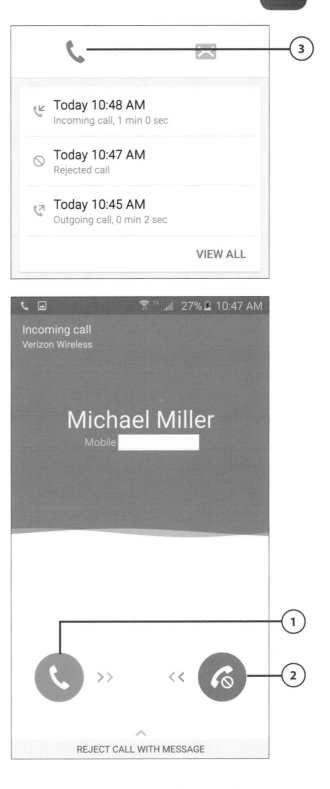

Answer a Call

Dialing out is easy enough. What do you do when someone calls you?

1 Touch and drag the green Answer icon in any direction to answer the call.

2 If you don't want to answer this call, you can reject it and send it automatically to voice mail. To do this, tap and drag the red Reject icon in any direction.

Answering When Active

If you're on the Home screen or your phone is currently locked when you receive a call, you see the screens shown with this task. If, on the other hand, you're using another app when the call comes in, you see the Answer and Reject icons in a pop-up window.

Options During a Call

When you're talking to someone on your phone, you have several options available to you.

(**1**) To change the volume level of the caller, press the Up or Down Volume keys on the left side of the phone.

(**2**) Tap Speaker to start using the speakerphone. Tap this button again to switch back to normal phone use.

(**3**) Mute the call so that the other person can't hear what you're saying by tapping Mute. Tap Mute again to unmute the call.

(**4**) To input any numbers during a call (if you're calling your bank, for example), tap Keypad to redisplay the onscreen keyboard.

(**5**) Tap the red End icon to disconnect the call.

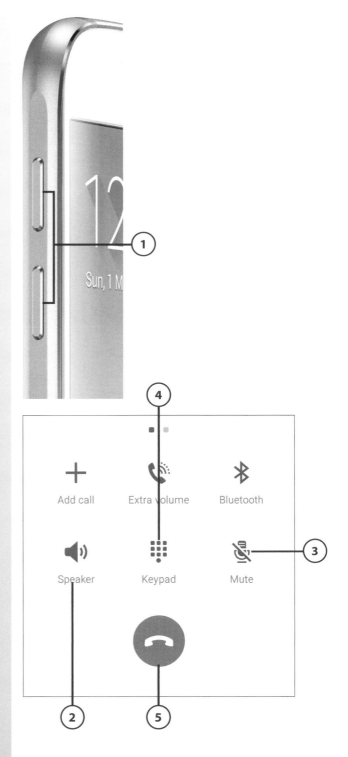

>>>Go Further
WHAT'S MY NUMBER?

In this era where every phone number is stored in your phone, and all you have to do is tap an icon to call someone, there's little incentive to memorize a person's phone number. If you're like me, this means that you don't remember anyone's phone number anymore. We rely on our smartphones to do the remembering for us.

It also means, if you're also like me, that you probably don't even remember your own phone number. You don't have to give it out to people; they see your number on their own smart-phones when you call, and add it to their own contacts list.

So, what is your phone number? The easiest way to find out is swipe down from the top of the screen to display the notification panel and then tap Settings. From the Settings screen, scroll to the System section and tap About Phone. On the next screen, tap Status. On the last screen, scroll down to the My Phone Number section, and there it is! (You might want to write it down, or even create a contact for yourself.)

Using Speed Dial

Your new Samsung phone lets you store up to 100 numbers in a Speed Dial list. With Speed Dial, phoning a person is as easy as tapping one or more number keys.

Create a Speed Dial Entry

You add numbers to Speed Dial from within the Phone app.

1. From the Phone app's dialing screen, tap More.

2. Tap Speed Dial to display the Speed Dial screen.

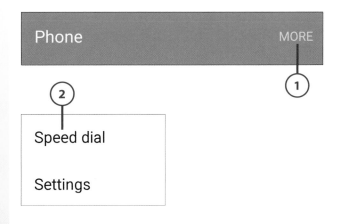

3 Tap the + icon next to the first open Speed Dial position.

4 Tap the name of the contact you want to add. The person is now added to your Speed Dial list.

Voice Mail

By default, voice mail is assigned to the first Speed Dial position.

Remove a Person from Speed Dial

Samsung makes it easy to edit your Speed Dial List.

1 From the Phone app's dialing screen, tap More.

2 Tap Speed Dial to display the Speed Dial screen.

3 Tap the minus (–) icon next to the person you want to remove from Speed Dial.

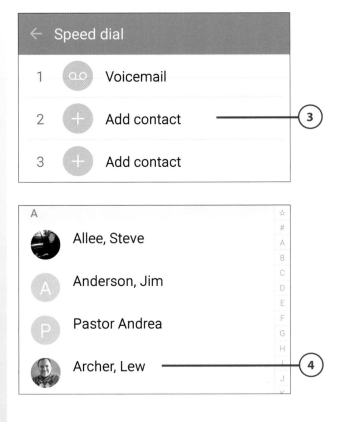

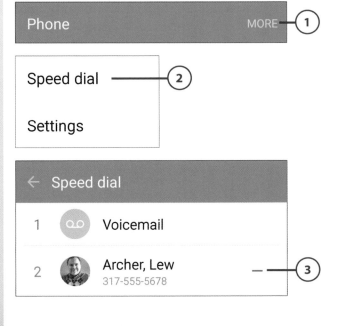

Make a Call with Speed Dial

The joy of Speed Dial is being able to call someone with just a tap or two on your phone's screen.

(**1**) From the Home screen, tap Phone to open the Phone app.

(**2**) Enter the Speed Dial number assigned to this person. When entering, tap and *hold* the last number. For example if this person is in Speed Dial slot number 2, tap and hold **2**. If this person is in Speed Dial slot 14, tap **1** then tap and hold **4**.

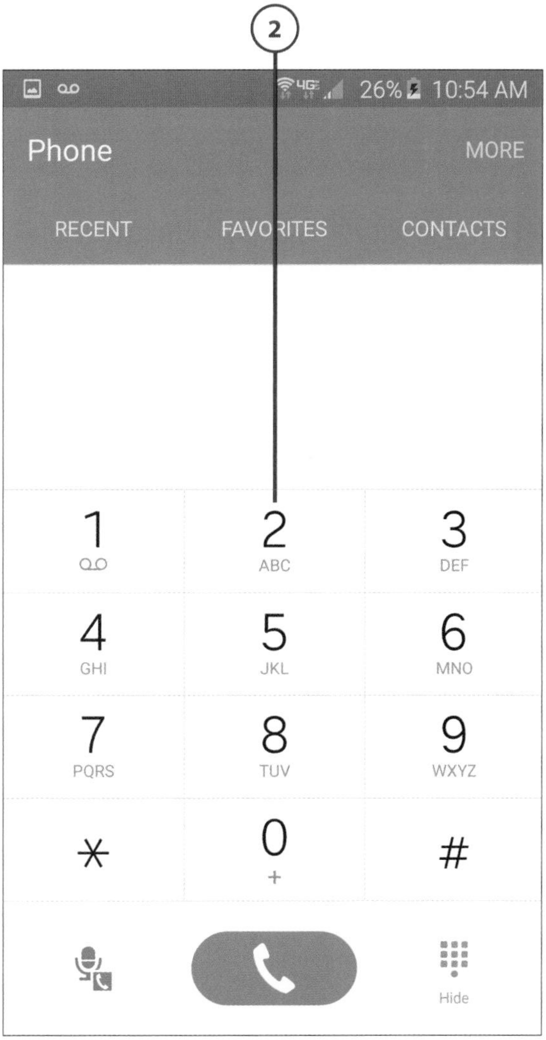

Phone

Phone		MORE
RECENT	FAVORITES	CONTACTS

1	2	3
	ABC	DEF
4	5	6
GHI	JKL	MNO
7	8	9
PQRS	TUV	WXYZ
✳	0	#
	+	

Hide

Handling Multiple Calls and Activities

Most mobile carriers let you handle two calls at once. This means answering an incoming call while you're on another, or placing a new call when you're already on the phone. You can even continue using your other smartphone functions—including Internet browsing—while talking.

Make a New Call While on Another

If your carrier supports this feature, you can make a new call while you're currently on an existing one.

1. While you're on a call, tap + Add Call to display the numeric keypad.

2. Tap the new number into the keypad.

3. Tap the green Dial icon.

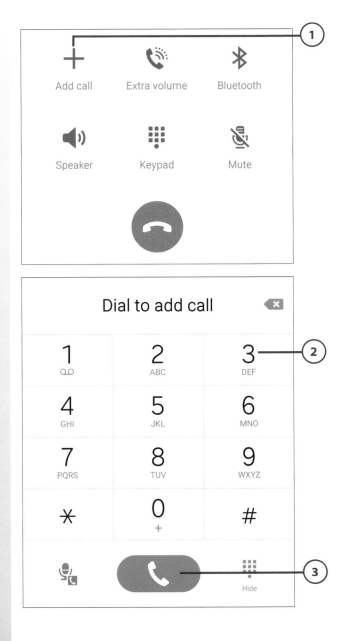

4 Tap Merge if you want to conference both callers into a single call. You will hear both callers at once—and they will hear each other, too.

Receive a New Call While on Another

Thanks to Call Waiting (supported by most carriers), you can answer an incoming call while you're on another call.

1 Slide the green Answer icon in any direction to answer the new call. This also places the existing caller on hold.

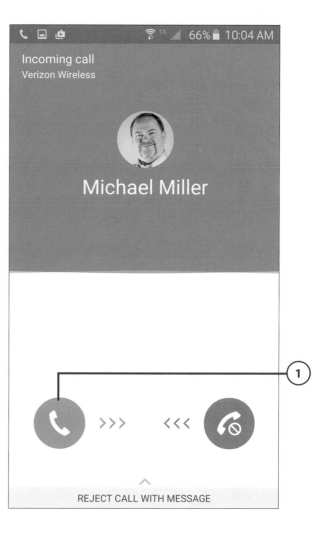

(2) Switch back to the original caller by tapping the previous On Hold entry.

>>>Go Further
USING OTHER SMARTPHONE FUNCTIONS DURING A CALL

Most carriers enable you to use other functions on your Samsung phone while you're engaging in a phone call. This multitasking can be quite useful; for example, you can look something up on Google to answer a question posed during the voice call.

To multitask in this fashion, simply press the Home key to return to the Home screen while you're talking. The voice call continues, and you can then tap any app icon to open and use that app.

In addition, your phone has several preset app options built into the Phone app. From within the call screen, swipe to the right and then tap the icon for Email, Message, Browser, Contacts, Calendar, or Memo.

To return to the call screen, swipe down from the top of the screen to display the notification panel and then tap Call Notification. To end the call from the notification panel, tap End Call.

Managing Your Call Log

All the calls you make and receive are recorded in your phone's call log, so you can easily review your call history. The call log even logs those calls you've missed.

View Recent Calls

You view your call log from within the Phone app.

(**1**) From within the Phone app, tap the Recent tab to display the call log, in reverse chronological order (newest first).

(**2**) Outbound calls are indicated with an upward arrow on the phone icon—green if answered, red if not answered. Incoming calls are indicated with a downward arrow on the phone icon—also green if answered, red if not answered. If the call was to or from someone on your contact list, you see that person's name. Tap a call to view more information.

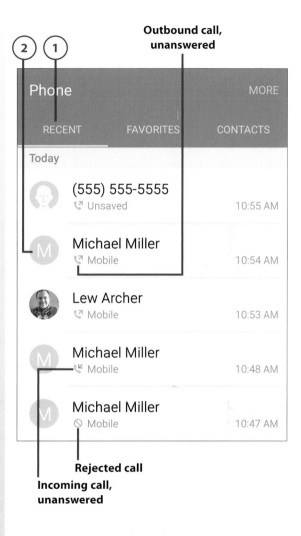

Outbound call, unanswered

Rejected call

Incoming call, unanswered

3 Recent calls to/from this number are displayed. Tap the green Dial (phone) icon to redial this person.

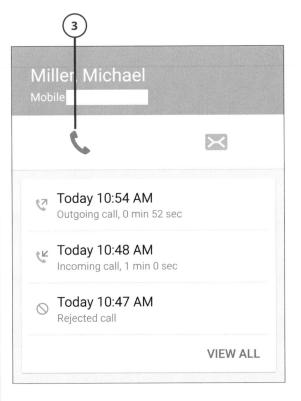

Save a Recent Call to Your Contact List

If someone calls you, or if you call someone else, you can add that person's information to your contact list from within the call log.

1 From within the Phone app, tap the Recent tab to display the call log.

2 Tap a call to view more information about that call.

3 Tap Create Contact to add this number to your contact list.

4 Tap Update Existing to update an existing contact with this new number.

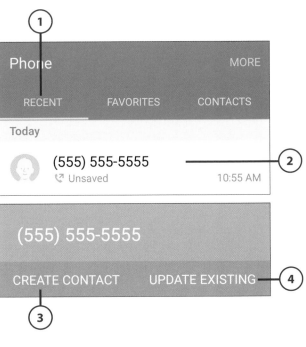

Delete a Call from Your Call Log

On occasion you'll receive calls from numbers you don't want to remember. (Or don't want anyone snooping through your phone to see.) Fortunately, you can delete any call from the call log.

1. From within the Phone app, tap the Recent tab to display the call log.

2. Tap More at the top of the screen.

3. Tap Edit.

4. Tap to check the call(s) you want to delete.

5. Tap Delete.

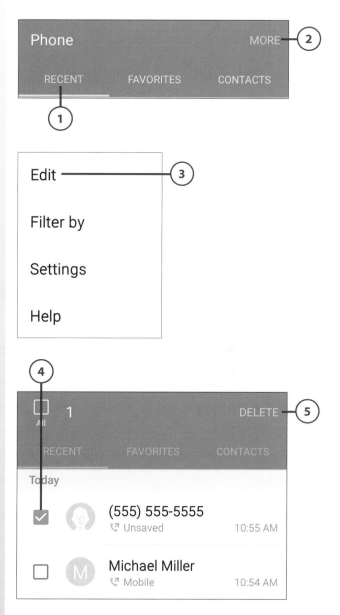

Reject Future Calls from a Given Number

It happens. Some telemarketer or scammer or debt collector gets hold of your mobile number, and you don't want that person to keep calling you. Fortunately, you can add any number to an Auto Reject list, so if you receive a call from that number, it's automatically rejected without you having to answer it.

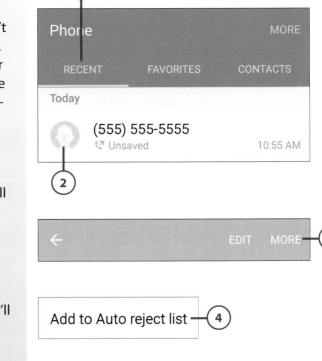

1. From within the Phone app, tap the Recent tab to display the call log.

2. Tap a call from the number you want to reject.

3. Tap More.

4. Tap Add to Auto Reject List. You'll never hear from this number again.

Rejecting Mistakes

If you accidentally add a number to the Auto Reject list, you can remove it from that list at a later time. From within the Phone app, tap More and then tap Settings. On the Call Settings screen, tap Call Rejection and then tap Auto Reject List. Find the number you rejected by mistake and tap the minus (–) sign.

Using Voice Mail

Your mobile carrier provides voice mail service in addition to your normal voice calling. Voice mail is like a digital version of a traditional answering machine; it lets callers leave you messages when you don't answer the phone.

Your voice mail is not stored on your phone; it's on your mobile carrier's system. For this reason, you actually have to dial into your voice mail to hear your messages.

Set Up Your Voice Mail

When you first sign up with a mobile carrier, you need to set up your voice mail account. This voice mail account follows you from phone to phone (it's specific to your mobile phone number and account), so if your new Samsung Galaxy S6 phone was added to an existing carrier account, there's nothing new to set up.

If you're a new customer with a mobile carrier, however, you do need to set up your voice mail. The process is different with different carriers, but works more or less like this.

(1) From within the Phone app, tap and hold **1** to access voice mail via Speed Dial.

(2) When connected, follow the voice prompts to create your password, record your name announcement, and record your voice greeting.

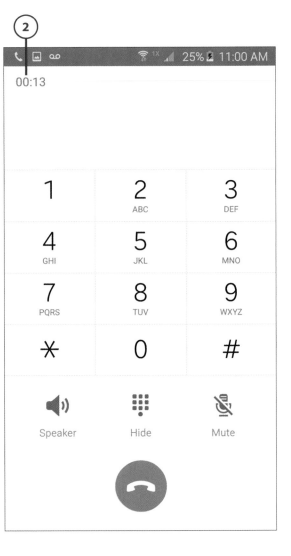

Check Voice Mail Messages

When you purchased your new Samsung Galaxy S6, your carrier should have set up your phone with the correct voice mail number. When you receive a new voice mail message, you'll see a notification to that effect; you can then dial into your voice mail account to listen to the message.

(1) Tap the notification to call your voice mail number *or…*

2 From within the Phone app, tap and hold **1** to access voice mail via Speed Dial.

3 When connected, follow the voice prompts to listen to or delete messages. (Some carriers launch their own voice mail app for managing voice mail messages; if so, tap the Play button to play the message.)

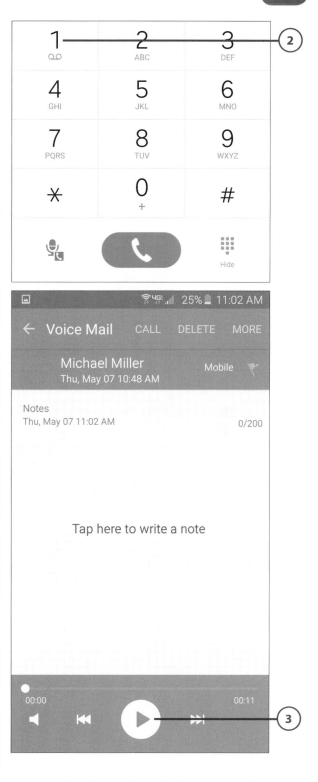

Configuring Call Settings

There are numerous things you can configure from within the Phone app. In addition, you can easily set different ringtones for your incoming calls.

Set Your Default Ringtone

You can choose from a number of different tones to ring when you receive incoming calls.

① From within the Phone app, tap More.

② Tap Settings to display the Call Settings screen.

③ Tap Ringtones and Keypad Tones

④ Tap Ringtones to display available ringtones.

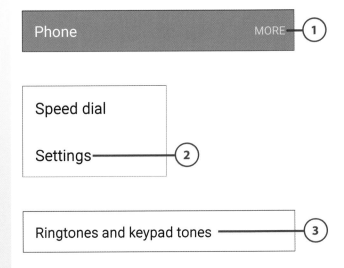

Phone   MORE ─①

Speed dial

Settings ──────── ②

Ringtones and keypad tones ──────── ③

← Ringtones and keypad tones

Ringtones
Over the Horizon

④

5 Tap to select the ringtone you want. When you tap a ringtone, you hear a preview of that sound.

6 To use a ringtone other than those built into your phone, scroll to the bottom of the list and tap Add Ringtone, then choose where you want to find the sound.

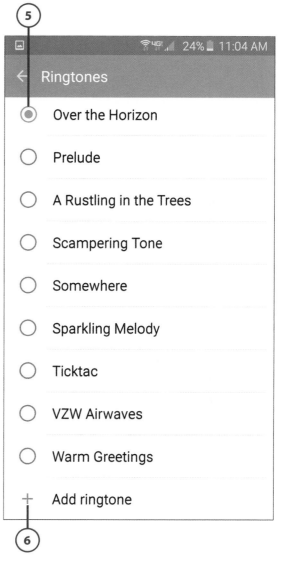

5

Ringtones

⦿ Over the Horizon

◯ Prelude

◯ A Rustling in the Trees

◯ Scampering Tone

◯ Somewhere

◯ Sparkling Melody

◯ Ticktac

◯ VZW Airwaves

◯ Warm Greetings

＋ Add ringtone

6

Assign a Unique Ringtone for a Specific Contact

In addition to your general ringtone for incoming calls, you can assign unique ringtones for different people in your contact list. This way you'll know who's calling just by the sound of the ring.

1. From within the Phone app, tap Contacts.

2. Tap the name of the person you want.

3. Tap Edit.

4. Scroll down the screen and tap Ringtone.

5. Tap to select the ringtone you want for this person.

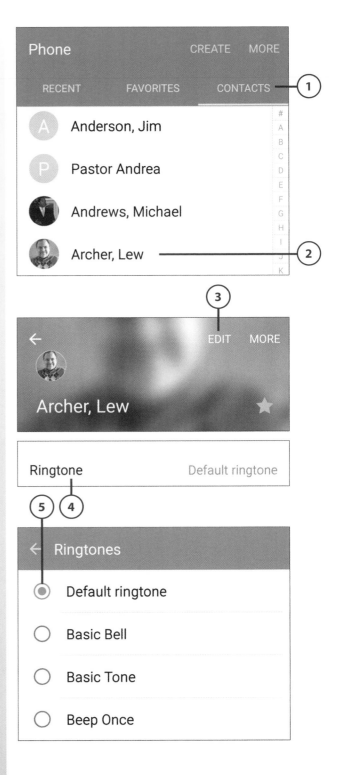

Configure Other Call Settings

Your Samsung smartphone has a number of settings you can configure to personalize the calling experience. All are accessible from the Call Settings screen.

1. From within the Phone app, tap More.

2. Tap Settings to display the Call Settings screen.

3. Click On the Swipe to Call or Send Messages switch to be able to initiate a call or message by swiping across a person's contact screen.

4. To automatically reject all calls from unknown numbers, tap Call Rejection, tap Auto Reject List, and then click On Unknown Number.

5. To answer calls with the Home key or voice commands, tap Answering and Ending Calls then tap On the appropriate switch.

6. To end calls by pressing the Power key, tap Answering and Ending Calls then tap On the Pressing the Power Key switch.

7. Tap On Automatic Answering to answer calls automatically after two seconds when you're using a headset or Bluetooth device.

8. Tap On Show Caller Information to display your history with a given caller.

Phone   ADD   MORE   (1)

Edit

Reorder Favorites

Settings ——— (2)

🖻   📶 4G 📶 24% 🔋 11:06 AM

← **Call settings**

Phone settings

Swipe to call or send messages
Make calls or send messages by swiping right or left across a contact's information in Contacts, or a log item in Phone.   ON (3)

Call settings

Call rejection ——————— (4)

Answering and ending calls ——— (5) (6)

Automatic answering
Answer incoming calls automatically after 2 seconds while a headset or a Bluetooth device is connected.   OFF (7)

Show caller information
Display my history of communication with the caller.   OFF (8)

Call alerts

Ringtones and keypad tones

9. To have your phone vibrate when a call is answered or ends, tap Call Alerts and then tap On the appropriate switch.

10. To *not* sound tones when a call is connected or ended, tap Call Alerts then tap Off the appropriate switch.

11. To turn on or off call forwarding, tap Call Forwarding and make the appropriate selection.

12. To improve the sound quality of your phone when using a hearing aid, tap More Settings then tap On Hearing Aids.

13. To change the alert sound when you receive a voice mail message, scroll to the Voice Mail section, tap Alert Sound, and make a selection.

14. To have your phone vibrate when you receive a voice mail message, go to the Voice Mail section and tap On Vibrate.

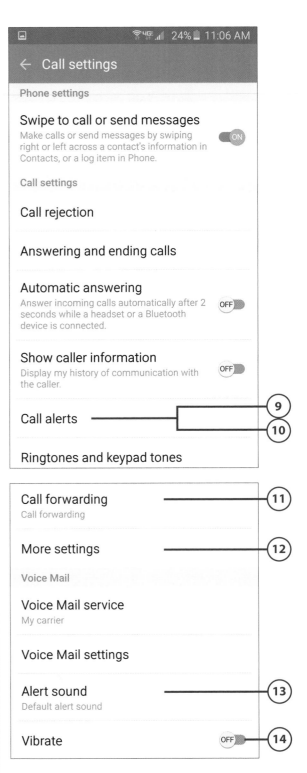

Connecting via Headset or Car Speaker

If you do a lot of talking on the phone, you might find it more convenient to use a wired or wireless headset instead of holding your Galaxy S6 to your ear. In addition, if your automobile offers Bluetooth functionality, you can do your calling over your car's audio system.

Connect a Wired Headset

Connected a wired headset is as easy as plugging it in. You can connect either phone headsets for making and receiving calls, or earbuds or head-phones for listening to music.

(1) Plug your headset/earplugs/headphones into the headset jack on the bottom of the phone.

(2) For headset operation, consult the directions that came with your headset.

Connect a Bluetooth Headset

Many people prefer to use wireless headsets, which not only eliminate the connecting wires but also let you walk a short distance away from your phone, if you want. Wireless headsets connect via Bluetooth technology, which is built into your Galaxy S6 phone.

(1) Swipe down from the top of the screen to display the notification panel.

(2) Tap the Settings icon to display the Settings screen.

3. In the Wireless and Networks section, tap Bluetooth to display the Bluetooth screen.

4. If Bluetooth is turned off, tap On the switch at the top of the screen.

5. Make sure that your Bluetooth headset is turned on and placed in discoverable mode. (Consult your headset directions on how to do this.) It should appear, along with any other nearby Bluetooth devices, in the Available Devices section. If not, tap Refresh at the top of the Bluetooth screen.

6. Tap the name of your wireless headset. Your phone now attempts to pair with this device. When prompted to confirm the pairing request, tap OK. If automatic pairing is unsuccessful, enter the passcode supplied by the wireless headset.

Connect to Your Car via Bluetooth

If your car includes Bluetooth functionality, you can connect your phone to your car's audio system via Bluetooth. You can then make and receive phone calls over your car's audio system and microphone.

1. Swipe down from the top of the screen to display the notification panel.

2. Tap the Settings icon to display the Settings screen.

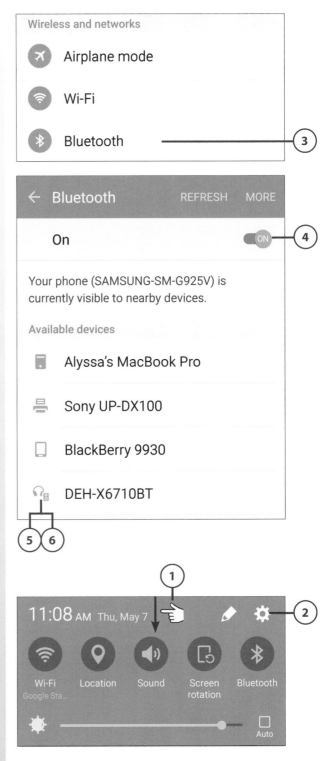

3. In the Wireless and Networks section, tap Bluetooth to display the Bluetooth screen.

4. If Bluetooth is turned off, tap On the switch at the top of the screen. This makes your phone discoverable by your car.

5. In your car, follow the manufacturer's instructions to begin the Bluetooth pairing process. In most instances, your car recognizes your phone and asks you to enter a passcode on your phone. Enter this code as instructed.

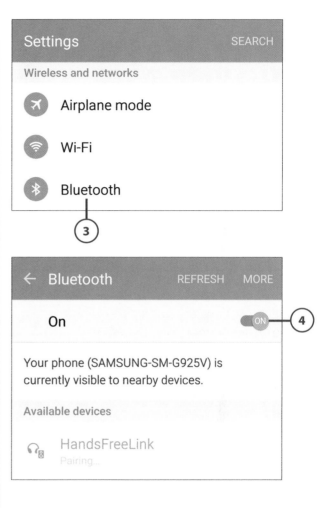

Settings — SEARCH

Wireless and networks

✈ Airplane mode

📶 Wi-Fi

❊ Bluetooth

3

← Bluetooth — REFRESH — MORE

On — ON — 4

Your phone (SAMSUNG-SM-G925V) is currently visible to nearby devices.

Available devices

🎧 HandsFreeLink
Pairing...

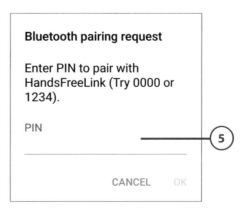

Bluetooth pairing request

Enter PIN to pair with HandsFreeLink (Try 0000 or 1234).

PIN — 5

CANCEL — OK

(**6**) Your phone now attempts to pair with your automobile. When pairing is successful, you may be prompted to share your phone's contacts with your car. If so, tap Allow.

Bluetooth Audio

Many cars also let you listen to music stored on your phone over the car's audio system, via the same Bluetooth connection. Learn more in Chapter 18, "Listening to Music."

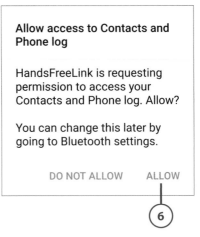

Allow access to Contacts and Phone log

HandsFreeLink is requesting permission to access your Contacts and Phone log. Allow?

You can change this later by going to Bluetooth settings.

DO NOT ALLOW   ALLOW

(**6**)

Call from Your Car

Answer call

End call

Voice dial

When your Galaxy S6 is connected to your car via Bluetooth, you can initiate a call in one of two ways.

First, you can simply start the call on your phone. You should be able to hear the sound over your car's audio system; if not, from the Galaxy S6's Phone app, tap Speaker to switch to car audio.

Second, you can initiate the call from your car. Each manufacturer has its own unique call functionality, but you should be able to press a button on your car's steering wheel or dashboard and then use voice commands to dial your favorite contacts. (Some cars also let you dial from a touchscreen display on the dash-board.) You need to set up these voice commands in advance, of course; consult your car's instruction manual for more details.

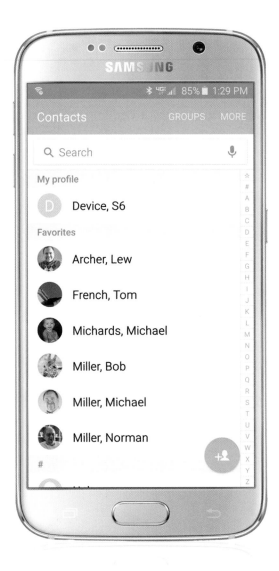

In this chapter, you find out how to use your phone's Contacts app. Topics include the following:

→ Adding and Editing Contacts
→ Using the Contacts App
→ Linking to Other Contacts
→ Working with Groups

Managing Your Contacts List

Although you can enter phone numbers manually each time you want to make a call or send a text, it's a lot easier to store the numbers of your friends and family in a contacts list and access that list when you want to reach out to your contacts. Samsung's Contacts app lets you store all sorts of useful information in addition to names and phone numbers. You can also store a person's street address and email address, as well as link to that person's profile on Facebook, Twitter, and other social networks.

Adding and Editing Contacts

All of your contacts are stored in your phone's Contacts app. This app is accessible from the favorites section at the bottom of every Home screen.

Add a New Contact

You can add new contacts manually or when you receive a phone call from a new person.

1. Tap Contacts at the bottom of any Home screen to open the Contacts app.

2. Tap the round Add icon at the bottom of the screen.

3. When prompted where to save the contact to, tap Phone.

4. Enter the contact's name (first and last) into the Name box.

5. Enter the contact's phone number into the Phone Number box. (By default, this is listed as a mobile number; to identify it as a home, work, or other type of number, tap Mobile next to the phone number and then make another selection.)

6. Enter the person's email address into the Email box. (By default, this is listed as a home email address; to identify it as a work or other type of email address, tap Home next to the address and then make another selection.)

7. Add secondary phone numbers or email addresses by tapping the + next to that section and then entering the necessary information.

8. Tap Add Another Field to add other types of information for this contact.

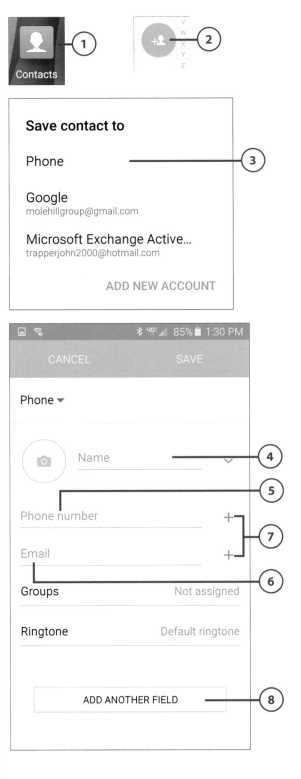

Contacts

Save contact to

Phone

Google
molehillgroup@gmail.com

Microsoft Exchange Active...
trapperjohn2000@hotmail.com

ADD NEW ACCOUNT

85% 1:30 PM

CANCEL   SAVE

Phone ▾

Name

Phone number

Email

Groups   Not assigned

Ringtone   Default ringtone

ADD ANOTHER FIELD

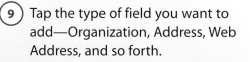

9 Tap the type of field you want to add—Organization, Address, Web Address, and so forth.

10 Tap Add.

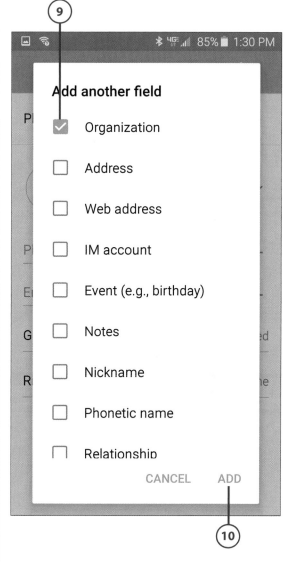

(11) The new field is now added to the main contact screen. Enter the appropriate information.

(12) Tap Save when you're done entering information.

(13) You see the contact screen for this person. Tap the back arrow to return to the main contacts list.

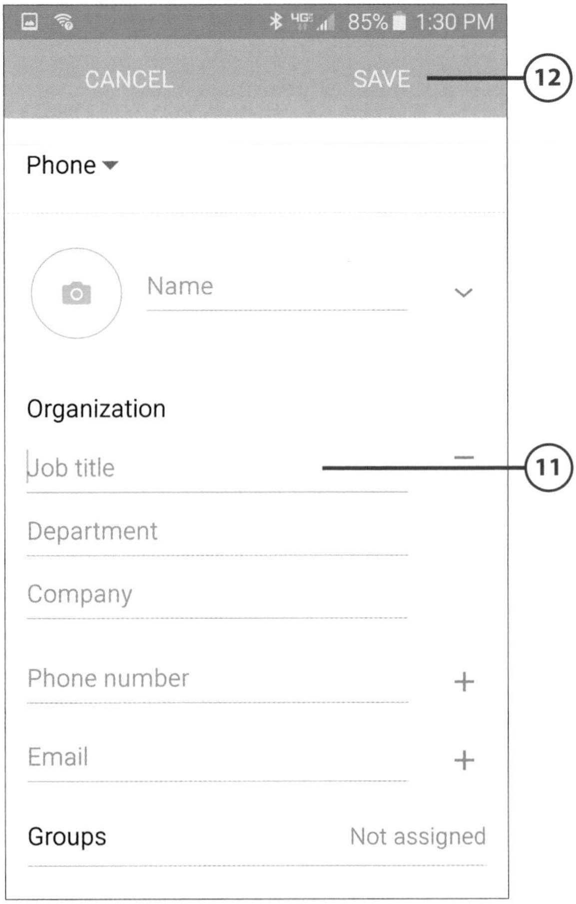

Phone ▼

Name

Organization

Job title ─── (11)

Department

Company

Phone number +

Email +

Groups   Not assigned

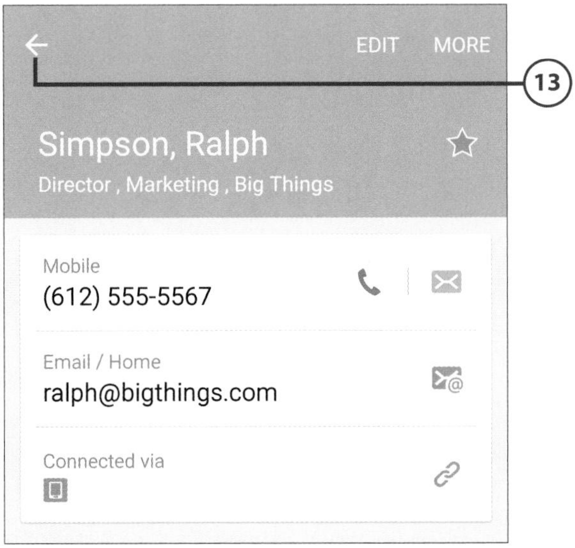

← EDIT MORE ─── (13)

Simpson, Ralph ☆
Director , Marketing , Big Things

Mobile
(612) 555-5567 📞 | ✉

Email / Home
ralph@bigthings.com ✉

Connected via 🔗

Add a New Contact from a Call

If you receive a call from someone new, you can quickly add that person to your contacts list.

(1) From the Home screen, tap the Phone icon to open the Phone app.

(2) Tap the Recent tab to display the call log.

(3) Tap the call from the person you want to add.

(4) Tap Create Contact to open a new contact screen.

(5) Enter additional information about this caller—name, email address, and so forth.

(6) Tap Save.

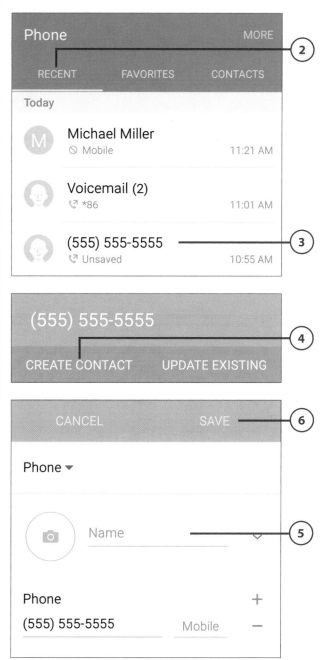

Edit Contact Information

You can, at any point, edit the information for any person in your contact list.

(1) From within the Contacts app,
navigate to and tap the name of
the contact you want to edit.

(2) Tap Edit on the person's contact
screen.

(3) Tap the field you want to edit and
make your changes.

(4) Tap Save when done.

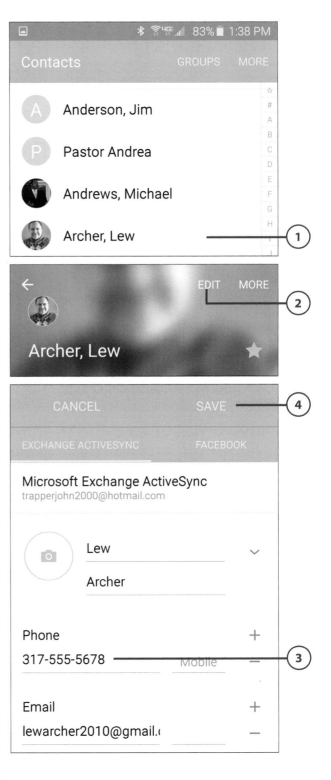

Star Favorite Contacts

You can designate the people you call or email the most as favorite contacts. All contacts marked as a favorite display together in the Favorites section at the top of your contacts list.

(1) From within the Contacts app, navigate to and tap the name of the contact you want to mark as a favorite.

(2) When the person's contact screen appears, tap the star icon, which turns gold. This contact is now favorited.

People Edge and Contact Colors

If you have a Galaxy S6 Edge (not the regular S6), you can activate the People Edge feature to display your priority contacts in color on the Edge screen. Learn more about this in Chapter 2, "Using the Galaxy S6 Edge."

Assign a Unique Ringtone to a Contact

If you often get calls from a specific contact and want to be alerted when this person is calling, you can assign a unique ringtone to that person.

(1) From within the Contacts app, navigate to and tap the name of the contact you want to edit.

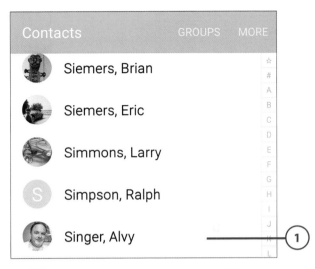

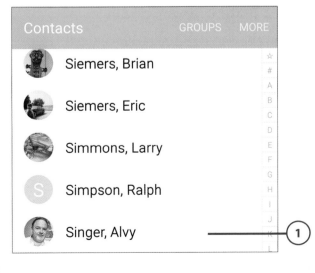

(2) Tap Edit on the person's contact screen.

(3) Scroll down the screen and tap Ringtone.

(4) Tap to select the ringtone you want for this person.

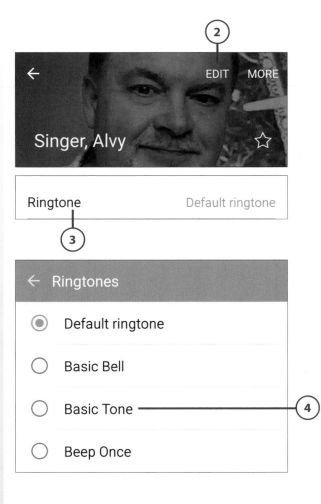

Add a Photo to a Contact

You can also add a person's picture to their contact information. This way you see the person's picture onscreen when they call you.

(1) From within the Contacts app, navigate to and tap the name of the contact.

(2) Tap Edit on the person's contact screen.

(3) Tap the camera icon next to the person's name. The camera screen opens.

(4) Tap the Camera button to take a picture of this person (assuming he or she is right in front of you) *or…*

(5) Tap the Picture icon to upload a picture of this person that's stored on your phone. Your photo gallery opens.

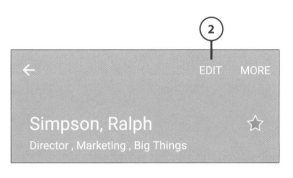

6. Scroll to and tap the picture you want to use.

7. Use your fingers to move, pinch, or spread the photo to better fit within the circle.

8. Tap Save.

9. Tap Save on the contact's page. The photo is added to this contact (not shown).

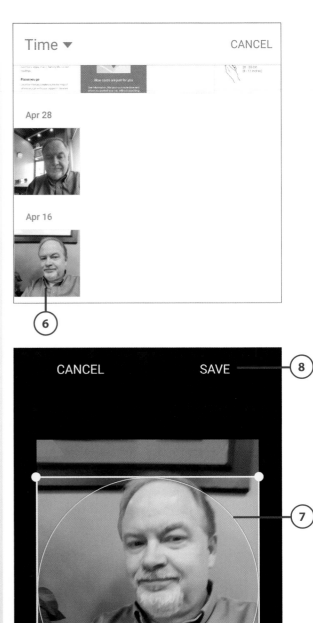

Delete a Contact

Sometimes you find you no longer communicate with a given person, and don't need (or want!) them in your contacts list. Fortunately, it's easy to delete contacts from your list.

1. From within the Contacts app, tap and hold the name of the contact you want to delete.

2. The screen changes to display check boxes beside each contact, with the current contact selected. Tap to select any other contacts you want to delete.

3. Tap Delete at the top of the screen.

4. Tap Delete in the prompt box.

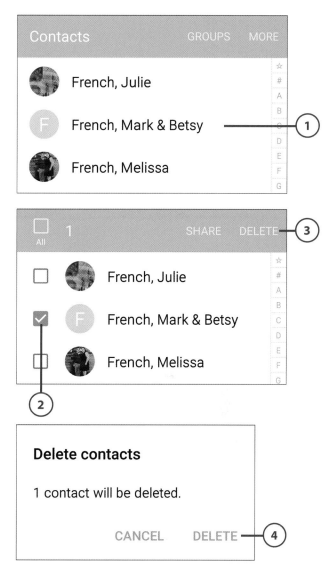

Using the Contacts App

After you've added your contacts to the Contacts app, there's a lot you can do with them—including making phone calls and sending texts and emails directly from a person's contact page.

Sort Contacts

By default, the contacts in your contacts list are sorted alphabetically by last name. You can, however, choose to sort your contacts by first name instead.

1. From within the Contacts app, tap More.

2. Tap Settings to display the Settings screen.

3. Tap Sort By.

4. Tap First Name to sort by first name.

5. Tap Last Name to sort by last name.

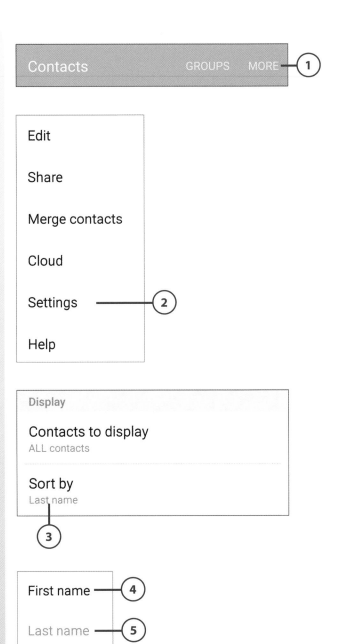

Change the Display Format

By default, the Contacts app displays your contacts in the First, Last name format. You can, if you like switch to the Last, First format.

1. From within the Contacts app, tap More.

2. Tap Settings to display the Settings screen.

3. Tap Name Format.

4. Tap Last, First to display last name first.

5. Tap First, Last to display first name first.

Contacts   GROUPS   MORE ──(1)

Edit

Share

Merge contacts

Cloud

Settings ──────(2)

Help

Display

Contacts to display
ALL contacts

Sort by
Last name

Name format
Last, first

(3)

First, last ──(5)

Last, first ──(4)

Search for Contacts

If you have a lot of contacts in your list, it might become cumbersome to scroll down until you find them. If this is a problem for you, you can use the Contact app's search function to search for specific contacts.

1. At the top of the contacts list, enter some or all of a person's name into the search box. Matching contacts display underneath the search box.

2. Tap a contact to view that person's contact screen.

Contact a Contact

You can call, text, or email a contact directly from his or her contact screen.

1. In the Contacts app, tap the name of the person you want to contact.

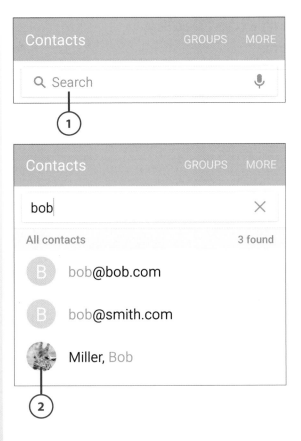

2 Tap the Phone icon to initiate a voice call with this person. This opens the Phone app and dials this person.

3 Tap the Message icon to send a text message to this person. This opens the Messages app with this person selected.

4 Tap the Email icon to send an email to this person. This opens your Email app with a new message started.

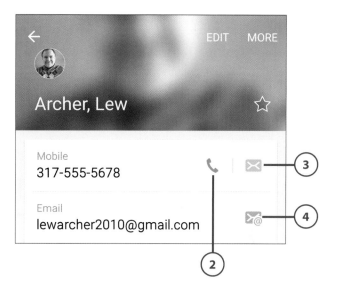

It's Not All Good

No Icons

You'll only see the Phone, Message, and Email icons if you have information of that type entered for a contact. If you have not entered a person's email address, for example, you won't see an Email icon and won't be able to email this person from within the Contacts app.

Linking to Other Contacts

By default, the Contacts app contains only those contacts you've manually added to your phone. However, you can add various social media accounts to your Galaxy S6, and your friends from those social networks are automatically added to your contacts list.

Add a New Account

When you first started using your Samsung Galaxy S6, you were prompted to enter your Google Account information. This makes it easier to use various Google and Android-related functions. It also adds your Gmail contacts (if you have a Gmail account) to your main contacts list.

You can connect your other social media accounts, including Facebook and Twitter, to your contacts list. You can also add contacts from your various email accounts. This way your contacts from across all your networks are housed and accessed from the same app.

1. Swipe down from the top of the screen to display the notification panel.

2. Tap Settings to display the Settings screen.

3. Scroll to the Personal section and tap Accounts to display the Accounts page.

4. If you've already connected your Google Account, you see listings for Email (Gmail, actually) and Google (your Google Account). If these are not displayed, you can add them manually.

5. Tap Add Account.

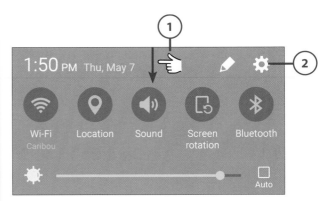

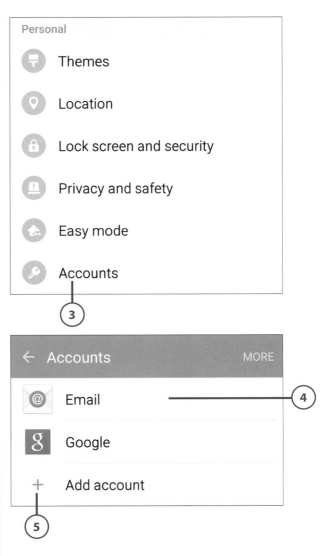

6) Tap the type of account you want to add.

7) If prompted to sign into the account, do so.

8) If prompted to sync information between this account and your phone, tap yes or okay. The contacts from this new account are now added to the Phones app. If the social network account had a profile picture for this person, that picture is used as his or her contact picture.

Account Types

You can add the following types of accounts to your phone: Amazon, Email, Facebook, Google, LDAP, LinkedIn, Microsoft Exchange, Personal Email (IMAP or POP3), Samsung Account, or Twitter. You can also opt to sync your apps with Foursquare or Google+. In addition, some mobile carriers offer their own apps and accounts that can be added.

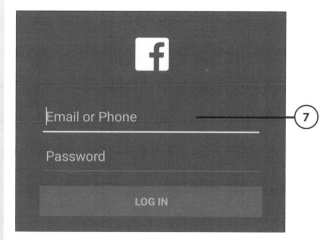

Merge Contacts from Different Accounts

If you have the same friends on different social networks, or on different email lists, you might end up having multiple contacts for them in the Contacts app. If this happens, you can merge multiple contacts for the same person into a single contact.

1. From within the Contacts app, tap More.

2. Tap Merge Contacts.

3. Tap to select two or more contacts that you know are for the same person.

4. Tap Merge. The selected contacts are merged into a single contact.

Delete Accounts

You might find that you don't actually want all the contacts from your various accounts synced into a single contacts list; too many contacts can sometimes be overwhelming. If this is the case, you can opt to disconnect a given account from your phone.

1. Swipe down from the top of the screen to display the notification panel.

2. Tap Settings to display the Settings screen.

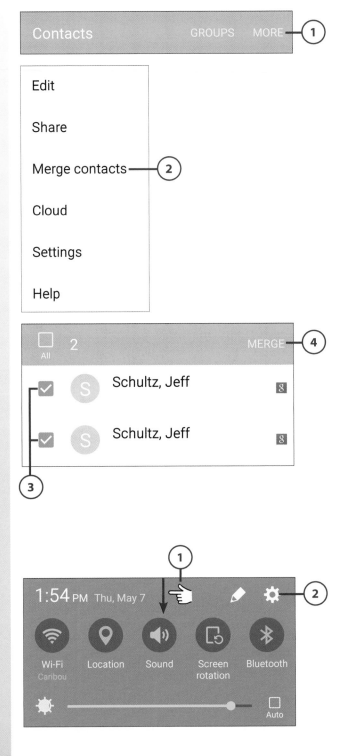

3 Scroll to the Personal section and tap Accounts to display the Accounts page.

4 Tap to select the account you want to delete.

5 Tap More.

6 Tap Remove Account.

7 Tap Remove Account in the prompt box.

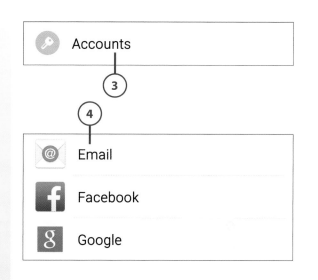

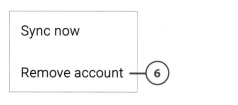

Sync now

Remove account

Remove account

Removing the account will delete all of its messages, contacts, and other data from the phone. Continue?

CANCEL   REMOVE ACCOUNT

Working with Groups

There's one more thing you can do from the Contacts app. If you regularly send emails or texts to a group of people—members of a golf league, say, or friends in a book club—you can create a contacts group. You can then send messages or emails to everyone in the group with a single action; you don't have to enter every single name separately.

Create a Group

You create new groups from within the Contacts app. In fact, the app comes with several common groups preloaded—Auction Winners, Coffeehouse Friends, Co-Workers, Family, Friends, My Contacts, Newsletter, Special Friends, Starred in Android, and YouTube.

1. From within the Contacts app, tap Groups to display the Groups screen. You see a list of existing groups.

2. Tap Add to add a new group.

3. Type a name for the group into the Group Name box.

4. If you want to add members now, Tap Add Member. (See the "Add Contacts to a Group" section for more information.)

5. Tap Group Ringtone and make a selection to set a default ringtone for messages from members of this group.

6. Tap Save.

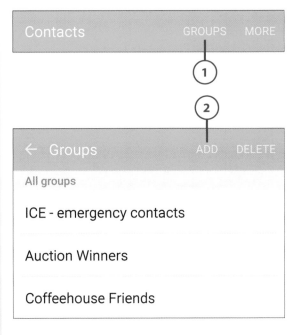

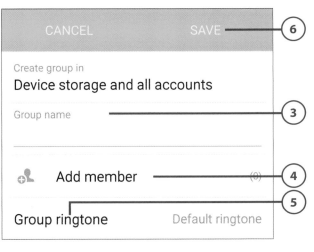

Add Contacts to a Group

You add new members to a group from your main contacts list.

1. From within the Contacts app, tap Groups to display the Groups screen.

2. Tap the group you want to add members to.

3. Tap Add to display your contacts list.

4. Tap to select those contacts you want to add.

5. Tap Done. The selected contacts are now added to the group.

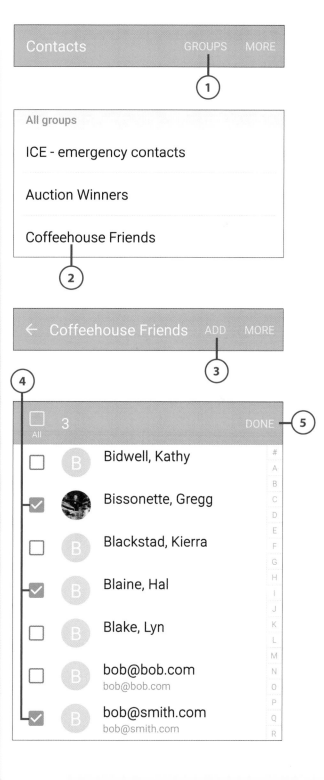

Send a Text Message to a Group

You can use your messaging app to send a text message to all the members of a group.

(1) From within your messaging app, create a new message.

(2) Enter the name of the group as the recipient.

(3) Type and send your message as normal. It is sent to all members of the group for whom you have mobile phone numbers.

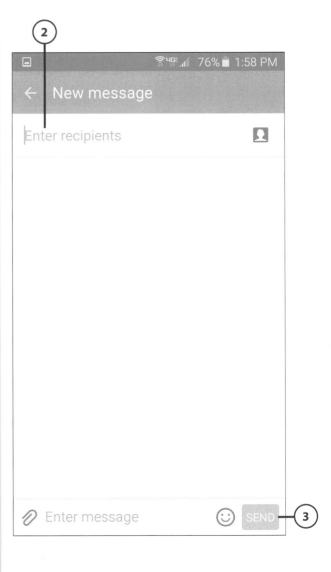

Send an Email to a Group

You can also send group emails to members of a group.

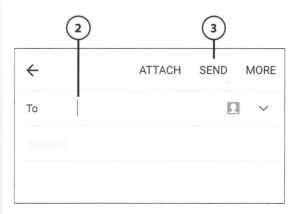

1 From within your email app, create a new message.

2 Enter the name of the group as the recipient.

3 Type and send your message as normal. It is sent to all members of the group for whom you have email addresses.

In this chapter, you see how to send and receive text and multimedia messages on your phone. Topics include the following:

→ Choosing a Messaging App
→ Sending and Receiving Messages
→ Sending and Receiving Multimedia Messages
→ Working with Priority Senders
→ Configuring the Messages App

9

Texting Friends and Family

These days, an increasing number of people use their phones less for voice calls and more for text messaging—what we colloquially call texting. It's easy to pop off a short text message while you're in the middle of doing something else; you can even participate in multiple text sessions with different people at the same time.

Of course, to be a proficient texter you need nimble fingers, proficiency with your phone's onscreen keyboard, and a decent messaging app. Although this book can't help you with your fingers, it does examine the most popular text messaging app and how to get the most out of it.

Choosing a Messaging App

Before you start sending texting, you need to choose a messaging app for your phone. You can choose from the messaging apps preinstalled on your Galaxy S6 or S6 Edge, or you can download a separate messaging app from the Google Play Store.

Examining Messaging Apps

Every Samsung smartphone comes with the Messages app preinstalled. This is a good, solid app that does everything you need it to do. There are also several well-regarded messaging apps available in the Google Play Store. The following table details some of the more popular of these apps.

App Icon	Name	Price
	Chomp SMS	Free
	Handcent SMS	Free
	Hello SMS	Free
	Textra SMS	Free

All of these apps are free, so feel free to download and experiment with them. Just open the Play Store app and search for the app you want.

In addition, it's likely that your mobile carrier has installed its own messaging app on your phone. For example, Verizon installs the Verizon Message+ app on phones it sells to its customers; AT&T installs the AT&T Messages app.

Most of these apps work in a similar fashion, so it's difficult to go wrong, whichever app you choose. The examples in this book use the default Messages app that Samsung installs on all of its smartphones.

>>>Go Further

SMS AND MMS

Text messages are technically SMS messages. SMS stands for Short Messaging Service, and it lets you send and receive text messages to and from other mobile phones.

When you send and receive pictures or videos via messaging, you're using MMS. This is short for Multimedia Messaging Services, which enables non-text attachments to be sent along with text messages. Most messaging apps support both SMS and MMS messages.

SMS and MMS messages are sent over your mobile carrier's network. You might have to subscribe to a separate service or level to send and receive messages. Some plans offer a set number of messages for a flat price; others offer unlimited messaging. If your plan limits the number of messages you can send or receive, take care not to go over this limit, or you'll incur excess messaging charges.

Set a Default Messaging App

If you have more than one messaging app installed on your phone, you need to tell your phone which one you want to use by default. You can then add this app to the Favorites area of your Home screen. (Your other messaging apps will still be available from the Apps screen.)

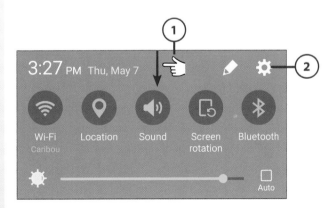

1. Swipe down from the top of the screen to display the notification panel.

2. Tap Settings to display the Settings screen.

3 Scroll to the Device section and tap Applications to display the Applications screen.

4 Tap Default Applications to display the Default Applications screen.

5 Tap Messages.

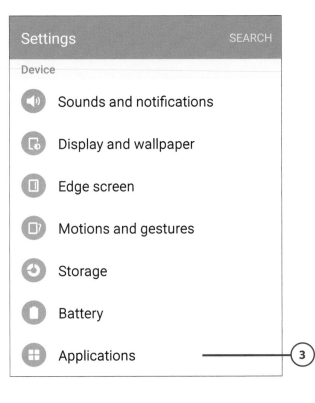

6 Tap to select the messaging app you want to use.

Displaying the Messages Shortcut

After you select your default messaging app, you might need to add a shortcut to that app to your Home screen. Tap Apps to display the Apps screen; then tap and drag the icon for your messaging app onto the appropriate Home screen—or onto the favorites area at the bottom of every Home screen.

6

Messages

◉ ✉ Messages

○ 💬 Hangouts

○ 💬 Message+

CANCEL

Sending and Receiving Messages

Sending and receiving texts is easy. (If it wasn't so easy, people wouldn't text so much!) And although it's likely that your children and grandchildren do a lot more texting than you ever will, you need to know how to text if you want to keep in touch.

Send a Text Message

A text message is nothing more than a line or two of text—or even just a single word!

1 From your phone's Home screen, tap the Messages icon to launch the Messages app.

2 Tap the Compose button to display the New Message screen and onscreen keyboard.

3 Type the name of the person you want to text into the Enter Recipients box. Separate multiple names with semicolons (;) or...

4 Tap the Add Recipient icon to display your contacts list.

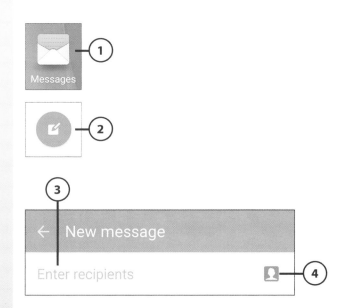

1

Messages

2

3

← New message

Enter recipients 👤 —**4**

(5) Tap to select one or more recipients for this text. The recipients' names appear at the top of the screen.

(6) Tap Done to return to the New Message screen.

(7) Tap in the Enter Message area and use the onscreen keyboard to type your message.

(8) Tap Send to send the message.

(9) Tap the back arrow at the top of the screen to return to the main Messages screen.

Exit Before Sending

If you exit the Messages app before sending a message, that message will be saved as a draft you can send at a later time.

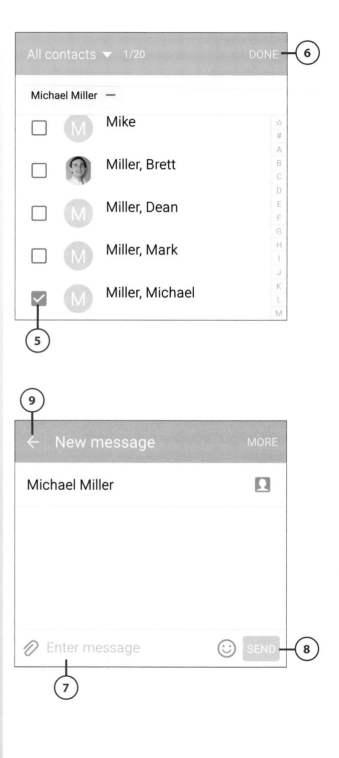

Read and Reply to a Message

When someone sends you a text, you receive a notification to that effect. (You also see new message icon in your phone's status bar.) You can read and respond to the text from the notification or from the Messages app.

(1) From the notification, tap View *or...*

(2) Swipe from the top of the screen to view the notification panel and then tap the message *or...*

(3) From the main screen of the Messages app, tap the message you want to read.

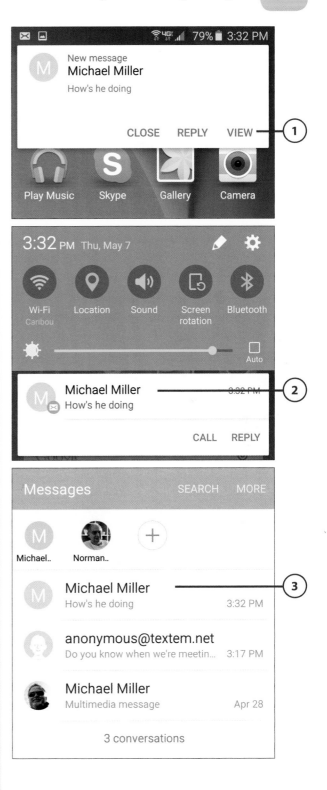

4 You now see all recent messages to and from this person or group of people. (This is called a *conversation*.) Your messages appear on the right side of the screen; the other person's messages appear on the left.

5 Reply to this message by tapping in the Enter Message area and, when the onscreen keyboard appears, type your message.

6 Tap Send.

7 Return to the main Messages screen and tap the back arrow at the top of the screen.

Use Emoji

Some people like to enhance their messages with little icons called emoji. As mentioned in Chapter 1, "Getting Started with Your Samsung Galaxy S6," an emoji is a small picture or icon used to express an emotion or idea. For example, if you like a person's text, you might reply with a smiley face or thumbs-up emoji instead of (or in addition to) a text message. If there's something you don't like, respond with a frowning face or thumbs-down emoji. You get the idea.

1 From within a message or conversation, tap the Emoji icon in the Enter Message area. This displays a collection of emoji.

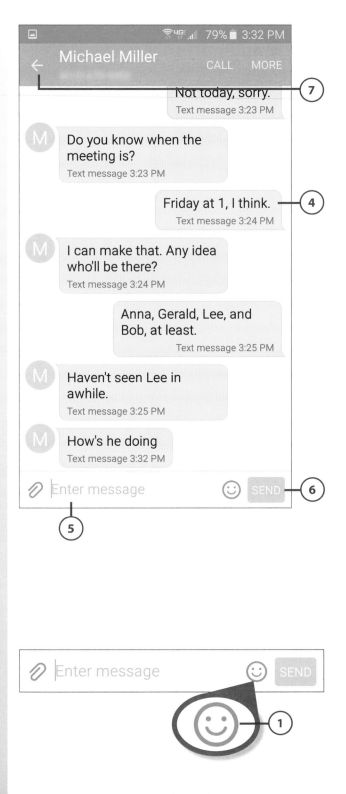

(**2**) Tap the appropriate tab to view a certain type of emoji.

(**3**) Tap the emoji you want to insert.

(**4**) Finish typing any text you want.

(**5**) Tap Send.

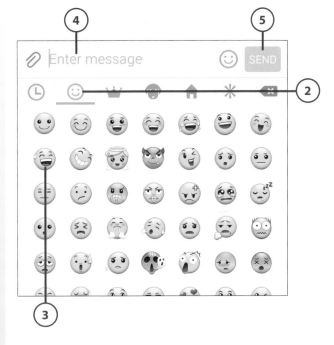

Delete Conversations

All your conversations are displayed on the main Messages screen. If you want to clean up this screen a bit, you can delete older conversations. (In fact, it's a good idea to delete your older conversations periodically, especially those that include videos or photos, to free up storage space on your phone.)

(**1**) From the main Messages screen, tap More.

(**2**) Tap Edit.

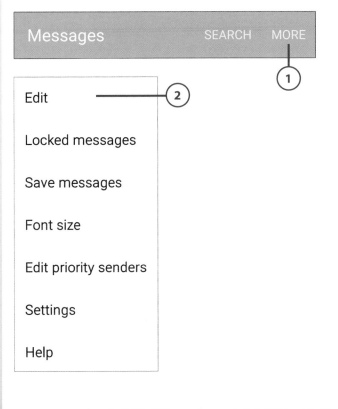

(**3**) Tap to select those conversations you want to delete.

(**4**) Tape Delete.

(**5**) When prompted to delete the conversation, tap Delete.

			DELETE SAVE
All	1		

Michael.. Norman..

☐ **Michael Miller**
How's he doing   3:32 PM

☑ **anonymous@textem.net**
Do you know when we're...   3:17 PM

☐ **Michael Miller**
Multimedia message   Apr 28

Delete conversation

1 conversation will be deleted.

CANCEL   DELETE

>>>Go Further
TEXTING ETIQUETTE

Just what should you text—and how? There is some very real etiquette involved in texting.

First, you don't have to use complete sentences. You don't have to use proper punctuation. You don't even have to use correct spelling. Texting is all about quickness and immediacy, and sometimes that means sending a single word or typing without capitalizing any letters. In the world of texting, it's better to be fast than to be precise. It's okay to make mistakes.

Second, don't write long-winded texts. Texts are short messages, with the emphasis on *short*. You don't have to write in complete paragraphs and sentences. Write enough words to get your point across, then tap the Send button. That's enough.

Third, about that fast thing. When somebody texts you, they expect an immediate response. If they didn't want an immediate response, they would email you instead. Think of texting as carrying on a conversation, but by typing instead of talking. You don't want to leave unnecessary gaps in the conversation.

Fourth, don't bombard your friends with too many texts. Yes, the kids text all the time about nothing much in particular, but you're not a kid and you're not texting other kids. (Unless you're texting your own kids or grandkids, of course, then all bets are off.) Text your friends and family when there's something important to share. Otherwise, don't.

Fifth and finally, don't text and drive. In many states it's against the law. In every state, it's just plain dangerous. Texting in the car requires you to take your eyes off the road, even if just for a second or two—and that's long enough for bad things to happen that you won't have time to respond to. Ignore the dinging of those incoming texts and keep focused on your driving. You can answer any text you receive at your next stop.

Sending and Receiving Multimedia Messages

An MMS message is a text message with some form of media attached. Most often, this means sending a photo or video along with your text message.

Attach a Photo or Video File

You can send lots of different types of files in an MMS message—images, videos, audio, memos, calendar events, contact information, and even maps. This section focuses on photos and videos, as they're most common.

(1) From within the Messages app, tap the Compose button to display the New Message screen and onscreen keyboard.

2 Select the recipient and enter any text for the message, as normal.

3 Tap the File icon to display the Attach panel.

4 Tap the type of file you want to attach. To attach a photo, tap Image. To attach a video, tap Video.

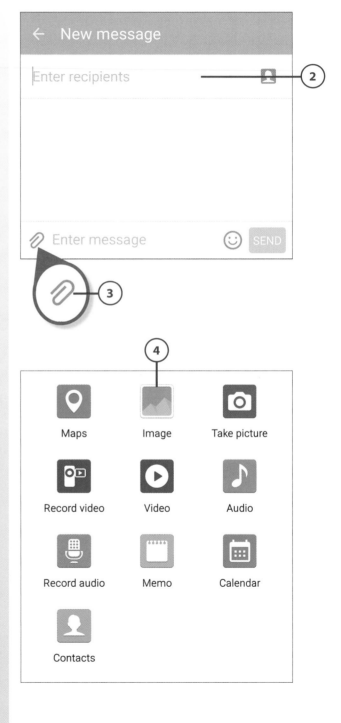

5 If prompted to select an app to complete the action, tap Gallery.

6 Tap to select the image or video you want to send.

7 Tap Done.

8 The image or video thumbnail is added in the message area. Tap Send to send the message.

Shoot and Send a Photo

You're not limited to sending photos stored in your phone's gallery. You can also shoot a new photo on the spot to send with your text.

1. From within the Messages app, tap the Compose button to display the New Message screen and onscreen keyboard.

2. Select the recipient and enter any text for the message, as normal.

3. Tap the File icon to display the Attach panel.

4. Tap Take Picture. The Camera app opens.

New message

Enter recipients ——————— 2

Enter message 😊 SEND

3

4

Image   Maps   Take picture

Record video   Video   Audio

5 Aim at your subject and then tap the Camera button.

6 You see a preview of your picture. If you like what you see, tap OK. (If you don't like the picture, tap Retry and try again.)

7 The photo appears in the message area. Tap Send to send the message.

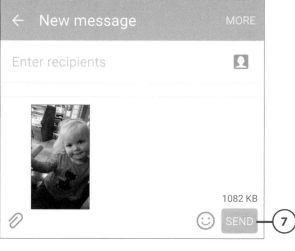

Shoot and Send a Video

Shooting and sending a new video is similar to sending a photo.

1. From within the Messages app, tap the Compose button to display the New Message screen and onscreen keyboard.

2. Select the recipient and enter any text for the message, as normal.

3. Tap the File icon to display the Attach panel.

4. Tap Record Video. The Camera app opens.

New message

Enter recipients

Enter message   SEND

Image   Maps   Take picture

Record video   Video   Audio

(5) Aim at your subject and then tap
the Video Camera button to start
recording.

(6) Tap the Stop button to stop
recording, or just let the
recording stop by itself—you can
record videos only up to three
seconds in length.

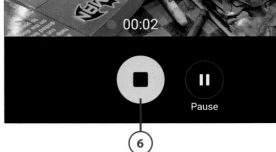

(**7**) You see a preview of your video. Tap Play to play the video.

(**8**) If you like what you see, tap OK. (If you don't like the video, tap Retry and try again.)

(**9**) A thumbnail of the video appears in the message area. Tap Send to send the message.

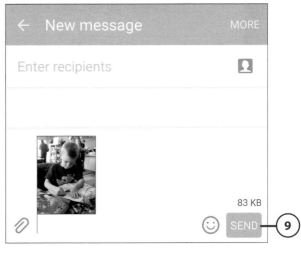

Send a Map of Your Current Location

There's one more type of item you might want to text from time to time. If you want to let someone know exactly where you are, you can text them a map of your current location.

1 From within the Messages app, tap the Compose button to display the New Message screen and onscreen keyboard.

2 Select the recipient and enter any text for the message, as normal.

3 Tap the File icon to display the Attach panel.

4 Tap Maps.

New message

Enter recipients — **2**

Enter message SEND

3

4

Image   Maps   Take picture

Record video   Video   Audio

(5) You see a map of your current location. Tap Done.

(6) A thumbnail of your map appears in the message area. Tap Send to send the message.

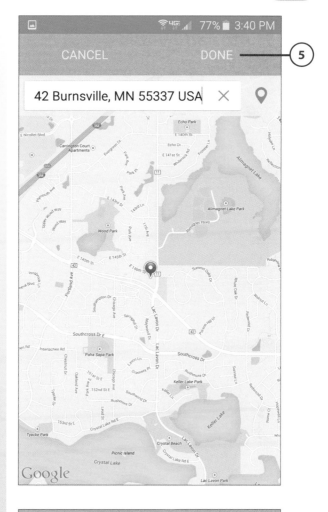

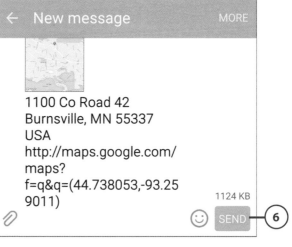

View Photos and Videos You Receive

What do you do if someone sends you a photo or video via text? Look at them, of course!

(1) Tap a picture to view it fullscreen.

(2) Tap a video to watch it fullscreen.

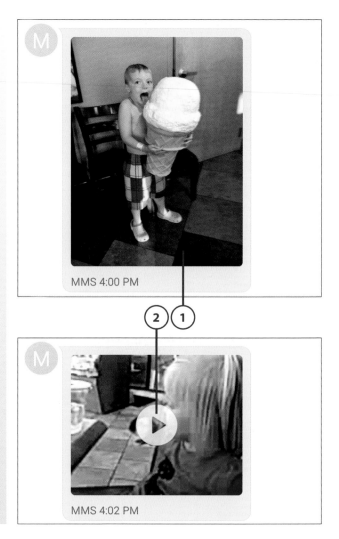

Working with Priority Senders

If you find yourself texting with the same people over and over, you set those folks as *priority senders*, which makes it easier to send messages to them.

Set Priority Senders

You can designate any person in your contacts list as a priority sender—and have multiple priority senders in your Messages app.

(1) Add your first priority sender by tapping More in the main screen of the Messages app.

(2) Tap Add Priority Senders to display your contacts list.

(3) Tap to select a contact you want to set as a priority sender.

(4) Tap Done.

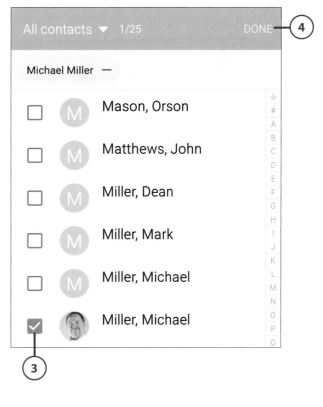

5 Add additional priority senders by tapping the + at the top of the main Messages screen and then repeating steps 3 and 4.

Text to Priority Senders

Priority senders appear at the top of the Messages screen. You can add other priority senders by tapping the + button.

1 From the main screen in the Messages app, tap the priority sender you want to text.

2 If you've previously texted this person, you see your past conversation. Otherwise, you see the New Message screen.

3 Enter your text as normal.

4 Tap Send.

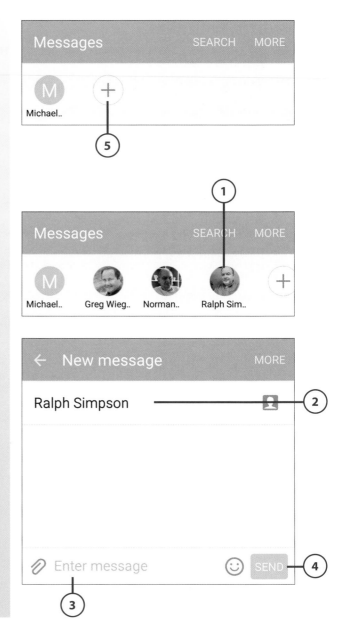

Configuring the Messages App

There are several settings in the Messages app you can configure to personalize your texting experience. In particular, you can personalize the display and font size to make your texts easier to read.

Personalize the Display

The first thing you can configure is the text display itself—the backgrounds and bubbles you see on the main Messages screen.

(1) From the main screen in the Messages app, tap More.

(2) Tap Settings to display the Settings screen.

(3) Tap Backgrounds and Bubbles.

| Messages | SEARCH | MORE |

(1)

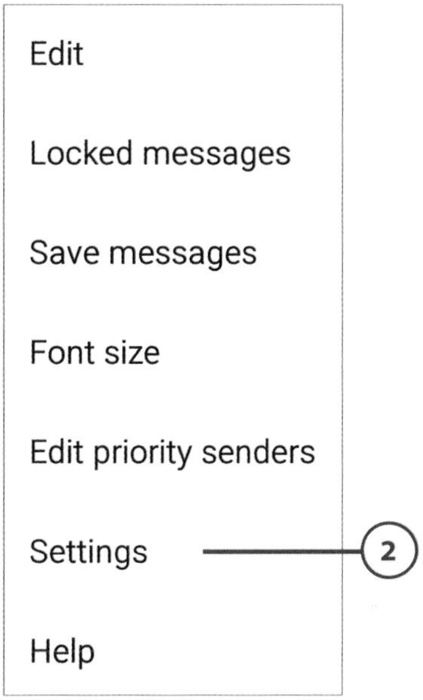

Edit

Locked messages

Save messages

Font size

Edit priority senders

Settings ———————(2)

Help

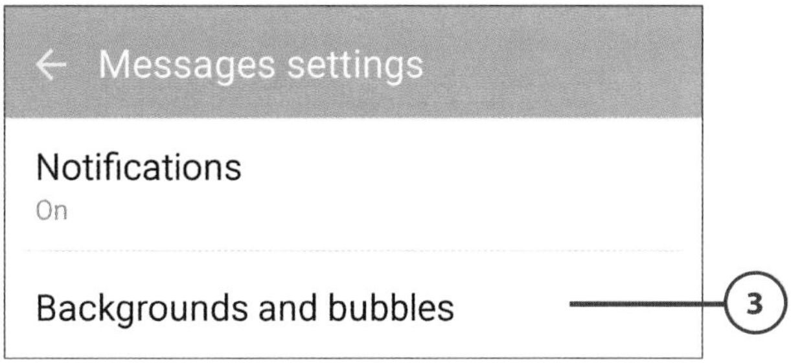

← Messages settings

Notifications
On

Backgrounds and bubbles ———————(3)

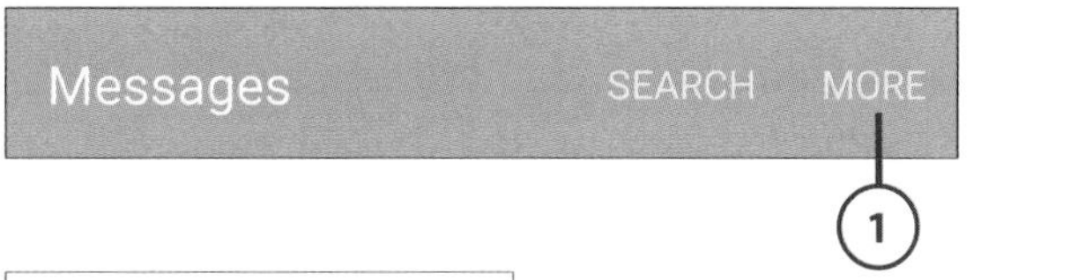

4 The top of the screen displays your current selections. At the bottom of the screen are two scrolling bands. Swipe the top band to view different bubble styles, then tap the style you want.

5 Swipe the bottom band to view different background styles, then tap the background you want.

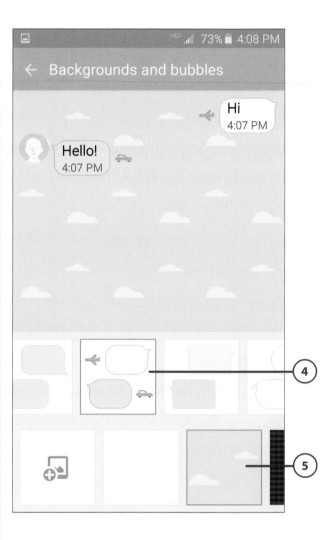

Change Font Size

You might find that the default font size in the Messages app is too small to read comfortably. Fortunately, it's easy to increase the size of the font to make it easier to read.

1 From the main screen in the Messages app, tap More.

② Tap Font Size to display the Font Size panel.

③ Tap to select the size you want, from Tiny to Huge.

Resizing on the Fly

You can also resize message text when you're reading a message. Just press the Volume Up or Down keys on the side of your phone to increase or decrease the font size, accordingly. In addition, you can pinch or stretch the screen with your fingers to make the text smaller or larger.

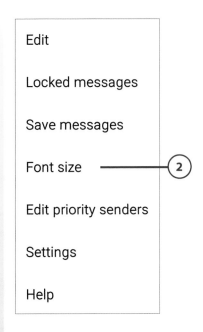

Edit

Locked messages

Save messages

Font size

Edit priority senders

Settings

Help

Font size

○   Use device font sizes

○   Tiny

○   Extra small

◉   Small

○   Medium

○   Large

○   Extra large

○   Huge

CANCEL

Inbox ▼
MillerWriter

SEARCH   MORE

Unread 0   Last synced 5:25 PM

Sherry Miller   3:44 PM
Good afternoon
Mike: Hope your day has been productive bet...   ☆

Jared Rendell   12:26 PM
Re: Service bulletin and @Grace announc...
Hey, Just an note, but its really important. Yo...   ☆

Michelle Newcomb   12:15 PM
Re: My S6 for Seniors
Hi. Can you put the chapters when they are re...   ☆

Doodle   12:14 PM
Doodle: "GraceAbounds Rehearsals" Upd...
Michael Miller just participated. View this poll...   ☆

Michael Miller (via Doodle)   12:13 PM
GraceAbounds Rehearsals
Michael Miller invites you to participate in the...   ☆

Doodle   12:13 PM
Doodle: Link for poll "GraceAbounds Reh...
Hi Michael Miller, You have initiated a poll "Gr...   ☆

Doodle
Welcome to your Doodle account
Welcome! Check out what you can do with yo...

In this chapter, you learn how to send and receive email on your new Samsung Galaxy S6 or S6 Edge. Topics include the following:

→ Using Samsung's Email App
→ Using Gmail

Sending and Receiving Email

Email is an essential part of most people's lives. It's how we communicate with friends and families, as well as with co-workers and organizations we work with. Because your new Samsung smartphone connects to the Internet, you can use it to send and receive email messages.

Using Samsung's Email App

The default email app for Samsung smartphones is called, simply, Email. You can configure the Email app to work with AOL Mail, Microsoft Exchange, Outlook.com, Yahoo! Mail, and IMAP/POP3 email services.

Add a New Account

Before you can use the Email app, you need to configure to work with your various email accounts. In most instances, all you need to know to do this is your email address and password.

① From your phone's Home screen tap the Email (*not* Gmail!) icon to open the Email app.

② The first time you use the Email app, you'll be prompted to set up your email account. On subsequent uses, tap More to add additional accounts.

③ Tap Settings to display the Settings screen.

④ Tap + Add Account.

⑤ Tap the type of account you want to add—AOL, Corporate, Outlook.com, Yahoo! Mail, or Other. (There may also be an option for the email account provided by your carrier.)

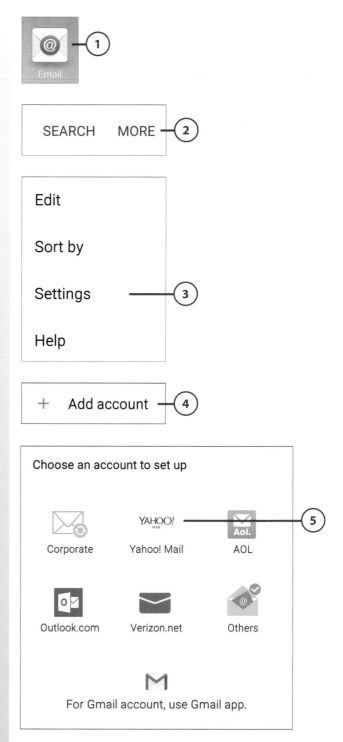

(**6**) Enter your email address into the Email Address box.

(**7**) Enter your email password into the Password box.

Outlook.com

If you select Outlook.com, you need to pull down the Select Service list to select from Outlook.com, Hotmail.com, MSN.com, or Live.com accounts—all owned by Microsoft.

(**8**) If you want this to be your primary email account when sending emails from your phone, select the Set This Account as the Default for Sending Emails option.

(**9**) Tap Next.

(**10**) The Email app now logs into your account, confirms the connection, and then displays the Sync Settings screen. In most cases you should leave the settings alone. Tap Next.

Register email accounts in just a few steps.

Email address ——————— (**6**)

Password ——————— (**7**)

☐ Show password

☐ Set this account as the default for sending emails. ——— (**8**)

NEXT ⟩ (**9**)

Period to sync Email

1 month ▾

Sync schedule

Every 15 minutes ▾

☑ Notify me when email arrives

NEXT → (**10**)

(11) Your account is now set up. If you want to change the name of the account, tap the current account name and type a new one.

(12) Tap Next to complete the configuration.

Your account has been set up. You can now change your account name and your name for outgoing email.

Account name (optional)
doctorwu_1997@yahoo.com ⟶ (11)

Your name (for outgoing email)
doctorwu_1997

NEXT ➤ (12)

Switch Between Accounts

If you have the Email app configured for more than one account, you can display the inbox for each account, or for all accounts combined.

(1) From the Email app's main screen, tap the Inbox down arrow.

(2) Tap a specific account to view that account's inbox.

(3) Tap Combined Inbox to view messages from all your accounts in a single inbox, identified by color.

(4) Tap Priority Senders to view messages from your designated priority senders.

(1)

Inbox ▼
MillerWriter   SEARCH   MORE

(2)
(3)

Combined view

📧 Combined inbox

📨 MillerWriter

📨 doctorwu_1997@yahoo.com

👤 Priority senders ⟶ (4)

⭐ Starred (2)

Read and Reply to Messages

Email messages you receive from other users are stored in your inbox. From there you can read and reply to these messages.

(**1**) Open the Email app, tap the Inbox down arrow, and select which account you want to view.

(**2**) All incoming messages in the selected account are displayed, the newest first. Unread messages have a white background; messages you've read appear with a shaded background. Each message displays the sender's name, the subject of the message (in bold), and the first line of the message. You also see the date or time the message was received. Scroll down to view more messages.

(**3**) Tap the message you want to read. The message opens on the next screen.

Spam and Phishing
For information about email spam and phishing, see the bonus task, "Email Apps and Spam" on the book's website at www.informit.com/title/9780789755445.

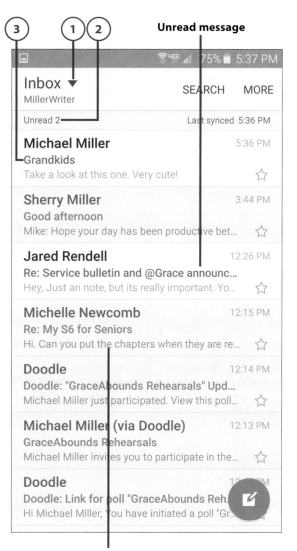

Unread message

Read message

4 By default, the Email app does not display images embedded in messages. To show images in a message, tap Show Images.

5 Tap Delete to delete this message after you've read it.

6 Tap the back arrow to return to the inbox.

7 Tap Reply to write a response to this message. (If the message was sent to multiple recipients, send your reply to all of them by tapping Reply All.)

Recipient

6

Sender   **Subject**

Date and time received

Message body

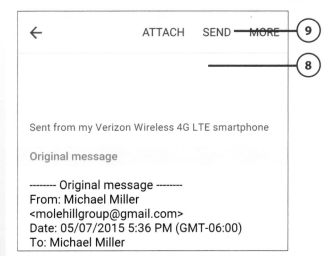

(8) You see the reply screen, with the sender's name or email address already added to the To: field and the original message displayed beneath. Use the onscreen keyboard to type your reply.

(9) Tap Send to send the email.

Create a New Message

It's also easy to create and send a new email message. You can enter the recipient's email address manually or automatically send to anyone in your contacts list.

(1) From the inbox screen, tap the New Message icon to open a new message.

(2) If you have multiple email accounts, tap the From down arrow to select which email account you want to send from.

(3) Tap in the To box and type the recipient's email address.

(4) The Email app displays matching contacts. Tap a name to select it, or finishing typing the name. If you want to send to more than one person, separate address with semicolons (;) or...

5 Tap the Add Recipient icon to display your contacts list.

6 Tap to select one or more recipients for this text.

7 The recipients' names appear at the top of the screen. Tap Done to return to the new message screen.

8 Tap in the Subject box and type the subject of this email.

9 Tap in the box beneath the Subject box and type your email message.

10 Tap Send to send the message.

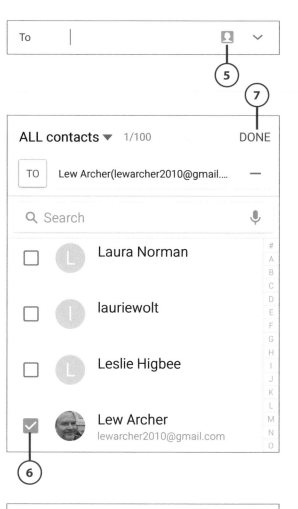

Send Photos and Other Attachments

You can send photos and other files stored on your phone via email. To send a file, you attach it to your message; these files are called *attachments*.

1. From within a new message, tap Attach to open the Attach panel.

2. Tap the type of file you want to attach—Images, Video, Audio, Memo, Calendar, Contacts, or Maps. To attach a different file type, tap My Files. You can also shoot a new photo or record new audio or video to attach.

3. Select the item you want to attach.

4. Tap Done.

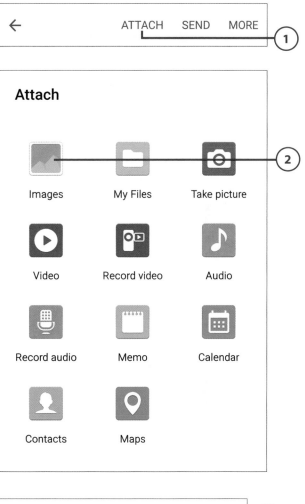

5 If you're attaching a photo, video, or other large file, you might be asked to resize the item. (Larger attachments take longer to upload and download, but resizing a photograph smaller reduces the picture quality.) Make a selection.

6 The item is added to your email. If you decide not to attach this item, tap the minus (–) sign.

7 Finish creating the message as normal and then tap Send.

Resize image

Original

Large (70%) ————————————— **5**

Medium (30%)

Small (10%)

← ATTACH SEND MORE **7**

To 👤 ⌄

From | MillerWriter ▼

Subject

Sent from my Verizon Wireless 4G LTE smartphone

1 item (1.5 MB/50.0 MB)

20150505_164441_resi... 1.5 MB —— **6**

Using Gmail

Google's Gmail is the most popular web-based email service today. If you added your Google Account to your phone, Gmail has already been set up for you. (Google uses your Gmail address to sign into your Google Account.) You can access Gmail from any computer, smartphone, or tablet, using any web browser. On the Samsung Galaxy S6, you access Gmail from the Gmail app.

Configure Your Google Account

When you first set up your Galaxy S6 or S6 Edge, you probably configured the phone to work with your Google Account. If you have not yet done this, you need to do so to use Gmail. (Your Google Account is linked to your Gmail address.)

(1) Swipe down from the top of the screen to display the notification panel.

(2) Tap Settings to display the Settings screen.

(3) Scroll to the Personal section and tap Accounts.

(4) Tap Add Account.

(5) Tap Google.

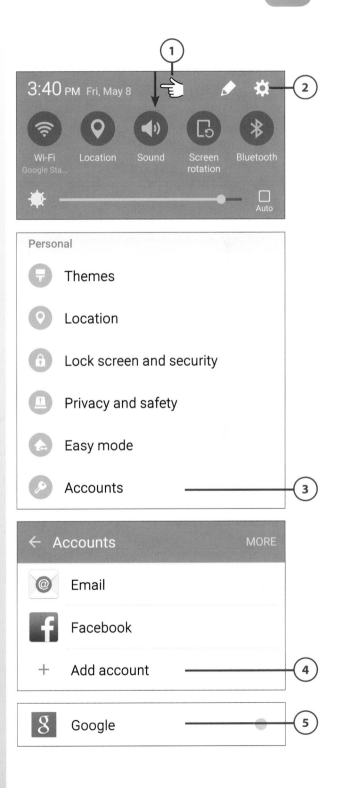

(6) Type your Gmail address into the
Enter Your Email box.

(7) Tap Next.

Creating a New Account

If you do not yet have a Google
Account, tap Or Create a New Account
and follow the onscreen instructions to
create an account. (It's free!)

(8) Enter your Gmail password into
the Password box.

(9) Tap Next.

(10) Tap Accept to agree to Google's
terms and conditions.

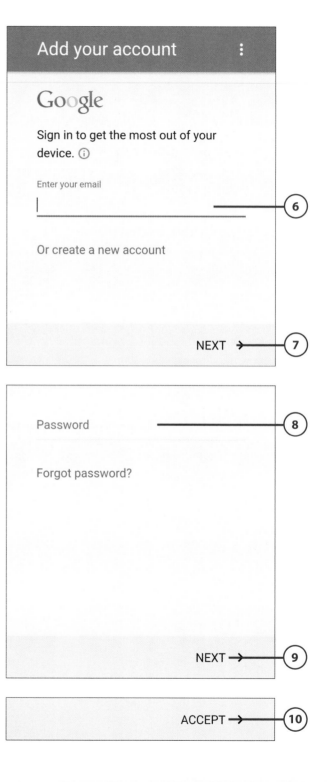

11 Tap Next to use Google to back up your phone's settings, apps, and data.

12 The next screen asks for your payment information. This is only necessary if and when you purchase apps, music, or videos from the Google Play Store. For now, tap Remind Me Later.

13 Tap Next. Your account is added to your phone and the Gmail app.

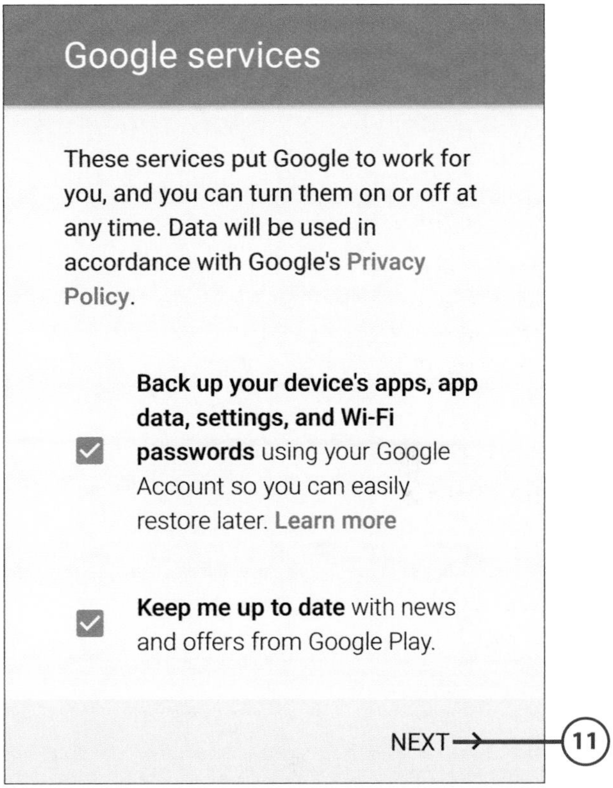

Google services

These services put Google to work for you, and you can turn them on or off at any time. Data will be used in accordance with Google's Privacy Policy.

☑ **Back up your device's apps, app data, settings, and Wi-Fi passwords** using your Google Account so you can easily restore later. Learn more

☑ **Keep me up to date** with news and offers from Google Play.

NEXT → **11**

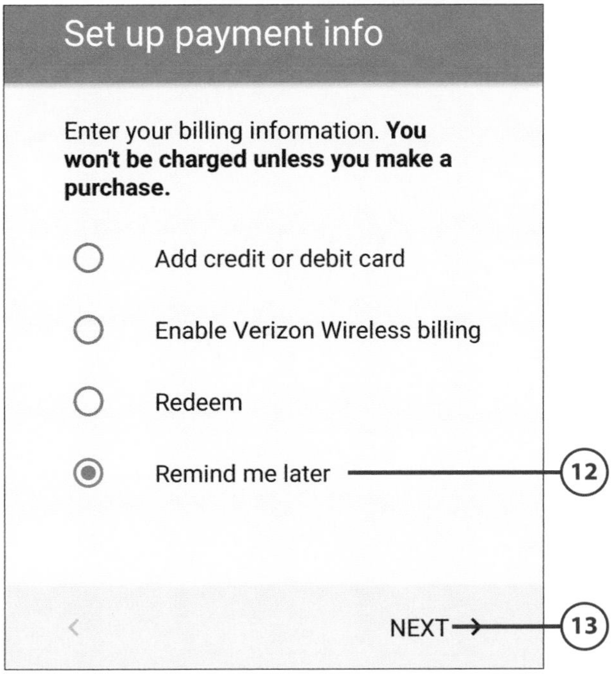

Set up payment info

Enter your billing information. **You won't be charged unless you make a purchase.**

○ Add credit or debit card

○ Enable Verizon Wireless billing

○ Redeem

◉ Remind me later ——— **12**

‹ NEXT → **13**

Read and Reply to Messages

Gmail organizes your inbox into three tabs, which show as separate screens on your phone. The Primary tab is where you see your most important messages. The Social tab displays messages related to your social networking activity. And the Promotions tab is where advertising messages most often end up.

1. From your phone's Home screen, tap the Gmail icon to open the Gmail app.

2. Tap the Options button to display the Options panel.

3. Tap the inbox you want to view—Primary, Social, or Promotions.

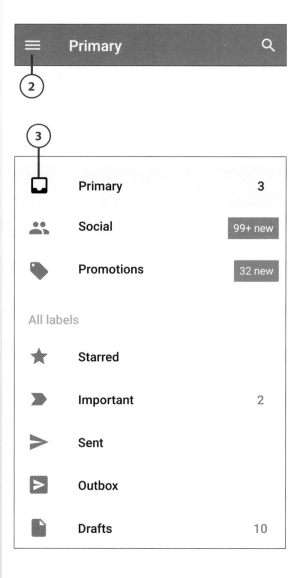

(4) The latest messages in the selected inbox are displayed. Unread messages appear in bold; messages you've read are not bolded. Each message displays the sender's name, the subject, the first line of the message, and the date or time it was received.

(5) Tap the message you want to read. The message opens on the next screen.

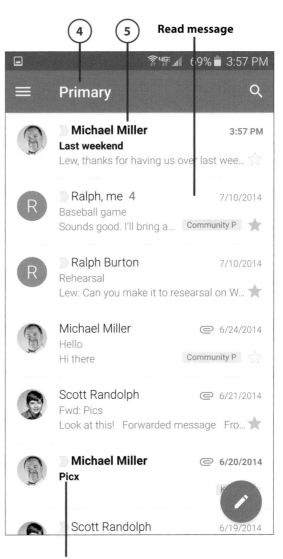

(4) (5)   **Read message**

≡ **Primary**   🔍

Michael Miller   3:57 PM
Last weekend
Lew, thanks for having us over last wee... ☆

Ralph, me 4   7/10/2014
Baseball game
Sounds good. I'll bring a...   Community P ★

Ralph Burton   7/10/2014
Rehearsal
Lew: Can you make it to researsal on W... ★

Michael Miller   📎 6/24/2014
Hello
Hi there   Community P ☆

Scott Randolph   📎 6/21/2014
Fwd: Pics
Look at this! Forwarded message Fro... ★

Michael Miller   📎 6/20/2014
Picx

Scott Randolph   6/19/2014

Unread message

6 Tap Delete to delete this message after you've read it.

7 Tap the back arrow to return to the inbox.

8 Scroll to the very bottom of the message and tap Reply to write a response to this message. (If the message was sent to multiple recipients, send your reply to all of them by tapping Reply All.)

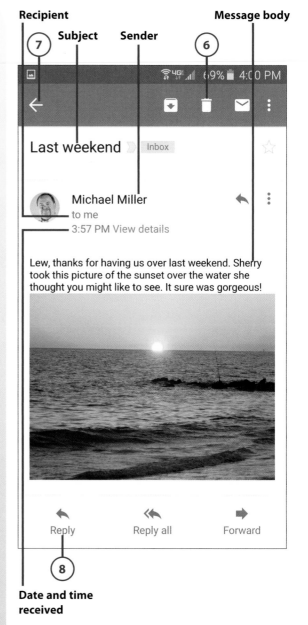

Recipient

Subject **Sender** **Message body**

7 **6**

Last weekend Inbox

Michael Miller
to me
3:57 PM View details

Lew, thanks for having us over last weekend. Sherry took this picture of the sunset over the water she thought you might like to see. It sure was gorgeous!

Reply Reply all Forward

8

Date and time received

9 You see the reply screen, with the sender's name or email address already added to the To: field and the original message displayed beneath. Use the onscreen keyboard to type your reply into the Compose Email box.

10 Tap Send to send the email.

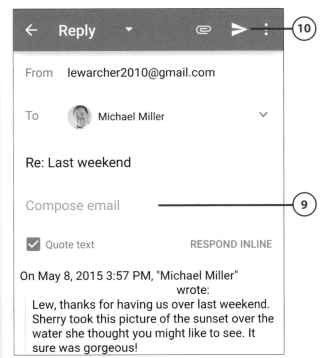

Create a New Message

It's equally easy to create and send a new email message.

1 From the inbox screen, tap the New Message icon to open a new message.

2 Tap in the To box and type the recipient's email address.

3 The Gmail app displays matching contacts. Tap a name to select it, or finishing typing the name. If you want to send to more than one person, separate the addresses with semicolons (;).

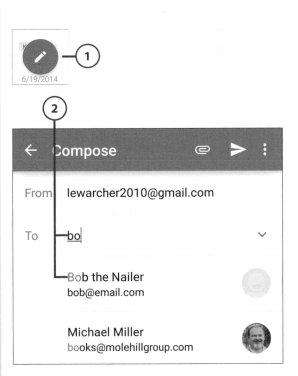

④ Tap in the Subject box and type the subject of this email.

⑤ Tap in the Compose Email box and type your email message.

⑥ Tap Send to send the message.

← **Compose** 📎 ➤ ⋮ ⑥

From   lewarcher2010@gmail.com

To   Bob the Nailer   ⌄

Subject ──────────── ④

Compose email ──────── ⑤

It's Not All Good

Sending Photos via Mobile Data

Photographs and videos attached to email messages are typically very large files. That may be fine when you're sending email when connected to Wi-Fi, but when you're sending email over a mobile data connection, those large files can quickly eat up the available data on your data plan. It's easy to send a handful of pics of your grandkids, or a video or two when you're on vacation; if you're not connecting via Wi-Fi, those attachments could use a lot of your available data, and possible send you over the limit.

A good rule of thumb is to wait until you have a Wi-Fi connection to send photos, videos, and other large attachments via email. That way you won't overuse your mobile data plan, and keep your costs down.

Send Photos and Other Attachments

You can also use Gmail to send photos and other files to your recipients, as attachments.

① ← **Compose**   📎 ➤ ⋮

Attach file ──────── ②

Insert from Drive

 ① From within a new message, tap the File (paperclip) icon.

 ② Tap Attach File.

3. Navigate to and tap the item you want to attach.

4. The item is added to your email. If you decide not to attach this item, tap the X.

5. Finish creating the message as normal and then tap Send.

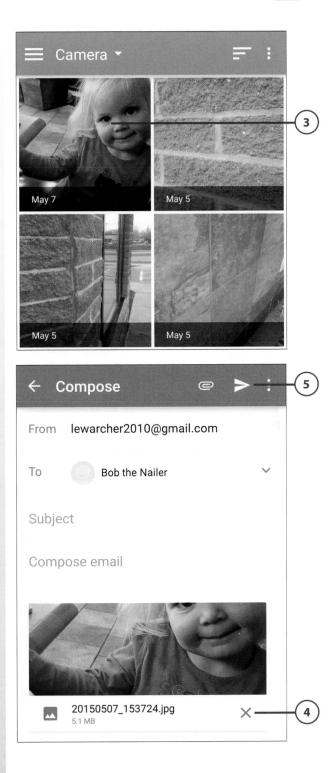

Browsing and Searching the Web

Your Samsung Galaxy S6 and S6 Edge smartphone is so much more than a regular phone. When you connect it to the Internet, either via Wi-Fi or your mobile carrier, it's a full-fledged computer and web browser that you hold in the palm of your hand. In fact, many people use their smartphones more than their computers to connect to the Internet. It's easy to see why!

Browsing the Web with Google Chrome

Your Galaxy S6 or S6 Edge comes with the Google Chrome browser preinstalled. The version of Chrome on your smartphone is very similar to the version you might be using on your personal computer, but it's customized to the smaller phone display.

Launch Google Chrome

To use Google Chrome to browse the Web, your phone must be connected to the Internet. If you don't have a Wi-Fi network or hotspot nearby, your phone automatically connects using your mobile carrier's data network.

Connecting to the Internet

Learn how to connect to the Internet in Chapter 5, "Connecting to the Internet (and Other Networks)."

---

1 From any Home screen, tap the Chrome icon to open Google Chrome.

2 The first time you launch Chrome, it opens to a blank page. If you've previously used the browser, it opens your last open page.

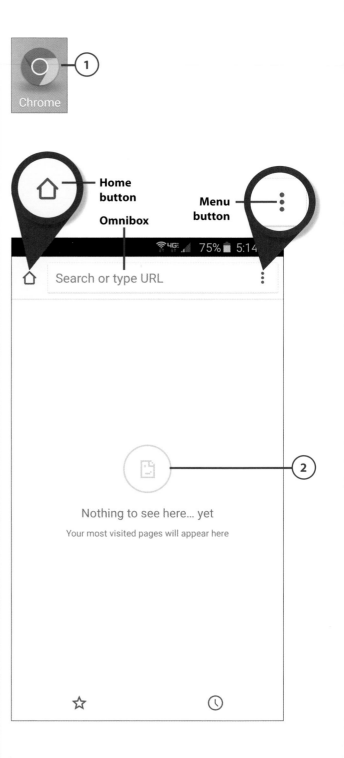

Home button

Menu button

Omnibox

Nothing to see here... yet

Your most visited pages will appear here

Enter a Web Address

To go directly to a given website or web page, you must enter the web address of that page into the Omnibox at the top of the browser screen.

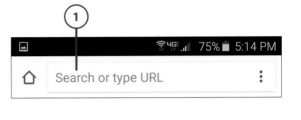

1. Tap within the Omnibox to display the onscreen keyboard. If the Omnibox is not visible (it slides up when not in use), drag down the web page until it appears.

2. Enter the address of the web page you want to visit.

3. As you type, Chrome might suggest matching web pages. Tap any page to go to it *or*…

4. Finish entering the full address and then tap Go on the keyboard to go to that page.

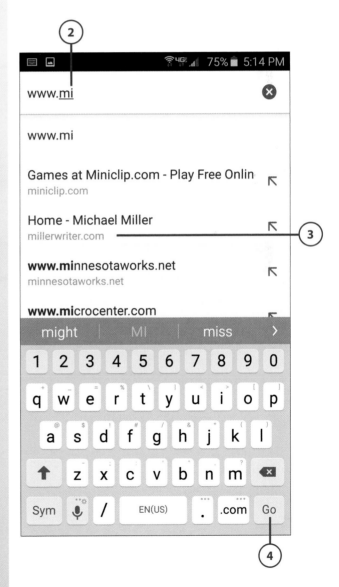

(5) The web page appears onscreen. Swipe up to scroll down the page.

(6) If a page has trouble loading, or if you want to refresh the content, you can reload the page. Begin by tapping the Menu button.

(7) Tap the Reload button.

>>>Go Further

WEB ADDRESSES

A web address is called a Uniform Resource Locator, or URL. Technically, all URLs start with either **http://** or (for secure sites) **https://**. You don't need to type this part of the URL, however; Chrome assumes it and enters it automatically.

The main part of most web addresses starts with **www** followed by a dot, then the name of the website, then another dot and the domain identifier, such as **com** or **org**. As an example, my personal website is **www.millerwriter.com**.

To make things easier, Samsung's onscreen keyboard includes a **www.** key you can use to start the URL. As you enter the rest of the address, this key changes to a **.com** key you can tap to finish things off.

Use Web Links

Pages on the Web are often connected via clickable (on your phone, tappable) links, called web links. A web link can be within a page's text (typically underlined or in a different color) or embedded in an image. Tap a link to go the linked-to page.

(1) On the current web page, tap the web link.

immortal *Plan 9 from Outer Space*): "We are all interested in the future, for that is where you and I are going to spend the rest of our lives." And the Internet of Things is our future. So buy the book and learn all about it! Click here for more.

(1)

(2) The linked-to page displays.

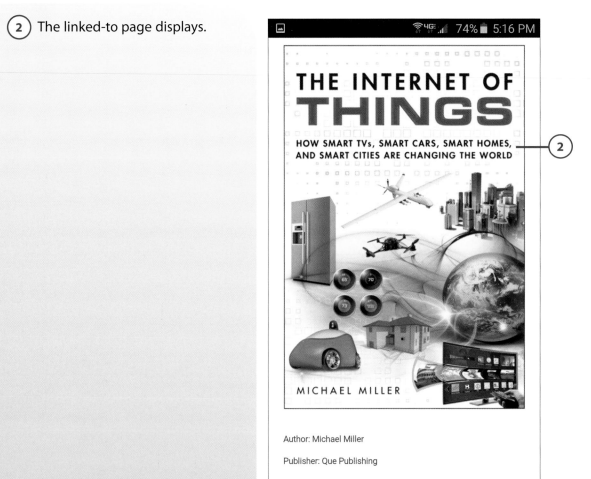

Author: Michael Miller

Publisher: Que Publishing

Published: March 2015

Revisit Past Pages

How easy is it to return to a web page you've previously viewed? Chrome keeps track of all your web browsing history, and revisiting a page is as easy as tapping it in the History list.

(1) Tap the Menu button.

(2) Tap History to display the History screen.

(3) Tap the page you want to revisit.

Working with Your Home Page

You can configure Chrome to display a Home page when it launches or when you tap the Home button.

Set Your Home Page

Your phone carrier might have created a default Home page for you. (For example, AT&T sets its own home. att.com page as your Home.) You can keep this page or set a different Home page.

1. Tap the Menu button.

2. Tap Settings to display the Settings screen.

3. Tap Home Page to display the Home Page page.

(4) Tap On the switch at the top of the page.

(5) Make sure that Default is *not* selected. If it is selected, tap it to deselect it.

(6) Enter the address of your desired Home page into the top box. (The **http://** is already entered for you.)

(7) Tap Done on the keyboard.

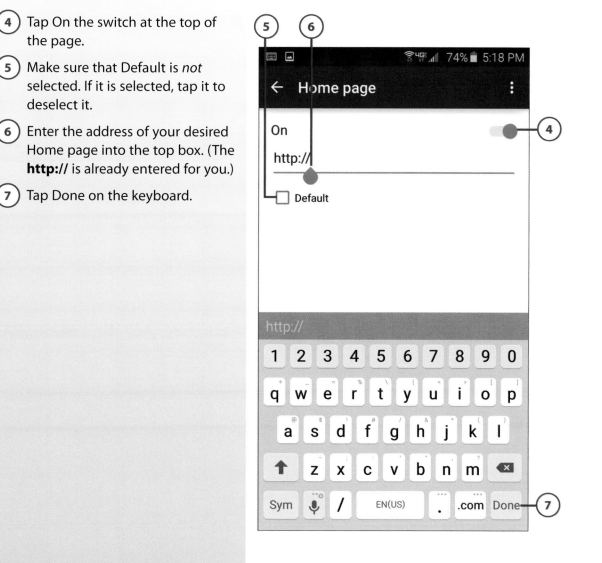

Go to Your Home Page

Your Home page is never more than a tap away.

(1) Tap the Home button.

② Your Home page displays.

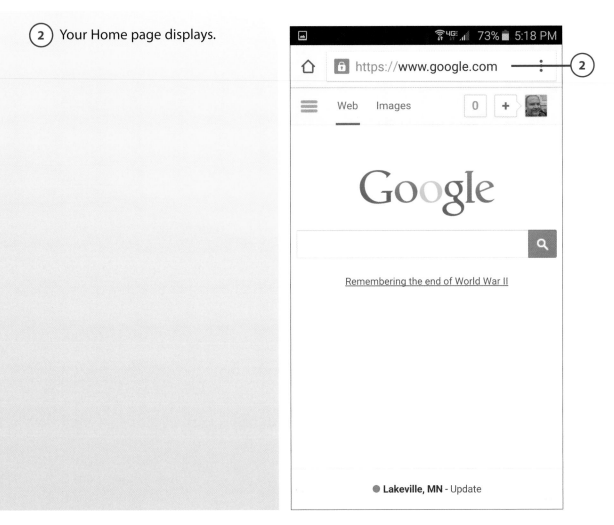

Using Tabs

Chrome is a tabbed browser, which means you can open several web pages at the same time, all in different tabs. You then switch from page to page by selecting different tabs within the browser.

Display Tabs as Tabs

By default, each tab displays as a separate app on your Galaxy S6 or S6 Edge. In this default mode, if you want to switch between open tabs, you have to tap the Recents key to view all running apps and then tap the app thumbnail that's running the tab you want.

Many users find this default behavior confusing, and would rather have all tabs available within the browser. You can make this happen by reconfiguring the proper setting.

(1) From within the browser, tap the Menu button.

(2) Tap Settings to display the Settings screen.

(3) Tap Merge Tabs and Apps.

(4) Tap Off the switch at the top of the screen. Tabs now appear within the browser screen; to return to tabs-as-apps operations, return to the Merge Tabs and Apps screen and tap On the switch.

⌂   Search or type URL   ⋮ —(1)

→   ☆   ↻

New incognito tab

Bookmarks

Recent tabs

History

Request desktop site   ☐

Settings   ———(2)

Help & feedback

Basics

Search engine
Google (google.com)

Merge tabs and apps   ———(3)
On

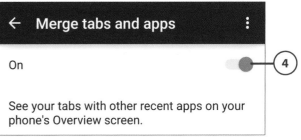

(5) You are cautioned that Chrome will separate tabs and apps. Tap OK.

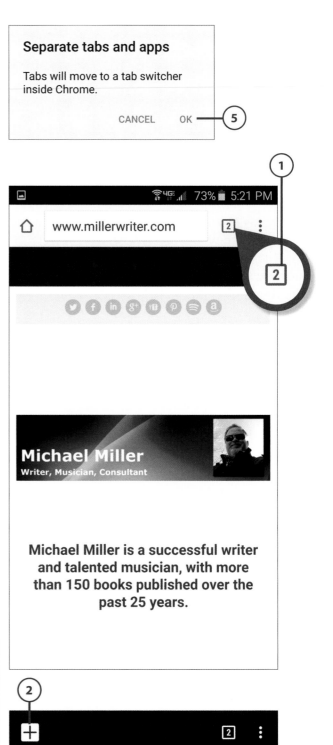

Separate tabs and apps

Tabs will move to a tab switcher inside Chrome.

CANCEL   OK ——— **5**

Open a New Tab

When you separate tabs and apps, Chrome displays a Tabs button at the top of the screen. The number within this button tells you how many tabs you have open. You use this button to open new tabs and switch between tabs.

When you open a new tab, you see Chrome's New Tab page. This page includes a Google search box and thumbnails that link to your most-visited web pages.

(1) Tap the Tabs button. All open tabs now appear in a stack.

(2) Tap the New Tab (+) button.

www.millerwriter.com

Michael Miller
Writer, Musician, Consultant

Michael Miller is a successful writer and talented musician, with more than 150 books published over the past 25 years.

(3) The new tab opens and displays the New Tab page.

It's Not All Good

Too Many Tabs

If you're like me, you go from one page to another in rapid succession. The temptation is to do so in separate tabs, and then leave all those tabs open. Before you know it, you end up with a half-dozen or more open tabs—which is not a good thing.

Not only are a lot of open tabs confusing to navigate (which page is where?), each tab you have open uses system resources. If you keep a half-dozen or so tabs open in the background, your phone's battery will drain much more quickly.

The best solution is to limit yourself to no more than two or three open tabs at a time. If you need to open another one, close an open one first. It's a lot more manageable!

Open a New Incognito Tab

Sometimes you want to visit web pages that you don't want others to see. Maybe you're shopping for a birthday present for your spouse that you want to keep secret. Maybe you want to view content that you simply want to keep private. To accommodate your need for privacy, Chrome offers Incognito browsing, a private browsing mode. Incognito mode is totally anonymous; the pages you visit in this mode are not tracked or stored in your browser history.

1. Tap the Menu button.
2. Tap New Incognito Tab.
3. A new Incognito tab opens. You can browse in this tab as you would normally.

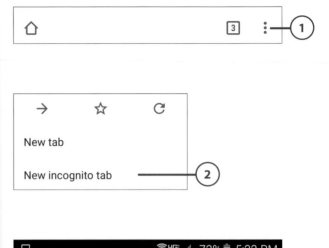

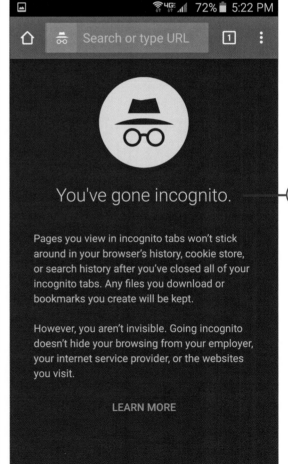

You've gone incognito.

Pages you view in incognito tabs won't stick around in your browser's history, cookie store, or search history after you've closed all of your incognito tabs. Any files you download or bookmarks you create will be kept.

However, you aren't invisible. Going incognito doesn't hide your browsing from your employer, your internet service provider, or the websites you visit.

LEARN MORE

Switch Between Tabs

When you have several different web pages open in different tabs, it's easy to switch back and forth between pages.

(1) Tap the Tabs button.

(2) You now see all your open tabs in a stack. Tap the tab you want to view.

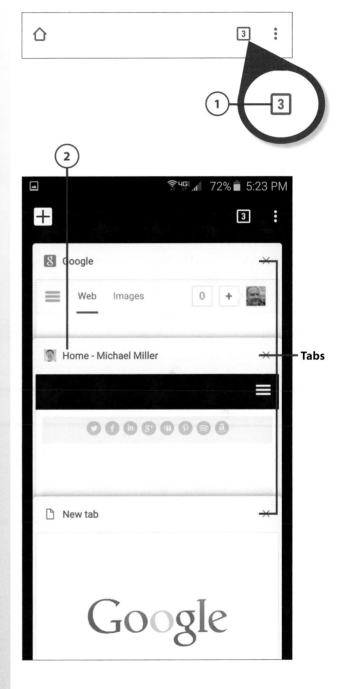

Tabs

Close a Tab

Closing a tab is equally easy.

1. Tap the Tabs button.
2. Tap the X for the tab you want to close.

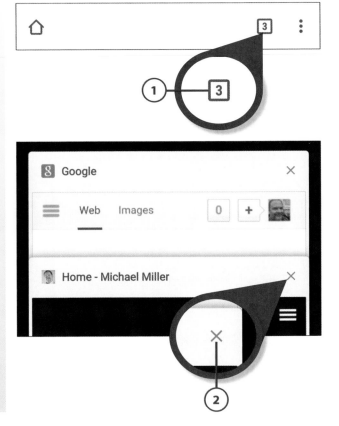

Bookmarking Favorite Pages

When you find a web page you like and expect to revisit, you can save that page as a *bookmark*. To return to the page, you don't have to re-enter the URL—just click the bookmark!

Create a Bookmark

Bookmarking a web page is as easy as tapping an icon.

1. Open the page you want to bookmark and then tap the Menu button.

2. Tap the star icon to display the Add Bookmark screen.

3. Accept or edit the bookmark name.

4. Bookmarks can be organized in folders. If you want to change where the bookmark is stored, tap Folder and select a new folder.

5. Tap Save.

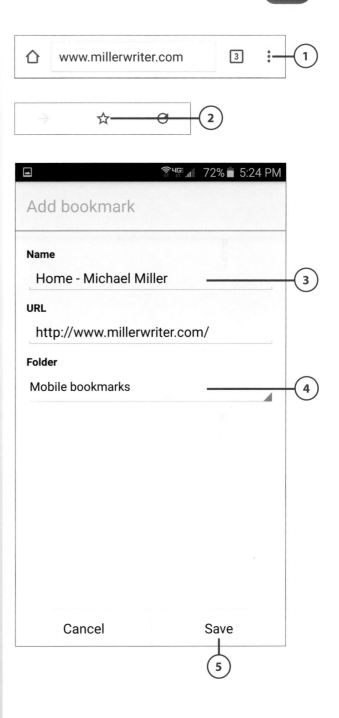

Revisit a Bookmark

When you want to revisit a book-marked page, just tap the item in your bookmark list.

(1) Tap the Menu button.

(2) Tap Bookmarks to display your bookmark folders.

(3) Tap the folder you want to view. Pages you've bookmarked on your phone are typically stored in the Mobile Bookmarks folder. Pages you've bookmarked on your desktop PC are typically stored in the Desktop Bookmarks folder.

(4) Tap the bookmark for the page you want to view. The page now opens in the Chrome browser.

⌂ 🔒 s://www.google.com/: ③ ⋮ ─(1)

★ C

New tab

New incognito tab

Bookmarks ─(2)

(4)

Bookmarks > Mobile bookmarks ─(3)

AARP - Health, Travel Deals, Baby Boo...

Breaking News, U.S., World, Weather, E...

Google

Home - Michael Miller

Samsung Mobile

>>>Go Further

SYNCHRONIZING BOOKMARKS—AND MORE

When you use the Chrome browser after signing into your Google Account (and you're always signed in on your S6 or S6 Edge), the pages you visit and bookmark are stored in your Google Account, online. When you open a Chrome browser on another device, such as your personal computer, you see the same browsing history and bookmarks on that device. (As long as you're signed into your Google Account, of course.)

This synchronization works both ways. Any new pages you visit using the PC version of Chrome also appear in your history when you next open Chrome on your smartphone. Likewise, any bookmarks you add when browsing Chrome on your PC appear when you access bookmarks on your smartphone.

This synchronization is a great way to maintain continuity between all the different devices you use. It's like using the exact same version of Chrome no matter which device you're using!

Making the Web More Readable

As our eyes age, we sometimes have trouble reading smaller type. Unfortunately, a lot of web pages are designed with very small type—especially on smartphone screens. Although sites well-designed for mobile use automatically resize the type for smaller screens, other sites become almost unreadable when viewed on your smartphone. Fortunately, there are ways to make these websites more readable.

Zoom Into a Page

The first thing you can do on many websites is to zoom into the page. This enlarges the entire page—which means you might need to drag your finger left and right to view the entire width.

1. Press two fingers together on the screen and then spread them apart to zoom in.

2. In some instances, you can zoom into a picture or other onscreen item by double tapping it.

3. Press two fingers apart on the screen and pinch them together to zoom back out.

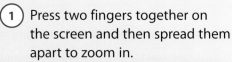

Rotate the Screen

The other way to make some web pages more readable is to rotate your phone so that your screen is horizontal (landscape orientation). This makes the web page wider, with larger type.

1. Rotate your phone 90 degrees to the left or right.

2. The web page enlarges to fill the width of the horizontal screen.

Searching the Web with Google

Google is not only the company behind the Chrome browser, it's also the most popular search engine in the world. You use a search engine, such as Google, to search for items and information on the Internet.

Enter a Query

You can query Google from Google's home page (www.google.com) or directly from the Chrome browser's Omnibox.

1. From within the Chrome browser, tap in the Omnibox to display the onscreen keyboard. Alternatively, you can go to **www.google.com** and tap within the search box there.

2. Start typing your query.

3. As you type, Google offers various search suggestions. Tap any suggestion to begin your search *or...*

4. Finish typing your query and tap the Go button on the keyboard.

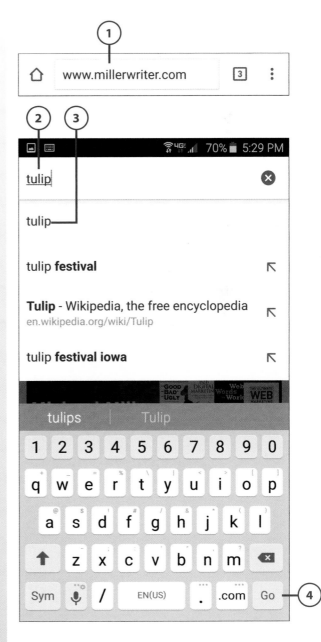

(5) Google displays its search results. Tap a link to go to that web page.

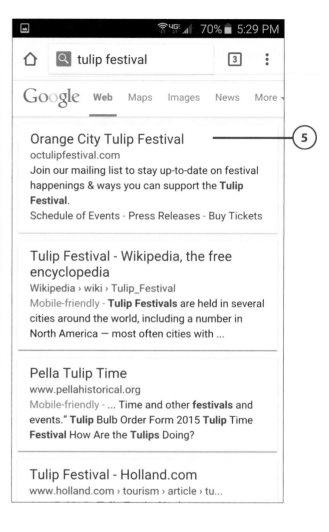

Fine-Tune Your Search Results

A Google search results page includes a list of links that match what you were searching for. You can tap to go directly to any listed web page, or use various Google features to fine-tune your search results.

1. By default, Google displays web page results. Display news results instead by tapping the News tab.

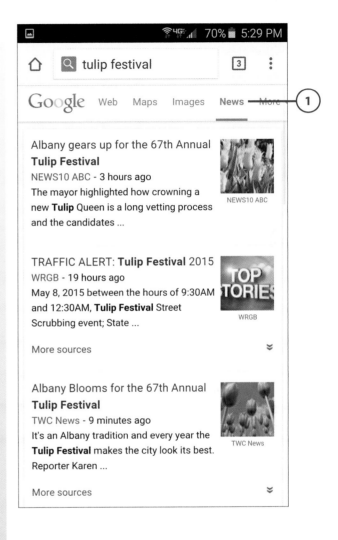

2 Display matching images by tapping Images.

3 Display matching videos, maps, shopping items, books, flights, or apps by tapping More and then tapping the appropriate selection.

4 Display additional search tools by tapping More and then tapping Search Tools.

5 Different types of search results offer different types of search tools. For Web results, tap Any Time to filter the results by time—Any Time, Past Hour, Past 24 Hours, and so forth.

6 For image results, you can filter results by color, type (Face, Photo, Clip Art, Line Drawing, or Animated), or time.

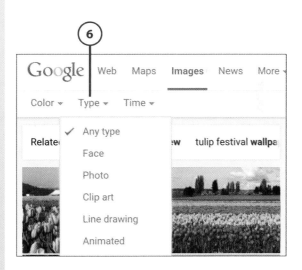

Controlling Your Phone with Voice Commands

You're probably used to using your fingers to control your phone. This dates back to the old rotary dial days, of course, when you needed to insert your index finger into the dial to make things work. Same thing in the touchphone days, when you had to push the buttons with your finger.

Now that we're working with smartphones and touchscreens, your fingers are as necessary as ever. Unless, that is, you know how to control your phone by talking to it. That's right, you can use voice commands not only to control your Samsung Galaxy S6 or S6 Edge, but also to search the Internet and find all sorts of information. It's a little like having your own HAL9000 (from the movie, *2001: A Space Odyssey*) in the palm of your hand.

Controlling Your Phone with Samsung's S Voice

In addition to the normal touchscreen interface, Samsung built voice control functionality into your Galaxy S6 phone. It's called S Voice, and you can use it to control basic phone operations as well as search the Internet for various types of information.

S Voice uses a natural language user interface to answer questions, make recommendations, and perform various operations. That means you can talk to it in plain English, and S Voice understands what you're asking and performs the appropriate operation. In a way, it's like the Siri personal assistant that Apple includes with its competing iPhones; you ask S Voice a question or tell it what to do, and it does what you've asked.

You can use S Voice to dial voice calls, dictate text messages, create tasks and events, play music, set alarms, and generate driving directions. You can also ask S Voice informational questions that can be answered based on information found on the Internet. Ask S Voice how far it is to the moon, or how old Kenny Rogers is, or how many miles there are in a kilometer. (Or is it vice versa?)

Set Up S Voice for the First Time

S Voice is activated by default on your new Samsung smartphone. Before you use it, however, you need to configure it to recognize your voice.

1. From your phone's Home screen, tap Apps to open the Apps screen.

2. Tap to open the Samsung folder.

3. Tap S Voice.

(4) The first time you launch S Voice, you're prompted to accept the terms of service. Tap to check okay.

(5) Tap Next.

(6) You are now prompted to record the wake-up command. Choose a phrase, such as "Hi there," "Hello S Voice," or "Honey, I'm home." Tap Start and say your phrase four times.

(7) Your setup is now complete. Tap Done to continue using your phone.

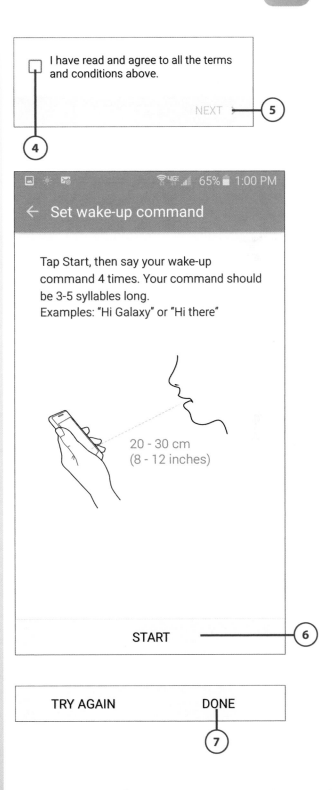

I have read and agree to all the terms and conditions above.

NEXT ▶ (5)

(4)

🚩 4G ⣿ 65% 🔋 1:00 PM

← Set wake-up command

Tap Start, then say your wake-up command 4 times. Your command should be 3-5 syllables long.
Examples: "Hi Galaxy" or "Hi there"

20 - 30 cm
(8 - 12 inches)

START ——— (6)

TRY AGAIN   DONE

(7)

Configure S Voice Options

By default, S Voice works when you start speaking to it. There are, however, some settings you might want to configure.

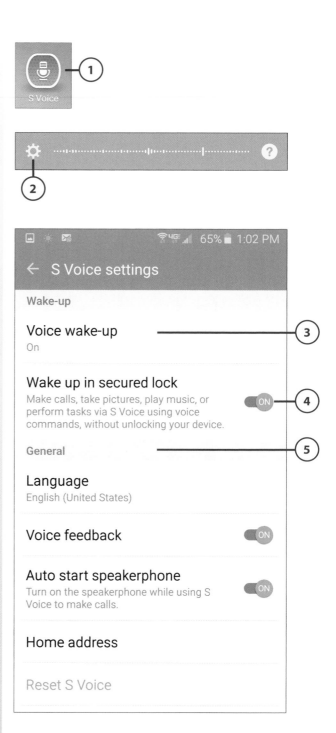

(1) From your phone's Home or Apps screen, tap S Voice.

(2) From the S Voice command bar at the bottom of the screen, tap Settings to display the S Voice Setting screen.

(3) By default, you can wake up S Voice by speaking the phrase you previously set. To turn off this functionality or change your wake-up command, tap Voice Wake-Up then make the appropriate changes.

(4) By default, you can use S Voice to make calls, take pictures, and perform other tasks without first unlocking your device. To turn off this functionality, go to the Wake Up in Secured Lock section and tap Off that switch.

(5) Configure any of the other settings in the General section, as desired. (The default settings work fine for most people.)

Add to Home Screen

If you use S Voice a lot, you might want to add a shortcut for the app to your Home screen. Open the Samsung folder, then tap and drag the S Voice icon up to your Home screen of choice.

Learn S Voice Commands

After you've set up S Voice, it's time to start using it—by talking to your phone. The following table details the commands you speak to initiate various operations.

Operation	Voice Command	Example
Control Wi-Fi and Bluetooth settings	Turn *setting* on/off	"Turn Wi-Fi off"
Find information	What or How or Why or When	"What is the largest ocean?" or "How old is George Clooney?"
Get directions	Navigate	"Navigate to art museum"
Hear news headlines	Read the news	"Read the news"
Local listings	Find	"Find coffeeshops"
Memo	Memo	"Memo *Buy milk*"
Music	Play	"Play *Proud Mary*" or "Play artist *Frank Sinatra*"
Open app	Open	"Open Calculator"
Post social network update	*Network* update	"Twitter update *Who remembers Perry Mason?*" or "Facebook update *Had a wonderful vacation glad to be heading home*"
Record voice	Record voice	"Record voice"
Schedule	New event	"New event *Collin's soccer game June twentieth at six pm*"
Search	Google	"Google *senior living in Arizona*"
Search contacts	Look up	"Look up *Olivia Jones*"

Operation	Voice Command	Example
Set alarm	Set alarm	"Set alarm for seven thirty am"
Set timer	Set timer	"Set timer for five minutes"
Task	Create task	"Create task *Star project due August second*"
Text message	Text	"Text Caleb the message *I'm on my way home*"
Voice dial	Call	"Call Bob"
Weather forecast	What is the weather	"What is the weather for today?"

Give S Voice a Command

Using S Voice is as easy as tapping the screen and speaking your command.

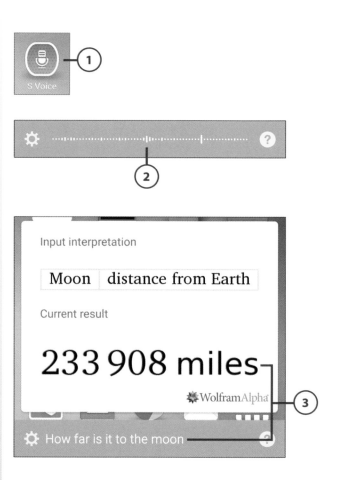

(1) From your phone's Home or Apps screen, tap S Voice to display the command bar at the bottom of the screen.

(2) Speak a command or ask a question.

(3) If you asked a question, S Voice speaks the answer and displays the answer onscreen.

Input interpretation

| Moon | distance from Earth |

Current result

233 908 miles

✹ WolframAlpha

✿ How far is it to the moon

Doing More with Google Now and OK Google

S Voice is pretty nifty, but there's an even better voice control app available—and built into your phone. Google Now is an intelligent personal assistant that taps into the power of Google Search. It offers information personalized to your own needs and organizes that information into onscreen "cards." You can access Google Now with normal touch commands or voice commands. Many people find its operation (and answers) superior to that of S Voice.

Google's voice operation functionality is called OK Google, because that's what you say to activate it. You can use Google Now and OK Google to set alarms and reminders, create events, check your schedule, dial voice calls, check your voicemail, dictate text messages, send emails, post to social networks, play music, search for web pages and images, shoot pictures, record videos, look up travel plans, track packages, check weather, calculate tips, define words, convert between units, solve math problems, and more. Practically anything you can do from Google's search site, you can do from your phone using voice commands.

You access both Google Now and the OK Google voice commands from the Google Search app that's preinstalled on your phone.

Set Up Google Now

Before you can use Google Now and OK Google commands, you have to configure both.

(1) From your phone's Home screen, tap Apps to open the Apps screen.

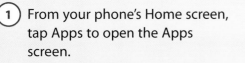

(2) Tap to open the Google folder.

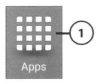

3 Tap Google Settings to open the Google Settings screen.

4 Tap Search & Now.

5 Tap Now Cards to display the Now Cards screen.

6 Tap On the Show Cards switch.

7 The cards setup wizard opens. Tap Set Up.

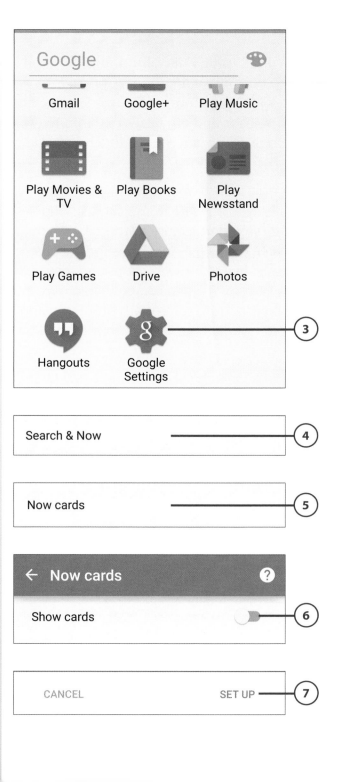

8   Tap Yes, I'm In.

9   You're taken to the Google Now app. Tap a card to display more similar items, or click an item to open it.

Add to Home Screen

If you use Google Now and OK Google a lot, you might want to add a shortcut for the app to your Home screen. Open the Google folder and then tap and drag the blue Google icon up to your Home screen of choice.

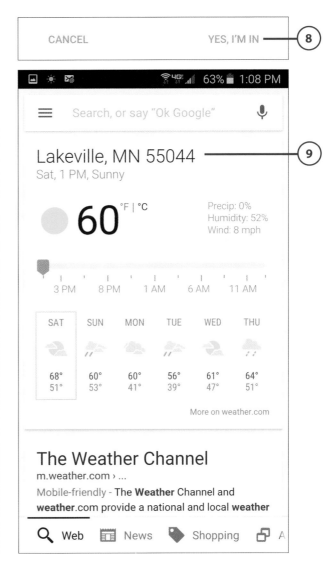

Learn OK Google Commands

The Google Search app displays Google Now cards, with information personalized for you. It learns what you like, based on searches you make, and displays news stories and other information it thinks you'll find interesting.

You also use the Google Search app to initiate voice searches and voice commands, by saying "OK Google." The following table details some of the more popular voice commands you can use.

Operation	Voice Command	Example
Calculate a tip	What's the tip	"What's the tip for thirty-seven dollars?"
Check the weather	What's the weather	"What's the weather like tomorrow" *or* "Do I need a jacket today?"
Check voicemail	Listen to voicemail	"Listen to voicemail"
Check your schedule	What's my day look like *or* When is *event*	"What's my day look like tomorrow?" *or* "When is my next meeting?"
Control Wi-Fi and Bluetooth settings	Turn on/off	"Turn on Wi-Fi"
Convert between units	What is *first unit* in *second unit*	"What is twenty-two miles in kilometers?"
Create a Google Calendar event	Create a calendar event	"Create a calendar event for lunch with Joan at Five Guys, Friday at noon"
Define a word	What does *word* mean	"What does defenestrate mean?"
Find a movie in a theater	What movie is playing *or* Where is *movie* playing	"What movies are playing this weekend?" *or* "Where is *The Avengers* playing?"
Find a radio station from Google Play	Play some music	"Play some music"
Find information	Where *or* How *or* When *or* What	"When was Abraham Lincoln killed?" *or* "How far is it to the moon?"
Find nearby places	Where is	"Where is the nearest coffeeshop?"
Find new music	What songs	"What songs does Taylor Swift sing?"
Find the time	What time is it	"What time is it in Paris?"

Operation	Voice Command	Example
Flashlight	Turn on/off my flashlight	"Turn on my flashlight"
Get directions	Navigate to *or* Directions to	"Navigate to the post office" *or* "Directions to Tenth and Main, Brownsburg, Indiana"
Identify a song	What's this song	"What's this song?"
Learn about a TV show	What's on TV	"What's on TV?"
Look up travel plans	Show me *or* Where is	"Show me my flights" *or* "Where is my hotel?"
Make a restaurant reservation	Book a	"Book a table for two at Luigi's on Friday night at eight pm"
Plan your trip	What are	"What are some attractions in San Diego?"
Play music	Play	"Play the Beach Boys" or "Play *California Dreaming*"
Post to a social network	Post to *network*	"Post to Facebook that I'm playing with my grandkids"
Read a book from Google Play	Read	"Read *To Kill a Mockingbird*"
Record a video	Record a video	"Record a video"
Search for images	Show me pictures	"Show me pictures of pickup trucks"
Search within apps on your device	Search for *thing* on *app*	"Search for Italian food on Yelp"
See your upcoming bills	My bill(s)	"My bills" *or* "My electric bill"
Send a Hangouts chat message	Send a Hangouts message	"Send a Hangouts message to Jacob"
Send an email	Send an email	"Send an email to Megan, subject *Meeting*, message, *Remember that the next meeting is changed to next Tuesday*, full stop"

Operation	Voice Command	Example
Set a reminder	Remind me	"Remind me to take out the trash"
Set an alarm	Set an alarm	"Set an alarm for seven thirty am"
Solve a math problem	What is	"What is one hundred forty-three divided by fifteen?"
Start a Hangouts video call	Start a video call	"Start a video call with Alethia"
Take a photo	Take a picture	"Take a picture"
Text message	Text	"Text Hayley that I'm on my way"
Track a package from a Gmail order confirmation	Where's my package	"Where's my package?"
Translate words or phrases	How do you say	"How do you say house in Chinese?"
Voice dial	Call	"Call Susie"
Watch a movie from Google Play	Watch	"Watch *Frozen*"

Give an OK Google Command

Using OK Google is much like using S Voice; tap the screen and speak a command.

1. From your phone's Home or Apps screen, tap Google to open the Google Now app.

2. Say "OK Google" or tap the microphone icon.

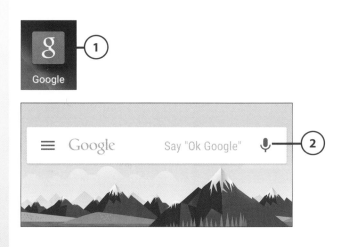

3 Google listens for your voice command. Speak a command or ask a question.

4 If you asked a question, OK Google speaks the answer and displays the answer onscreen.

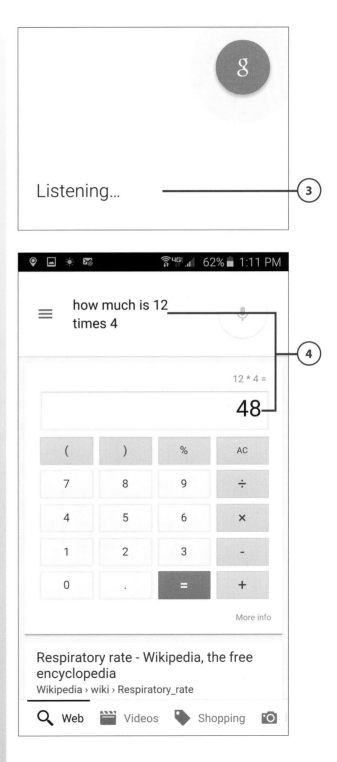

Using Google Voice Typing

Google also offers voice input for typing. This way you can speak the words you want to enter instead of typing them with the onscreen keyboard.

This feature, dubbed Google Voice Typing, is enabled by default.

Type with Voice Commands

Any time you see the onscreen keyboard, you can opt to speak your entry instead.

1. From the onscreen keyboard, tap the Microphone key.

2. Speak your text.

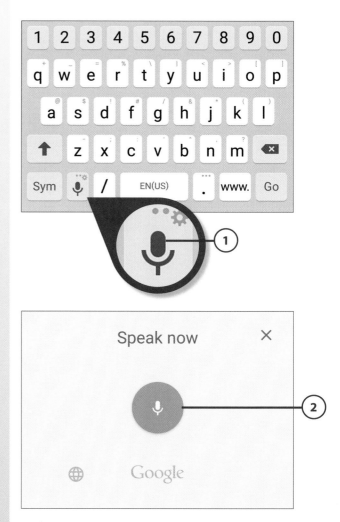

In this chapter, you see how to make video calls with Google Hangouts and Skype. Topics include the following:

→ Using Google Hangouts
→ Using Skype

Video Chatting on Your Phone

In addition to making traditional voice calls, you can also use your new Samsung Galaxy S6 or S6 Edge to make video calls. That's right, the age of video calling is here, and you can do it on your phone!

Using Google Hangouts

Video calling is a great way to keep in touch with distant friends and family. If you can't be there in person, you can talk via video chat on your smartphone. It's just like being there—and, because you do it over the Internet, it's completely free.

One of the most popular video calling apps comes from Google. Google Hangouts lets you make one-on-one video calls as well as participate in group video chats. You can even use Google Hangouts to make voice calls and text message with others.

Hangouts

In Google parlance, a Hangout is either a text or video chat. Instead of calling them chat sessions, Google calls them Hangouts. So that's that.

Make a Video Call

The Google Hangouts app is preinstalled on your Samsung smartphone.
When you're logged into your Google
Account (which you are by default),
it's easy to call someone else who's
using the same app on their phone or
computer.

Apps

Google

(1) From your phone's Home screen,
tap the Apps icon to open the
Apps screen.

(2) Tap to open the Google folder.

(3) Tap the Hangouts icon to open
the Google Hangouts app.

(4) You see the most recent
Hangouts in which you've
participated. To view details of a
given Hangout (or to start one
back up), tap the Hangout.

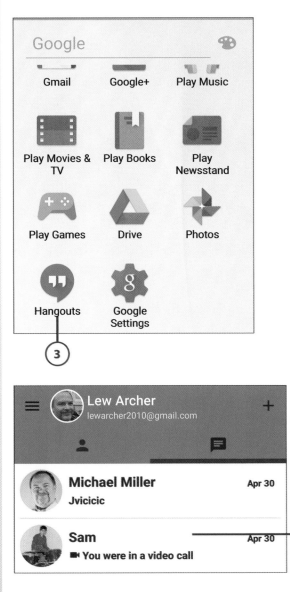

5 Start a new Hangout by tapping the Contacts tab. You see a list of your phone's contacts, with your most frequently messaged ones at the top.

6 Tap the name of a person that you wish to chat with. This displays a new Hangout screen.

7 Tap the video camera icon at the top of the screen. Google calls the other person to start a Hangout.

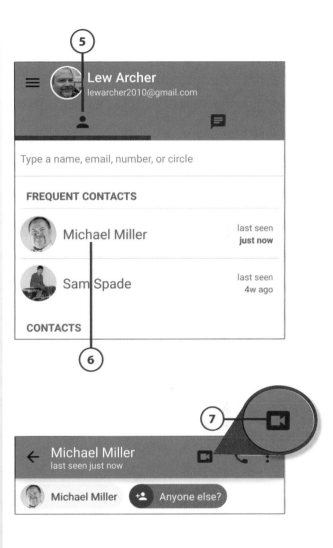

8 When the other person answers, you see that person's picture across the middle of the screen. Your picture appears at the bottom right. Start talking!

9 Tap the screen to display the Hangout controls at the top and bottom of the screen.

10 Tap the microphone button to mute the sound. Tap the microphone button again to unmute.

11 Tap the camera button to hide your video from the other person. Tap the camera button again to make your video visible.

12 Tap the red disconnect button to leave the Hangout.

Add to Home Screen

If you use Google Hangouts a lot, you might want to add a shortcut for the app to your Home screen. Open the Google folder then tap and drag the Hangouts icon up to your Home screen of choice.

Person you're chatting with   You

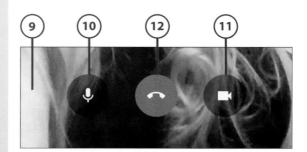

Add People to a Group Call

You can include multiple people in a group video Hangout. This is great for virtual meetings, or for impromptu family reunions.

(1) Start a video Hangout with the first person you're talking with.

(2) Tap the screen to show the Hangout controls.

(3) Tap the Menu button.

(4) Tap Add People.

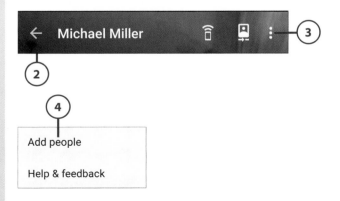

5 From your list of contacts, tap to select the person or people you want to add to your Hangout.

6 Tap OK.

7 When the person answers the call, she is added to the Hangout. Her picture appears at the bottom of the screen, and whomever is talking at the moment appears in the large video window.

8 Switch to display a specific participant's video by tapping that person's thumbnail at the bottom of the screen.

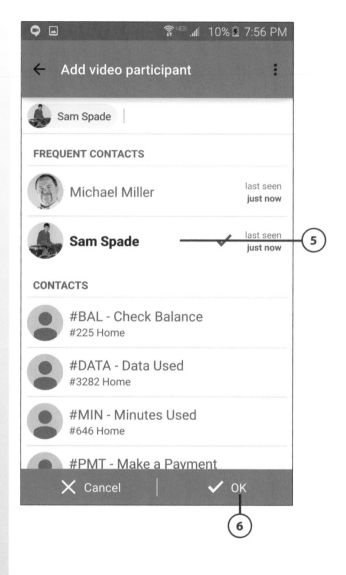

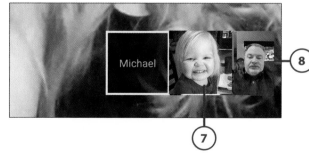

Participate in a Voice Call

If you'd rather not talk face-to-face, you can still use Google Hangouts to participate in voice calls with your contacts. A voice Hangout is just like a video Hangout, but without the picture.

(1) From within the Hangouts app, tap the Contacts tab.

(2) Tap the name of a person that you want to chat with. This displays a new Hangout screen.

(3) Tap the phone icon at the top of the screen. Google calls the other person to start a Hangout.

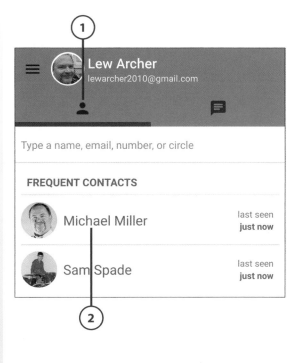

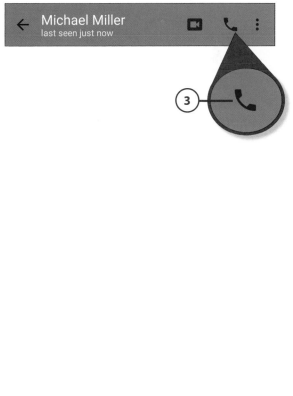

4 Start talking after the other person answers.

5 Tap the red disconnect button to end the call.

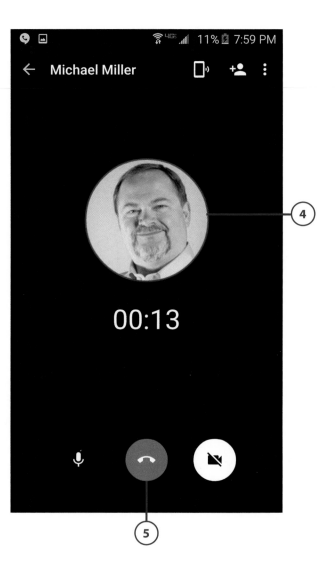

Participate in a Text Chat

You can also use Google Hangouts to participate in text chats. A text Hangout is like an exchange of text messages, but using the Google Hangouts service.

(1) From within the Hangouts app, tap the Contacts icon.

(2) Tap the name of a person that you want to chat with. This displays a new Hangout screen.

(3) Tap within the Send Hangouts Message box at the bottom of the screen and type your message.

(4) Tap the Send button.

(5) Your message appears on the right side of the screen. The other person's messages appear on the left. Continue messaging to participate in the conversation. When you're done, just quit— there are no buttons you need to tap to end the conversation.

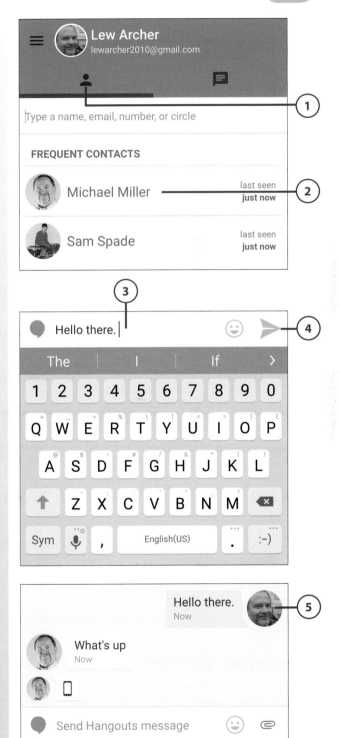

Using Skype

Google Hangouts is a popular app, especially among Google and Android users. But the most popular video chat service today is Skype.

To use Skype, you need to install the Skype app. You can do this from the Google Play Store; just search for Skype and then choose to download and install it. It's free.

Signing Up and Logging On

When you first install the Skype app, you're prompted to either log on with an existing Skype account (which you might have, from your computer) or create a new account. Follow the onscreen instructions to do so.

Make a Video Call

Skype automatically searches your phone's contacts list for those people who also have Skype accounts. You can then call any of these people directly—as long as you're both online at the same time. (And, in the case of people connecting via computer, that they have a webcam operating.)

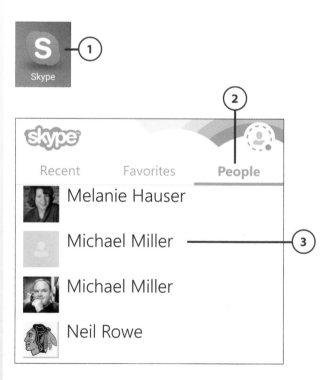

1. From your phone's Home screen, tap the Skype icon to open the Skype app.

2. Tap the People tab to see all your Skype contacts.

3. Tap the name of the person you want to talk with.

(4) If you have not yet connected with this person on skype, you're prompted to do so. Tap the Connect on Skype button.

(5) Accept or edit the invitation message.

(6) Tap the check mark to send the message. The other person must accept your contact request before you can chat with him.

(7) When the person accepts your request and is online, a green Available indicator appears under that person's name in the People list. Tap the person's name to proceed.

(8) Tap the video camera icon to initiate a video call.

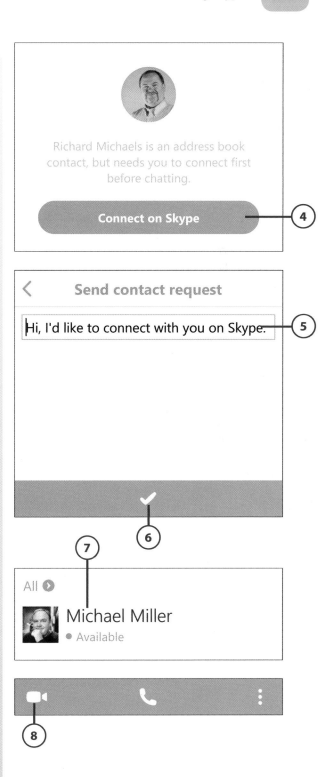

Richard Michaels is an address book contact, but needs you to connect first before chatting.

Connect on Skype ———(4)

<   **Send contact request**

Hi, I'd like to connect with you on Skype. ——(5)

✓ ——(6)

(7)

All ❯

Michael Miller
● Available

(8)

9 The person you're talking to appears on your phone's screen. A smaller thumbnail of you appears at the bottom right. Start talking!

10 Tap the screen to display the Skype controls.

11 Tap the microphone button to mute the sound. Tap the microphone button again to unmute.

12 Tap the camera button to hide your video from the other person. Tap the camera button again to make your video visible.

13 Tap the red disconnect button to leave the call.

Person you're   You
talking to

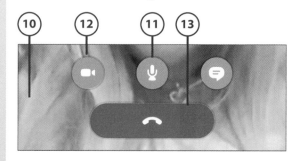

Participate in a Voice Call

Like Google Hangouts, Skype also lets you participate in voice-only calls. It's like making a phone call, but over the Internet.

(1) From within the Skype app, tap the People tab.

(2) Tap the name of a person that you want to chat with.

(3) Tap the phone icon. Skype now calls the other person.

(4) When the other person answers, start talking.

(5) Tap the red disconnect button to end the call.

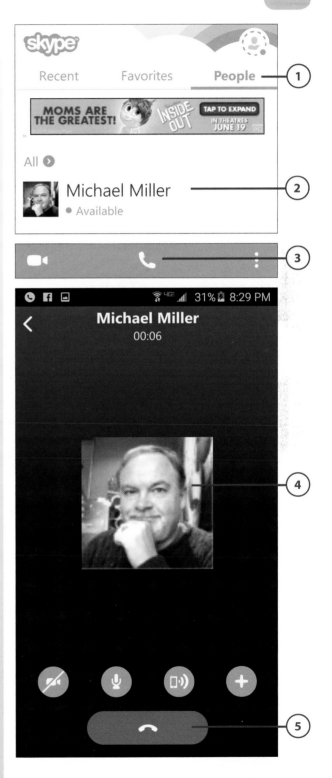

>>>Go Further
FREE CALLING

Many people (and younger users, too) like using Google Hangouts and Skype to make voice-only calls because they're free. Unlike traditional landline or mobile phone calls, which may incur hefty long-distance fees, you can talk to anyone over the Internet with Hangouts or Skype for zero cost. You just have to make sure both parties have Hangouts or Skype accounts and then you connect over the Internet for free. (That's if you're using Wi-Fi, of course; connecting over your carrier's data service can rack up very large data fees, very quickly.)

Participate in a Text Chat

Finally, you can use Skype to text message with other users.

1. From within the Skype app, tap the People tab.

2. Tap the name of a person that you want to chat with.

3. Tap within the Type a Message Here box at the bottom of the screen and type your message.

4. Tap the Send button.

5. Your message appears on the right side of the screen. The other person's messages appear on the left. Continue messaging to participate in the conversation. When you're done, just quit—there are no buttons you need to tap to end the conversation.

In this chapter, you get suggestions on how to use your new Galaxy S6 and S6 Edge to live healthier and manage your medicines and medical conditions. Topics include the following:

→ Using the S Health App

→ Discovering Other Health and Fitness Apps

Monitoring Your Health

Samsung cares about your health—really. The company's S6 and S6 Edge smartphones include a built-in heart rate monitor, which you can use just by placing a finger on the back of the case. Even better, Samsung includes the S Health app, which works in conjunction with the heart rate monitor to track and analyze your heart rate and other medical conditions.

But that's far from all. Many other companies offer health-related apps that help you turn your Galaxy S6 or S6 Edge into a full-fledged portable medical tracker. You can use your smartphone to manage your prescriptions (including alerting you when it's time to take your meds), track blood sugar and blood pressure, organize your medical charts and visits, and even look up detailed information about various medical conditions and medications. There are also fitness and yoga and dieting apps to help you live healthier, and apps you can activate if you ever have a medical emergency.

So if you want to live healthier, all you have to do is fire up your phone—and launch the right apps!

Using the S Health App

You use Samsung's S Health app to plan and track a variety of health goals and medical conditions. S Health can track your exercise regimen, sleep patterns, and meals—as well as your heart rate, blood pressure, blood glucose levels, and weight.

Best of all, S Health is free—and already installed on your Galaxy S6 or S6 Edge. It's a fun and easy way to stay as healthy as you can, all from the screen of your new smartphone.

Get Started with S Health

When you first use the S Health app, you need to configure it for your own personal use.

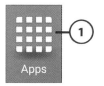

1. From the Home screen, tap Apps to open the Apps screen.

2. Tap to open the Samsung folder.

3. Tap to open the S Health app. You see the opening screen.

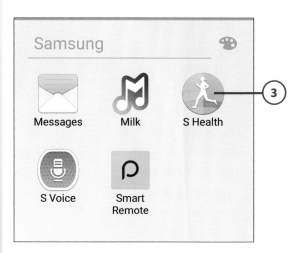

4 Tap to check both of the I Agree checkboxes.

5 Tap Next. (If prompted to sign into or create a new Samsung account, do so now.)

Add to Home Screen

If you use S Health a lot, you might want to add a shortcut for the app to your Home screen. Open the Samsung folder, then tap and drag the S Health icon to your Home screen of choice.

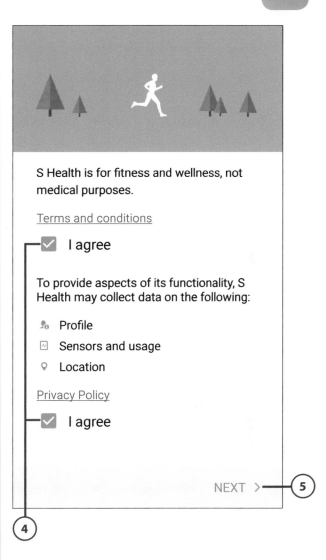

S Health is for fitness and wellness, not medical purposes.

Terms and conditions

☑ I agree

To provide aspects of its functionality, S Health may collect data on the following:

⚙ Profile

☲ Sensors and usage

◎ Location

Privacy Policy

☑ I agree

NEXT >

Configure Your Profile

To get the most out of S Health, you need to tell the app a little bit about yourself—including your gender, birthday, height, and weight.

1 From the Home or Apps screen, tap S Health to open the app.

2 Tap the profile picture or image at the top-left corner. Your My Page profile opens.

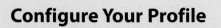

S Health

(3) Tap Edit to open the screen for editing.

(4) Tap Name to enter your name.

(5) Tap the camera icon and select the desired image to add a profile picture.

(6) Tap Male or Female in the gender section.

(7) Tap to enter your birthdate in the Birthday section.

(8) Tap to enter your height in the Height section.

(9) Tap to enter your weight in the Weight section.

(10) Tap the icon in the Activity Level section that best represents how active you are. If you're not at all active, tap one of the icons on the left. If you are very active, tap one of the icons on the right.

(11) Tap Save.

← My page

Profile   EDIT ─(3)

(6)(5)   (4)

CANCEL   SAVE ─(11)

[camera icon]   Name

Gender *   ◯ Male   ◯ Female

Birthday *   [DATE   ] ─(7)

Height *   ft, in ▼─(8)

Weight *   lb   ▼─(9)

Activity level *

[icon] [icon] [icon] [icon] [icon]
  1   2   3   4   5

Select your activity level. The more often you exercise, the higher your activity level will be.

(10)

(12) Tap the back arrow on the My Page screen to return to the main screen.

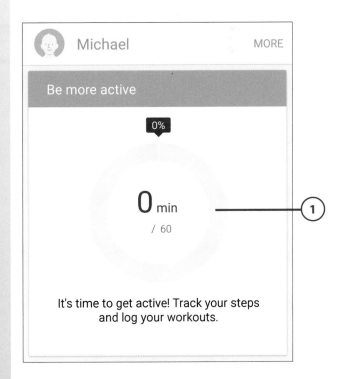

Select Activities to Manage

You need to tell S Health which activities you want to track.

(1) At the top of the main screen of the S Health app you see a graphical representation of your current day's activity. If this is your first time using the app, you see zero activity.

(**2**) Scroll down to see tiles for specific activities.

(**3**) Scroll to the very bottom of the screen and tap + Manage Items.

(**4**) Tap to select the Trackers tab. (It might be selected by default.)

(**5**) Tap On those activities and items you want to track—everything from walking and running to food and water, from weight and sleep to heart rate and blood pressure. Tiles are added to the main screen for those items you select.

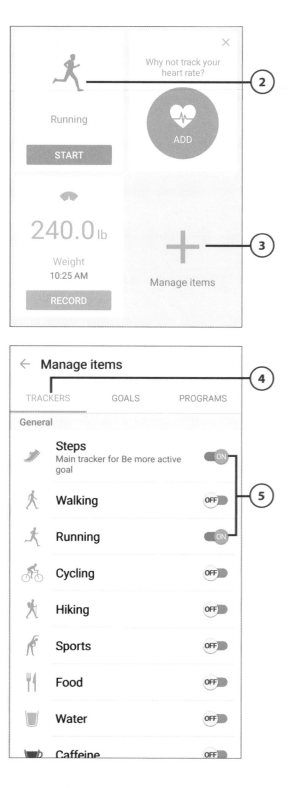

6 Tap to select the Goals tab.

7 Tap to select any of the stated goals—Be More Active, Eat Healthier, or Feel More Rested.

8 For each goal you select, enter specific goals.

9 Tap Start.

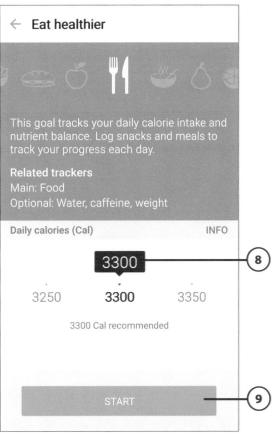

Monitor Your Pulse

Here's something cool and useful—your Galaxy S6 or S6 Edge has a heart rate monitor built in. You can use this feature to monitor your pulse—but first, you have to enable heart rate tracking.

(1) Scroll to the bottom of the main screen and tap + Manage Items.

(2) Tap to select the Trackers tab.

(3) Scroll to the bottom of the screen and tap On the Heart Rate switch.

(4) Tap the back arrow to return to the main screen.

(5) You see a new Heart Rate tile on the main screen. Tap Measure.

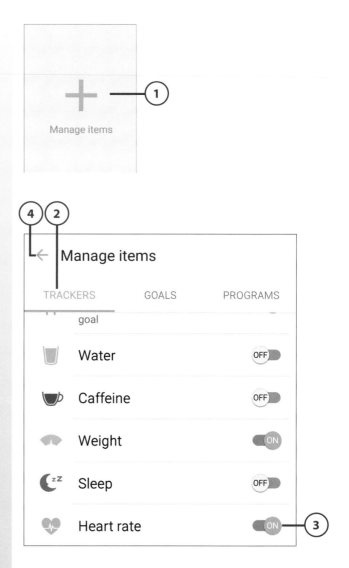

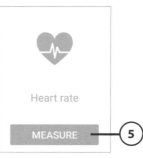

6 When prompted, place your index finger on the heart rate monitor on the back of your phone. Try to keep still and calm while the device monitors your pulse rate.

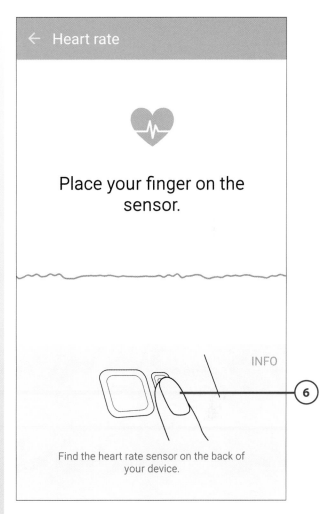

(7) S Health displays your measured heart rate.

(8) At the bottom of the screen, tap to select your current status: General, Resting, After Exercise, Excited, Tired, In Love, Surprised, Sad, Angry, Fearful, Unwell, or Before Exercise.

(9) Tap Save.

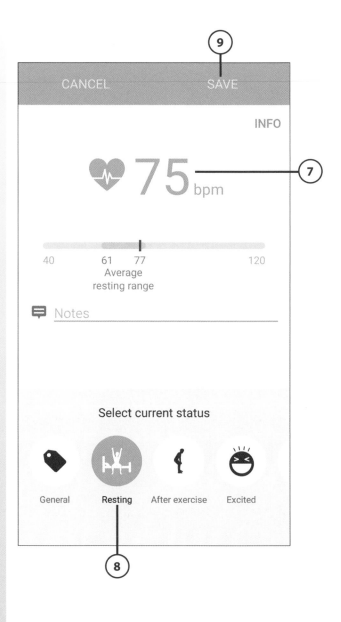

(10) Tap Trends on the main Heart Rate screen.

(11) You see a graph of your recent heart rate measurements.

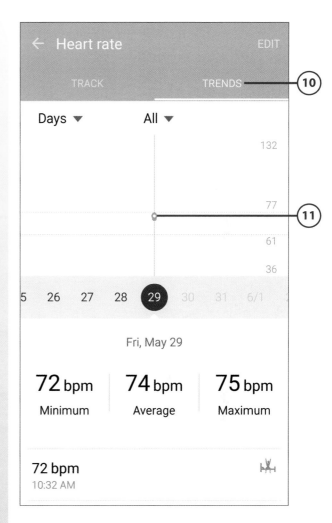

Track Your Blood Pressure

As you've just seen, your Galaxy S6 or S6 Edge can both record and track your heart rate. The S Health app can also track (but not record) your blood pressure levels over time.

(1) To track your readings, you must first configure the S Health app appropriately. Scroll down to the bottom of the main screen and tap + Manage Items.

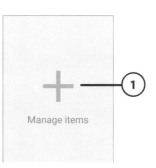

(**2**) Tap to select the Trackers tab.

(**3**) Scroll to the bottom of the screen and tap On the Blood Pressure switch.

(**4**) Tap the back arrow to return to the main screen.

(**5**) You see a new Blood Pressure tile on the main screen. Tap this tile.

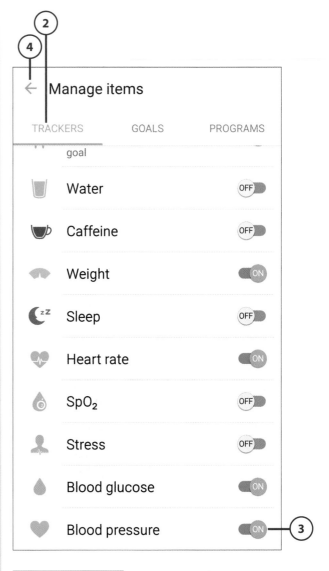

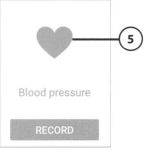

6 Enter your current blood pressure reading by tapping to select the Track tab.

7 Tap Record Manually.

8 Tap the date box at the top of the screen.

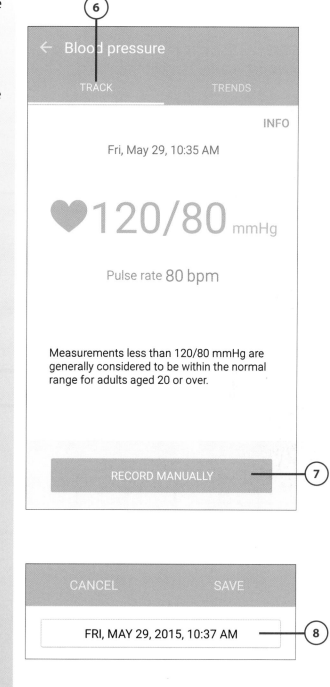

9 Enter the date and time of the reading.

10 Tap Done to return to the previous screen.

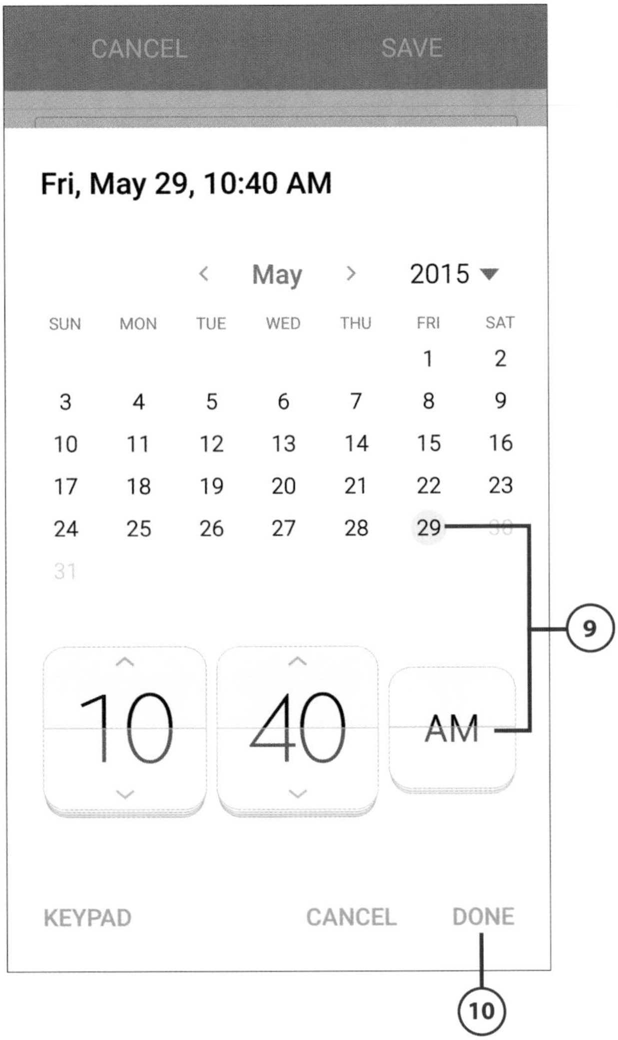

CANCEL   SAVE

Fri, May 29, 10:40 AM

	<	May	>	2015 ▼	

SUN	MON	TUE	WED	THU	FRI	SAT
					1	2
3	4	5	6	7	8	9
10	11	12	13	14	15	16
17	18	19	20	21	22	23
24	25	26	27	28	29	30
31						

10   40   AM

KEYPAD   CANCEL   DONE

(11) Tap and drag the appropriate controls to enter your systolic, diastolic, and pulse rate (optional) readings.

(12) Tap Save.

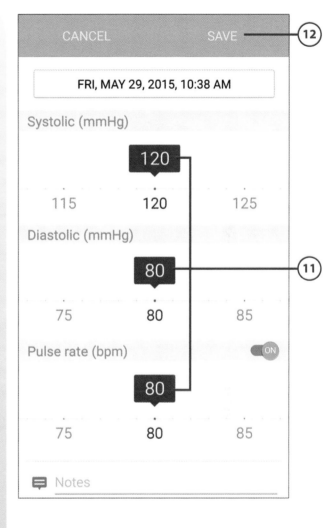

(13) You see the reading you just entered.

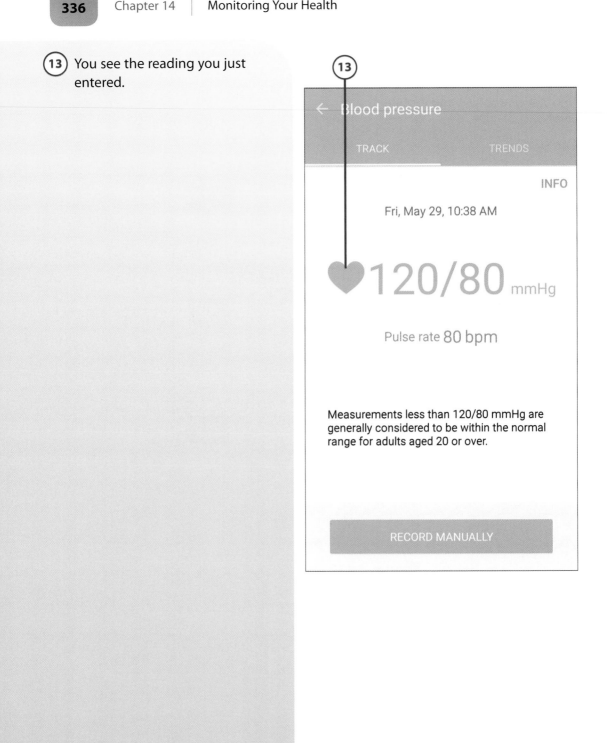

14 Tap to select the Trends tab. You see a graph of your blood pressure readings over time.

Track Automatically

By default, you have to enter blood pressure, blood sugar, and other data manually. You can, however, connect external measurement devices to your smartphone to input this data automatically.

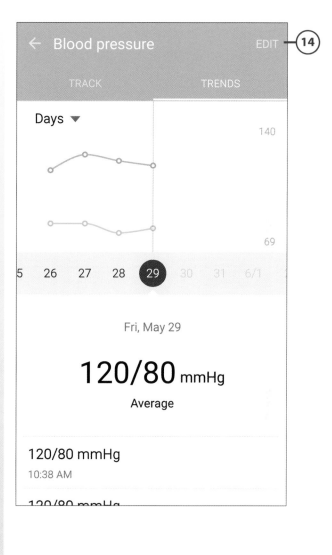

Track Your Blood Glucose Level

If you have Type I or Type II diabetes, it's important to monitor your blood sugar (glucose) readings. You can keep track of these readings in the S Health app.

1 To track your readings, you must first configure the S Health app appropriately. Scroll down to the bottom of the main screen and tap + Manage Items.

Manage items

(2) Tap to select the Trackers tab.

(3) Scroll to the bottom of the screen and tap On the Blood Glucose switch.

(4) Tap the back arrow to return to the main screen.

(5) You see a new Blood Glucose tile on the main screen. Tap this tile.

(2)
(4)

← Manage items

TRACKERS   GOALS   PROGRAMS

goal

🥛 Water   OFF

☕ Caffeine   OFF

👟 Weight   ON

🌙ᶻᶻ Sleep   OFF

💓 Heart rate   ON

💧 SpO$_2$ OFF

👤 Stress   OFF

💧 Blood glucose   ON ── (3)

❤ Blood pressure   ON

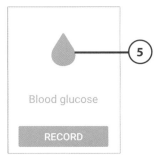

Blood glucose

RECORD ── (5)

6. Enter your current blood sugar reading by tapping to select the Track tab.

7. Tap Record Manually.

8. Tap the date box at the top of the screen.

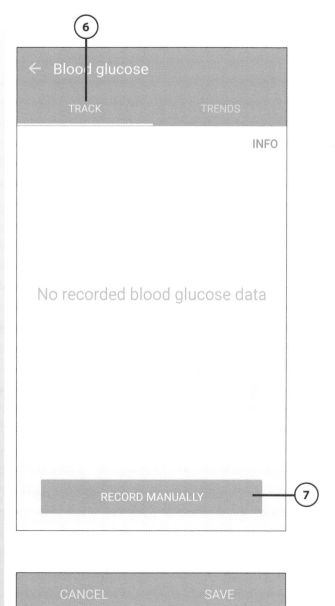

9 Enter the date and time of the reading.

10 Tap Done to return to the previous screen.

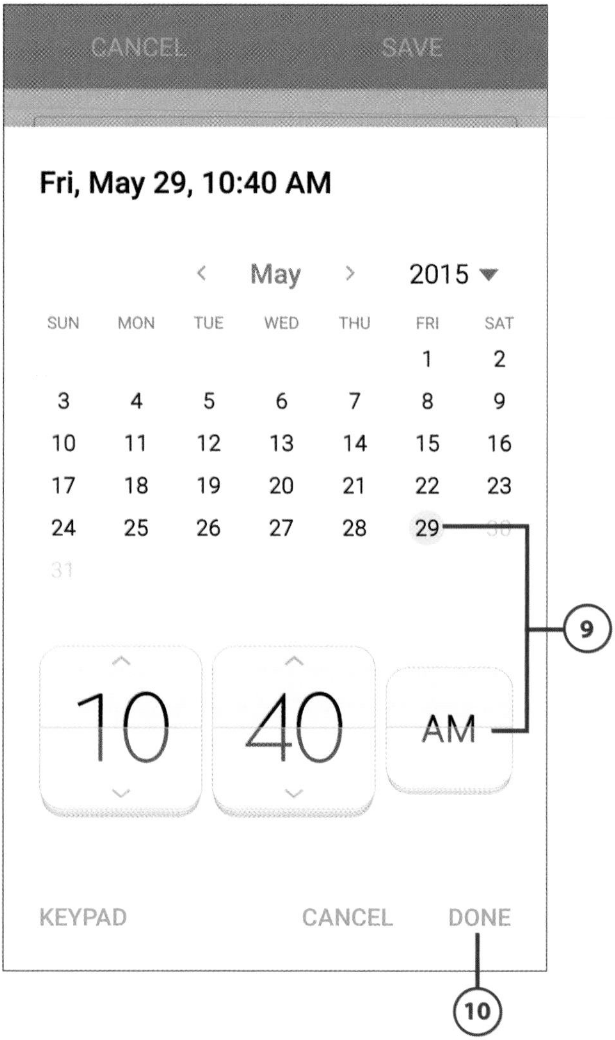

CANCEL   SAVE

Fri, May 29, 10:40 AM

<	May	>	2015 ▼	
SUN	MON	TUE	WED	THU	FRI	SAT
					1	2
3	4	5	6	7	8	9
10	11	12	13	14	15	16
17	18	19	20	21	22	23
24	25	26	27	28	29	30
31						

10   40   AM

KEYPAD   CANCEL   DONE

11 Tap and drag the control in the Blood Glucose section to record the measured blood glucose level.

12 Tap the icon in the Meal Tags section that represents when you took this reading—General, Before Meal, or After Meal.

13 Tap Save.

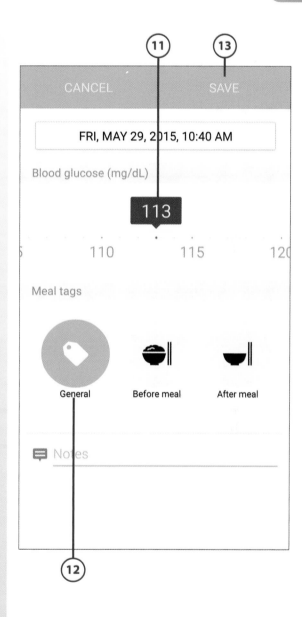

14 You see the reading you just entered.

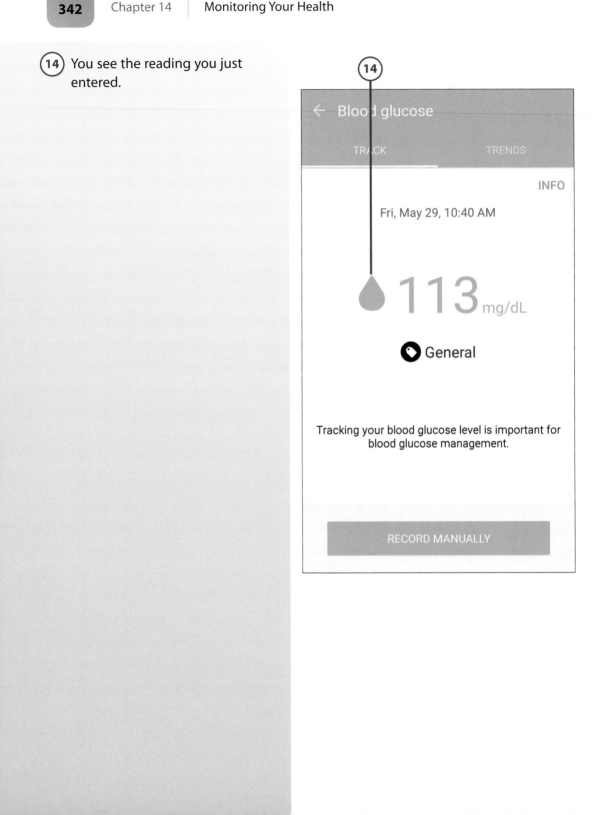

15 Tap to select the Trends tab. You see a graph of your blood sugar readings over time.

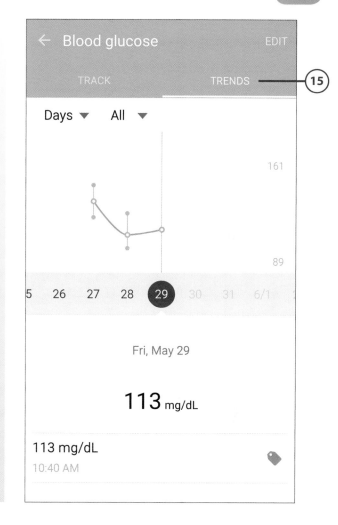

>>>Go Further

ORGANIZE YOUR TILES

Any goals you've activated in the S Health app are tracked at the top of the main screen. Tap and swipe left and right to scroll through progress graphs for multiple goals.

Beneath this section of the main screen are tiles for each activity or condition you're tracking. If you're tracking a lot of items, you'll have a lot of tiles displayed. To organize these tiles, tap and drag a tile to move it to a new position. You might like to put your exercise-related tiles all together, your meal-related tiles together, and the tiles that track your various health readings together.

Track Your Food Intake and Calories Consumed

Another useful feature of the S Health app is its ability to track your daily food intake and calculate the calories you consume.

(1) To track your intake, you must first configure the S Health app appropriately. Scroll down to the bottom of the main screen and tap + Manage Items.

(2) Tap to select the Trackers tab.

(3) Tap On the Food switch. (This may be on by default.)

(4) Tap the back arrow to return to the main screen.

(5) You now see a new Food tile on the main screen. Tap this tile.

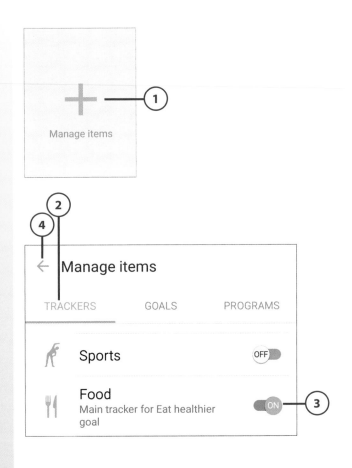

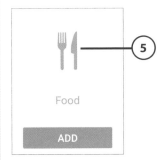

Tap to select the Track tab.

 Tap the icon for the meal or snack you're recording.

 Tap to select the Search tab then enter the name of the food you ate into the Search box *or…*

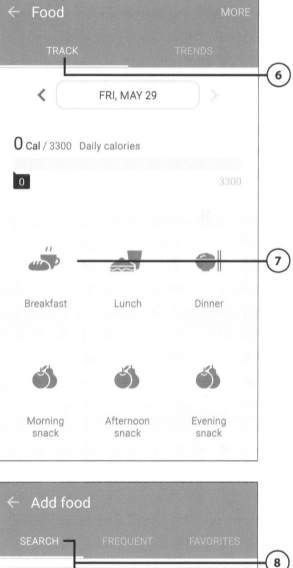

9 Tap to select the Frequent tab and tap the + by the food you ate *or...*

10 Tap to select the Favorites tab and tap the + next to one of your favorite meals. (This only appears after you've added some favorites.)

11 Repeat steps 8 through 10 to add more food.

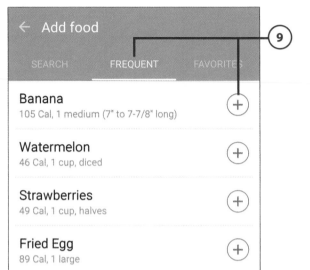

← Add food

SEARCH **FREQUENT** FAVORITES

Banana
105 Cal, 1 medium (7" to 7-7/8" long)

Watermelon
46 Cal, 1 cup, diced

Strawberries
49 Cal, 1 cup, halves

Fried Egg
89 Cal, 1 large

← Add food

SEARCH FREQUENT **FAVORITES**

Favorites

Breakfast egg
2 items, 139 Cal

Lunch sub sandwich
2 items, 217 Cal

Lunch burger
2 items, 599 Cal

Breakfast
2 items, 255 Cal

My food

ADD TO MY FOOD

12. Examine the details of this meal. If this is a meal you eat often, tap Add to Favorites.

13. Tap Done.

14. The calorie count for this meal is displayed on this day's track page.

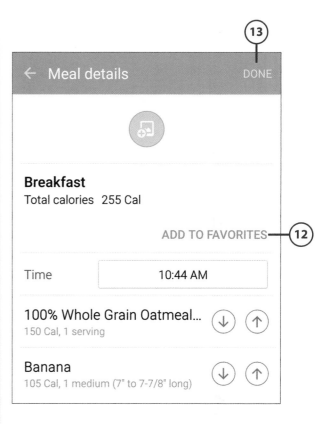

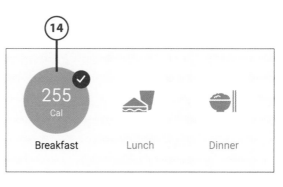

15 Tap to select the Trends tab. You see a graph of your calorie consumption over time.

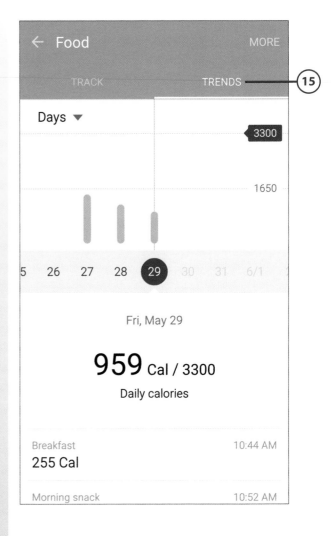

Track the Steps You Take

The S Health app includes a built-in pedometer for counting the steps you take. All you have to do is activate the pedometer and then start walking!

1 To activate the pedometer, you must first configure the S Health app appropriately. Scroll down to the bottom of the main screen and tap + Manage Items.

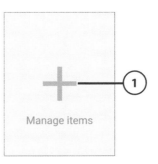

(2) Tap to select the Trackers tab.

(3) Tap On the Steps switch. (It might be on by default.)

(4) Tap the back arrow to return to the main screen.

(5) You see a new Steps tiles near the top of the main screen. This tile tracks the steps you take over time. To see more detail, tap this tile.

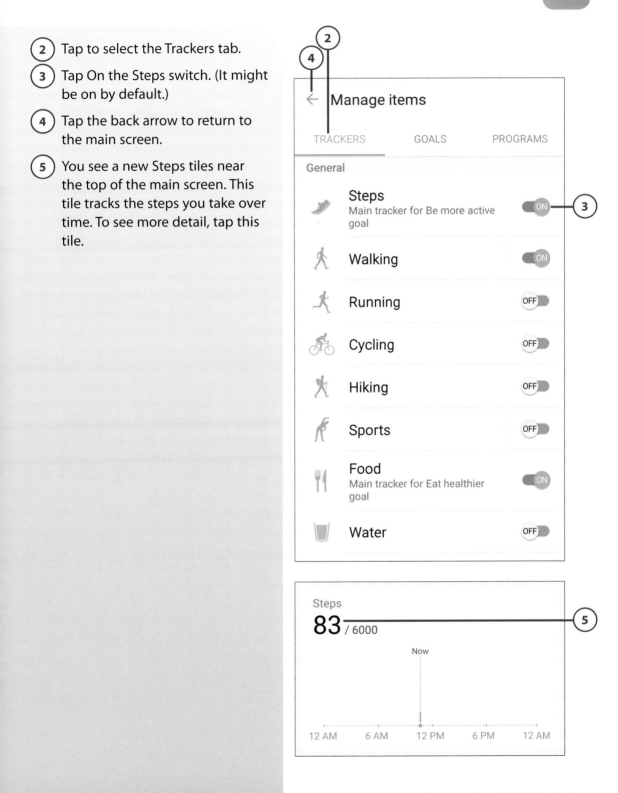

2

4

← Manage items

TRACKERS   GOALS   PROGRAMS

General

Steps
Main tracker for Be more active goal   ON — **3**

Walking   ON

Running   OFF

Cycling   OFF

Hiking   OFF

Sports   OFF

Food
Main tracker for Eat healthier goal   ON

Water   OFF

Steps
83 / 6000   **5**

Now

12 AM   6 AM   12 PM   6 PM   12 AM

(6) Tap to select the Track tab. This displays a graph of the steps you've taken today. The distance you've walked and calories burned are displayed beneath the graph.

Track Other Exercise

Walking is a rather low-impact type of exercise. If you're into more vigorous exercise and sports, the S Health app can track those, too. Just open the Manage Items screen and tap On those activities you want to track. Tiles for those activities will be added to the main screen; tap a tile to track and monitor that activity.

(7) Tap the Trends tab. This displays a day-by-day graph of the steps you've taken.

Discovering Other Health and Fitness Apps

For a list of some other health and fitness apps available, download the bonus task, "Health Fitness Apps" from the book's website at www.informit.com/title/9780789755445.

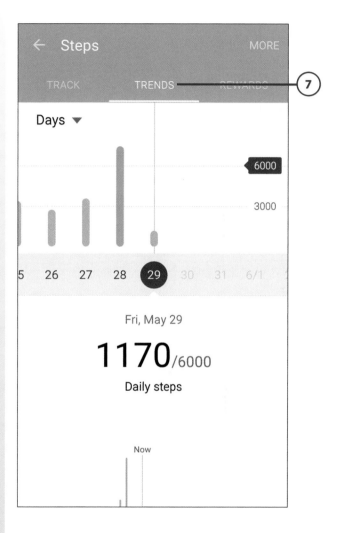

In this chapter, you learn how you can manage your daily activities with Samsung's Calendar app. Topics include the following:

→ Viewing Your Calendar

→ Creating Appointments and Events

→ Creating a To-Do List

Managing Your Calendar

What do you have to do today? You can use your Galaxy S6 or S6 Edge to manage your day-to-day activities, using the phone's built-in Calendar app. This chapter shows you how.

Viewing Your Calendar

Samsung includes the Calendar app with every new Galaxy S6 and S6 Edge smartphone. You use this app to view calendars and track your appointments and activities.

Change the Calendar View

The Calendar app can display yearly, monthly, and weekly views. Choose the view that's right for you.

1. From the Home screen, tap the Calendar icon to open the Calendar app.

2. By default, the Calendar app displays a monthly calendar of the current month. To highlight the current day, tap Today at the top of the screen.

3. Swipe left on the screen to view the next month.

4. Swipe right on the screen to view the previous month.

5. Tap the down arrow by the month at the top of the screen to change to a yearly, weekly, or daily calendar view.

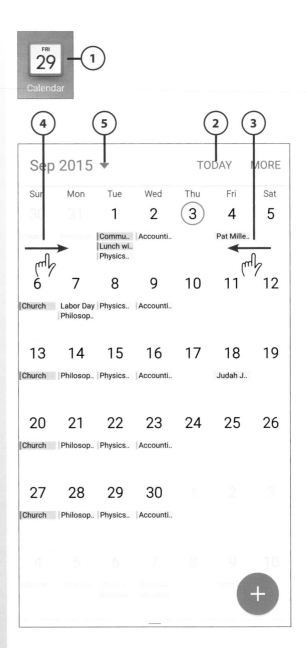

6 Select the view you want—Year, Month, Week, Day, or Tasks.

7 In Year view, you see thumbnail monthly calendars for all 12 months of the year. Tap a month to view a monthly calendar for that month.

8 In Week view, you see a grid of the days of the week (left to right) and the hours in each day (top to bottom).

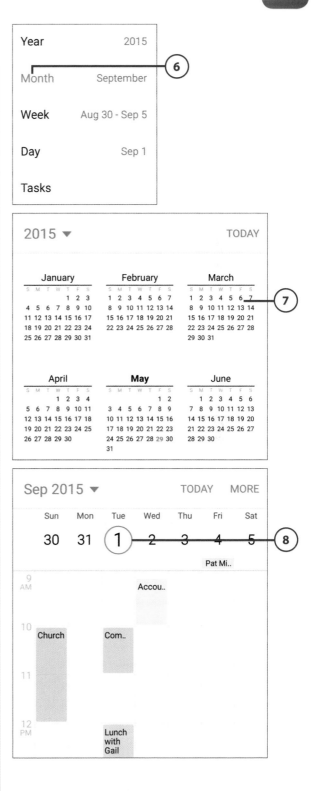

9 In Day view, you see the days of the week across the top of the screen, with all activities for the selected day (by time) beneath that. Tap another date to view the daily activities for that day.

View Calendar Items

You add activities and appointments to the basic calendar and can then view upcoming events.

1 From within the Calendar app, select your desired view. (The examples use monthly view.)

2 View a list of events for a given day by tapping that day on the calendar and then swiping up from the bottom of the screen or...

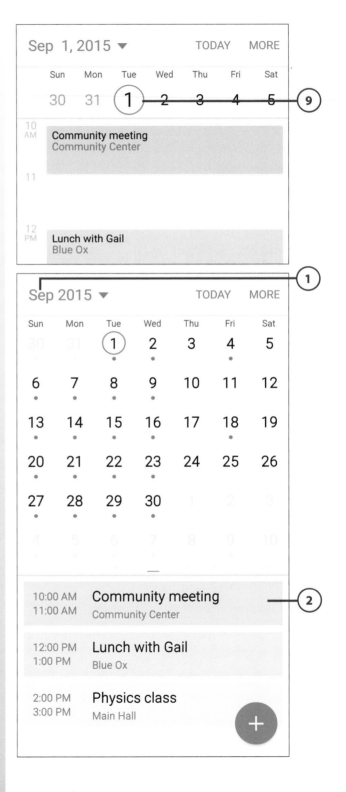

3 Tap a day on the calendar to view a pop-up with events for that day.

4 Tap an event to view details about that event.

5 You now see the item's details— start time, end time, location, and such. To delete this event, tap Delete.

	Sun	Mon	Tue	Wed	Thu	Fri	Sat
	30	31	1	2	3	4	5

1 Tuesday   ✕

10:00 AM 11:00 AM	Community meeting Community Center	12
12:00 PM 1:00 PM	Lunch with Gail Blue Ox	
2:00 PM 3:00 PM	Physics class Main Hall	19

← DELETE SHARE

Community meeting 🎨

🕐 All day   OFF

Start   TUE, SEP 1, 2015   10:00 AM

End   TUE, SEP 1, 2015   11:00 AM

Creating Appointments and Events

You use the Calendar app not just to display yearly, monthly, and weekly calendars, but also to create and track events on those calendars. An event might be a meeting or an appointment, or maybe a friend's birthday or your anniversary.

Create a New Event

You can set a new event to start and end at a specific time, or you can create an all-day event.

1. From the monthly or weekly view, tap the day you want the event to occur.

2. Tap the green + button to open the new event screen.

3. Enter the name of this event or appointment into the Title box.

4. Tap the color palette icon to assign a color to this event.

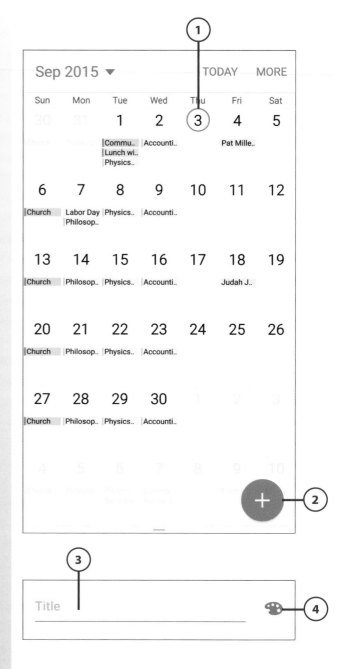

5 Tap a color.

6 If this is an all-day event, tap On the All Day switch. Otherwise, leave this switch in the Off position.

7 Tap the Start control.

8 Use the time controls to set the start time, along with AM or PM.

9 Tap End.

10 Use the time controls to set the end time, along with AM or PM.

11 If this event spans multiple days, tap the ending day on the calendar.

12 Tap Done to return to the event screen.

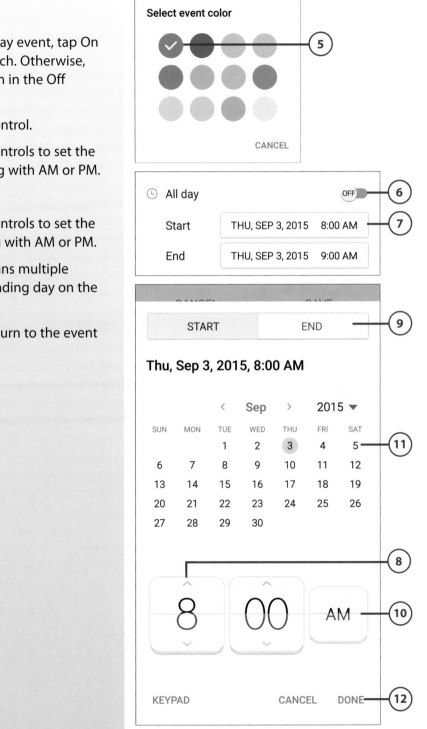

(13) By default, you'll receive an alert about this event 10 minutes in advance of the start time. To delete this alert, go to the notification screen and tap – (minus).

(14) If you want to add another alert for this event, go to the notification section and tap + (plus).

(15) By default, you will receive a notification on your phone about this event. If you'd prefer to receive notification via email, tap the Notification down arrow and then select Email instead.

(16) Tap when you want to receive the notification—anywhere from On Time (at the starting time of the item) to 1 day before.

(17) To enter a location for this event, tap Location and then enter an address, room number, or the like. Alternatively, you can tap Map to display a local map, and then tap the location on this map.

(18) Tap Save to save this event.

🔔 10 min before, Notification	— +

← **Reminder**

Alert type   Notification ▼

○ On time

○ 10 min before

○ 30 min before

○ 1 hour before

○ 1 day before

○ Customize

CANCEL   SAVE

Planning meeting

🕐 All day   OFF

Start   THU, SEP 3, 2015   8:00 AM

End   THU, SEP 3, 2015   9:00 AM

📅 ● Community Events

🔔 10 min before, Notification   — +

📍 Location   MAP

Create a Repeating Event

Events can repeat. For example, you can schedule a golf game to occur every Saturday morning at 10:00 am., or schedule a phone call to family on the first Wednesday of every month.

(1) Create a new event as described in the "Create a New Event" task.

(2) Tap Repeat.

(3) Tap how often this event recurs, from Daily to Yearly.

(4) For more detailed recurrences, tap Customize.

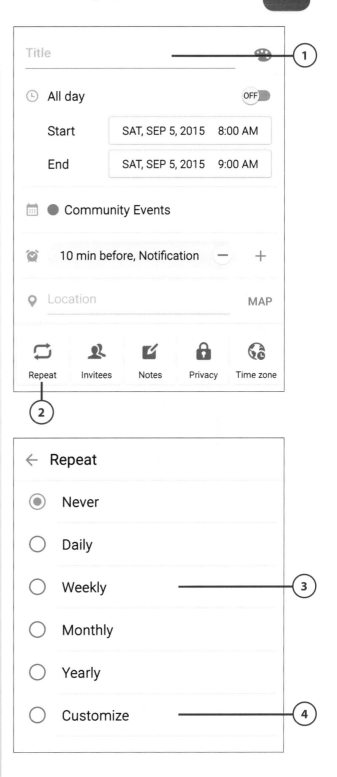

5 For events that repeat on a daily basis (every X number of days), select Daily and then enter the number of days.

6 For events that repeat on a weekly basis (a specific day each week, or every other week), select Weekly, enter the number of weeks between recurrences, and then tap the day of the week.

7 For events that repeat on a monthly basis (a specific day each month), select Monthly, select when each month the event occurs.

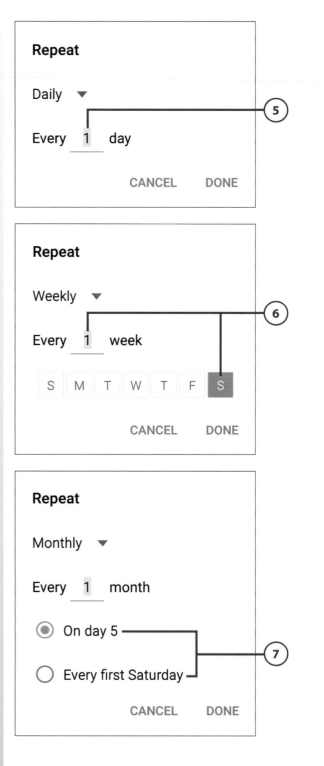

(8) For events that repeat just once a year (such as birthdays and anniversaries), select Yearly and enter the number of years.

(9) Tap Done to return to the new event screen.

(10) By default, recurring events repeat forever. To change this, tap the Forever down arrow and then tap either Until or Repetitions.

(11) Tap Save to save the event.

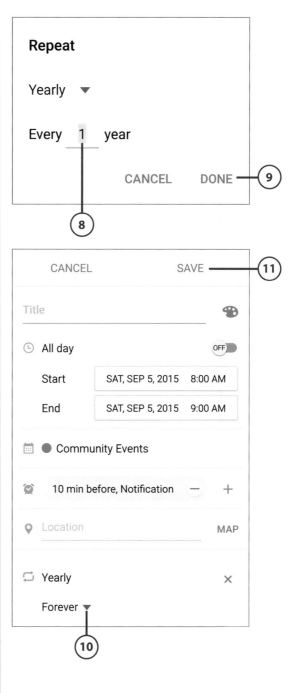

Invite Others to an Event

You can use the Calendar app to schedule group meetings, by inviting others to a given event.

1. Create a new event as described in the "Create a New Event" task.

2. Tap Invitees to display a new section on the screen.

3. Tap to enter individual email addresses or...

4. Tap the Contacts icon to display the Contacts screen.

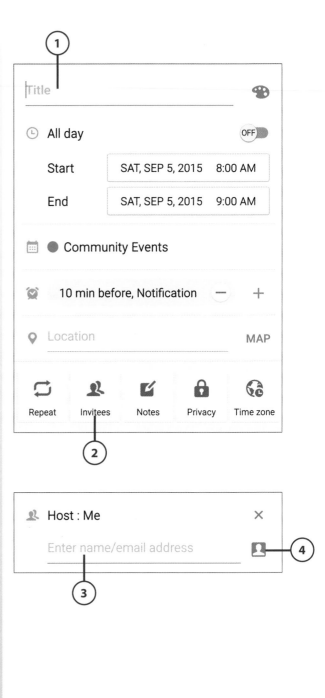

5 Tap one or more contacts to invite.

6 Tap Done.

7 Tap Save; invitations will be emailed to the people you've invited.

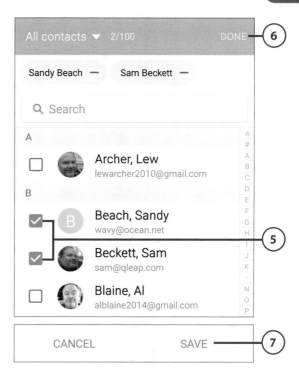

Creating a To-Do List

The Calendar app can also be used to manage your upcoming tasks, as a kind of digital to-do list.

Create a New Task

You create new tasks from the Tasks screen.

1 From any calendar screen, tap the date down arrow.

2 Tap Tasks to display the Tasks screen. A list of all current tasks opens.

(3) Create a new task by tapping Enter New Task and using the onscreen keyboard to enter the task or name of the task.

(4) As you type the name of the task, the screen changes to display additional options. If the task is to be completed today or tomorrow, click the Today or Tomorrow buttons.

(5) If the completion date is further out, tap the Expand button.

(6) Tap On the Due Date switch.

(7) Tap the date button to display an onscreen calendar.

(8) Tap the date you'd like to have this task completed.

(9) Tap Done.

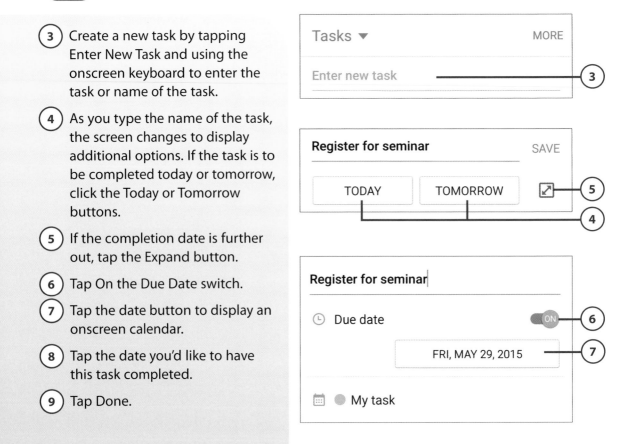

Tasks ▼	MORE
Enter new task —————————————————— (3)	

Register for seminar	SAVE
TODAY	TOMORROW	⬈ —(5)
└───(4)───┘	

Register for seminar|

🕐 Due date ————————————— ON —(6)

FRI, MAY 29, 2015 ——(7)

📅 ● My task

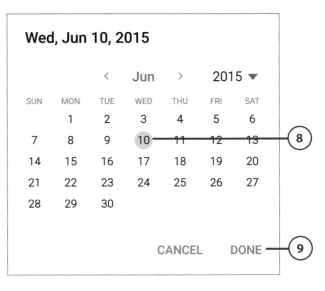

Wed, Jun 10, 2015

< Jun >   2015 ▼

SUN	MON	TUE	WED	THU	FRI	SAT
	1	2	3	4	5	6
7	8	9	10	11	12	13 |—(8)
14	15	16	17	18	19	20
21	22	23	24	25	26	27
28	29	30				

CANCEL   DONE —(9)

10 If you'd like to be reminded of this task's due date, tap Reminder.

11 Tap the date and time you'd like to be reminded.

12 Tap Done.

13 If this is a particularly important task, tap Priority to display a new Priority section.

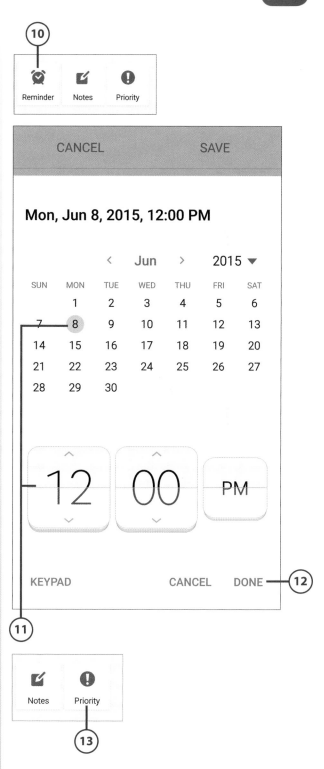

(14) Tap the down arrow in the Priority section and select either High, Medium, or Low priority.

(15) Tape Save to save this task.

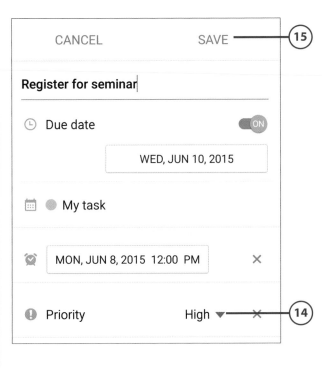

Manage Your Tasks

After you've created a list of tasks, you can mark off tasks as you complete them.

(1) From any calendar screen, tap the date down arrow.

(2) Tap Tasks to display the Tasks screen. A list of all current tasks opens.

3   View details about a given task by tapping that task.

4   Swipe the task to the left to postpone a task's due date by one day.

5   Tap the task's check box to mark a task as completed.

6   Swipe a task to the right to remove a completed task.

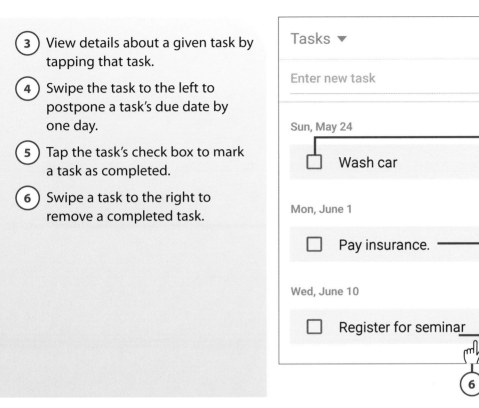

Personalizing Your Calendar

You can customize your calendar to your personal tastes. For more information, see the bonus task "Personalize Calendar" on the book's website at www.informit.com/title/9780789755445.

In this chapter, you discover how to find locations and generate driving directions using the Google Maps app. Topics include the following:

→ Viewing Maps
→ Finding Nearby Places
→ Generating Directions

Viewing Maps and Driving Directions

Your new Samsung smartphone comes with the Google Maps app. You use Google Maps to find nearby homes and businesses, as well as to generate driving directions to places you want to go.

Viewing Maps

At its most basic, the Google Maps app will display maps of just about any location in the developed world. You can look at maps of your neighborhood, city, state, or country. You can even use Google Maps to view current traffic conditions—so you'll know which routes to avoid!

Display Your Current Location

Google Maps works with the GPS functionality of your phone to track and display your current location.

Turn On Location Tracking

To get full use and benefit of the Google Maps app, you need to turn on location tracking on your phone. Swipe down from any screen to display the notification panel, then tap On the Location icon.

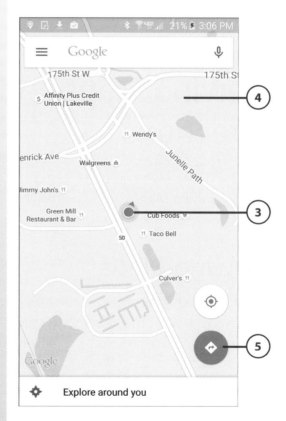

(1) From the Home screen, tap Apps to open the Apps screen.

(2) Tap the Maps icon to open Google Maps.

(3) By default, Google Maps uses your phone's GPS functionality to display your current location, as identified by a blue circle on the map.

(4) To move around the map, tap and drag the map in any direction.

(5) To return to your current location, tap the Location icon at the lower-right corner of the map screen.

6. To zoom into the current location, tap the screen with two fingers and then spread them apart.

7. To zoom out from the current location, pinch the screen with two fingers.

Add to Home Screen

If you use Google Maps a lot, you might want to add a shortcut for the app to your Home screen. Open the Apps screen then tap and drag the Maps icon up to your Home screen of choice.

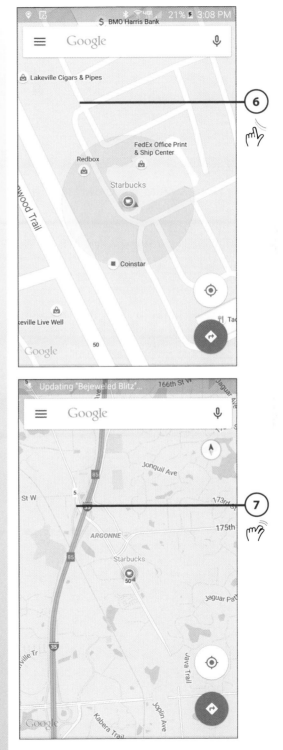

Display Traffic Conditions

If you live in a busy metropolitan area, or even just an area prone to traffic jams and slowdowns, you can use Google Maps to display current traffic conditions on the map. Green means traffic is moving just fine, orange means traffic is slow, and red means traffic is heavily congested or stopped.

1. From the main map screen, tap the Options button at the top-left corner.

2. Tap Traffic.

3. Current traffic conditions are now displayed on the map. (If no colors appear on a given road, that means no conditions are currently being reported.)

Change the Map Display

By default, Google Maps displays a typical street map. You can also choose to display public transit, bicycling, satellite, and terrain maps.

(1) From the main map screen, tap the Options button at the top-left corner.

(2) Tap the type of map you want to display.

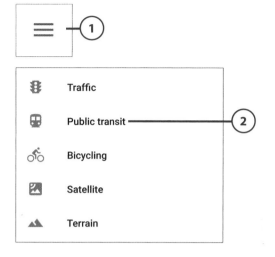

Public transit map

Bicycling map

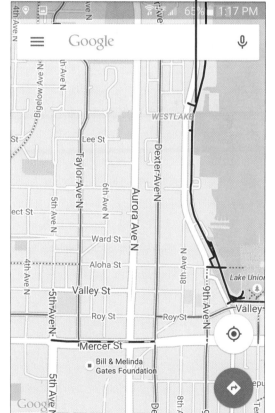

Satellite map

Terrain map

Around Downtown Phoenix

Around Lakewood

It's Not All Good

Draining the Battery

The Google Maps app is a lifesaver when you're not sure where you're going, or when you're just on a long trip. But know that the combination of the app and its use of location services puts a major drain on your phone's battery. Leave the Google Maps app running for an hour or more and you'll see your phone's battery level decrease significantly.

The solution is to either not use the app when you don't need it, or to keep your phone connected to your car's power. Do this with an external charger cable that connects to a 12 volt power outlet in your car. This way your phone will continually charge while you're driving, and the battery won't drain while you're navigating.

Finding Nearby Places

As you've discovered, it's easy enough to display a map of your current location. But what if you want to display a map of someplace else? Or find a restaurant or gas station nearby?

Enter a New Location

Google Maps can map street addresses, general location information (such as street intersections), cities and states, and even specific locations, such as museums, stadiums, and airports.

1) From the main map screen, tap within the Google search box and enter the location you want to map. Enter a street address, street name, intersection ("Fifth and Main"), city, or state. You can also enter the name of a building or location, such as "Yankee Stadium," "O'Hare Airport," or "Golden Gate Bridge."

2) Google now displays a map of that location, with the specific location pinpointed with a red pin.

3) To generate driving directions to this location from your current location, tap the Directions icon at the bottom right.

Voice Commands

If you're using Google Maps while driving, it is safer to speak your commands rather than type them. Tap the microphone icon in the Google search box and then speak the location you want to map, or the type of business or attraction you're looking for.

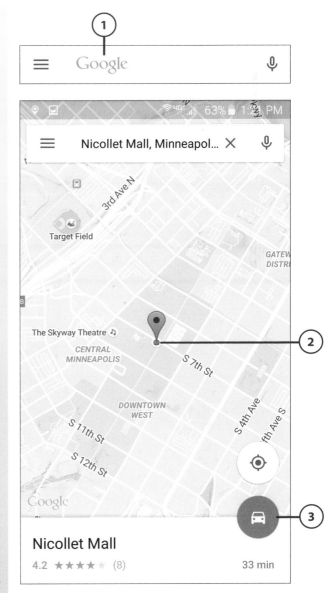

Find Nearby Businesses and Attractions

When you're traveling, you often want to find interesting and useful businesses and attractions near where you are. You might want to find nearby coffeehouses, restaurants, hotels, grocery stores, ATMs, or gas stations. Not surprisingly, Google Maps uses the power of Google to search for whatever it is you want—and then display the results on a map.

1. From the main map screen, tap within the Google search box to display a screen of search suggestions.

2. Tap Explore Nearby to view suggested businesses and attractions nearby.

3. Tap a tile to view more details about that business or attraction or...

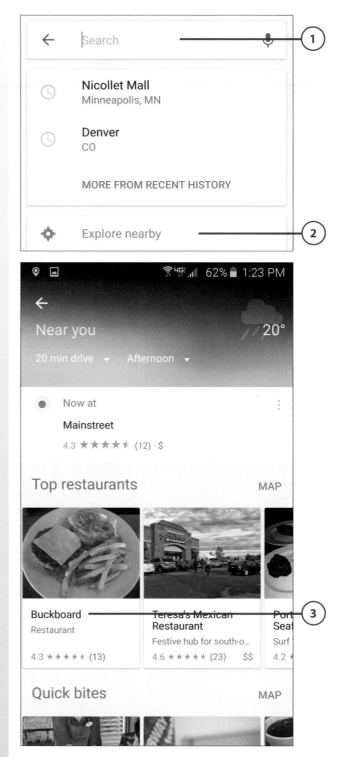

(4) Tap the appropriate icon to display nearby gas stations, groceries, pharmacies, and ATMs.

(5) Tap More to see additional types of businesses.

(6) Tap the type of business or service you're looking for *or*...

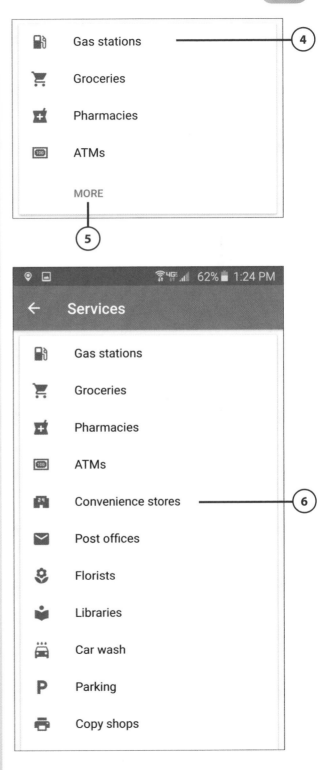

7. On the search suggestions screen, enter the type of business or service you want into the search box.

8. Matching businesses are displayed on the map and in a list on the bottom part of the screen. Tap an icon or listing to learn more about that business.

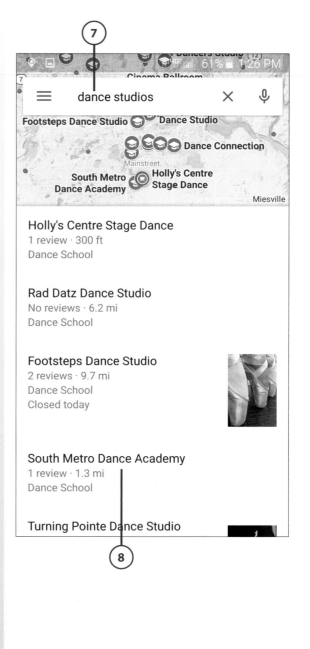

9 Tap the Call icon to call that business from your phone.

10 Tap the Website icon to display that business' website in the Chrome browser.

11 Tap the Directions icon to display driving directions to this business.

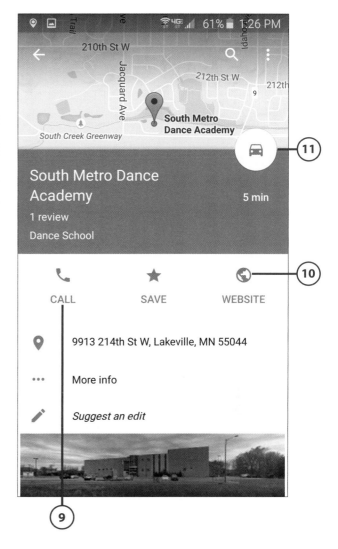

Generating Directions

If you don't know where it is that you need to go, you can use Google Maps to generate directions to get you there. Just follow the step-by-step (or turn-by-turn) instructions and you'll end up at the right place, every time.

Generate Driving Directions

To generate driving directions, all you have to do is tell Google Maps where you are and where you want to go.

1. From the main map screen, tap the Home icon to display your current location.

2. Tap the Directions icon to display the Directions screen.

3. Tap the car icon at the top of the screen to generate driving directions.

4. Tap within the Choose Destination box and enter the end destination.

5. Google now displays a map of what it feels is the best route to the destination. To view other routes, swipe left on the bottom part of the screen.

6. Tap the bottom part of the screen to view the turn-by-turn directions.

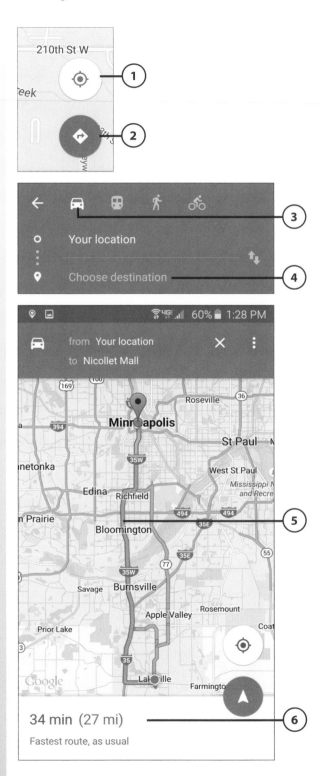

7 Tap the Start (up arrow) icon when you're ready to start driving.

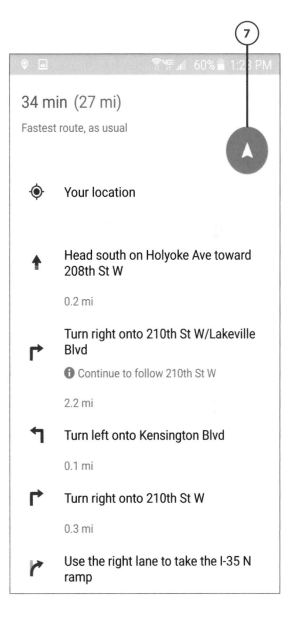

7

34 min (27 mi)
Fastest route, as usual

◉ Your location

↑ Head south on Holyoke Ave toward 208th St W

0.2 mi

↱ Turn right onto 210th St W/Lakeville Blvd

ⓘ Continue to follow 210th St W

2.2 mi

↰ Turn left onto Kensington Blvd

0.1 mi

↱ Turn right onto 210th St W

0.3 mi

↱ Use the right lane to take the I-35 N ramp

8 Google Maps displays a zoomed in map of your current location, with the next turn highlighted at the top of the screen. The app's built-in voice speaks your first instructions.

9 Start driving and follow the driving directions. The map updates itself as you move, and the app speaks additional instructions as needed.

Coming Back Home

After you've arrived at a destination, Google Maps can generate directions for getting back home. Just re-open the directions screen and tap the reverse arrows between your current location and destination. The app now generates directions to your original location.

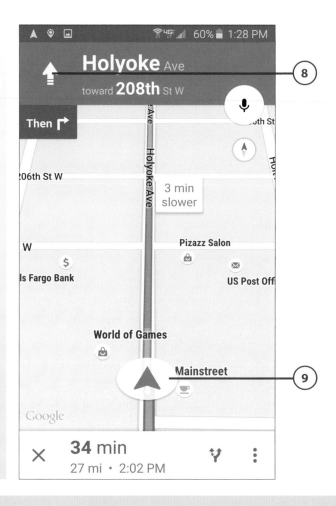

>>>Go Further
GOOGLE MAPS IN YOUR CAR

Google Maps is designed for use while you're driving. You can use the combination of Google Maps and your Galaxy smartphone much the same way you'd use a freestanding GPS navigation device. The screen provides turn-by-turn maps and directions while the app's voice directs you as to where to turn next.

If you have your phone synced to your car's audio system via Bluetooth, it gets even better. The voice commands sound through your car's speakers, and all you have to do is follow the instructions. The app even lets you know when you've arrived at your destination. (Learn more about connecting to your car via Bluetooth in Chapter 7, "Making Phone Calls.")

Generate Other Types of Directions

Google Maps isn't limited to generating driving directions. The app can also generate direction for mass transit, walking, and bicycling.

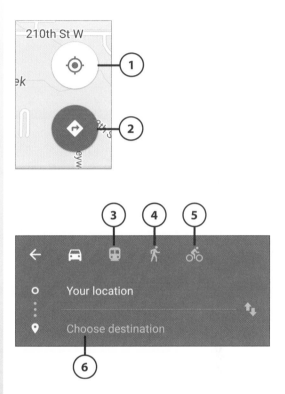

1. From the main map screen, tap the Home icon to display your current location.

2. Tap the Directions icon to display the Directions screen.

3. Tap the Mass Transit icon to generate directions via mass transit (train, subway, or bus).

4. Tap the Walking icon to generate walking directions.

5. Tap the Bicycle icon to generate directions via bicycle paths and streets.

6. Tap within the Choose Destination box and enter the end destination. Google generates the appropriate instructions and map based on your selected method of conveyance.

Mass Transit

If you select Mass Transit, Google Maps displays a list of transportation options based on departure and arrival time. Tap the option that best meets your transportation needs.

In this chapter, you find out how to shoot and share photos and videos with your Samsung Galaxy S6 or S6 Edge. Topics include the following:

→ Shooting Photos with Your Smartphone's Cameras
→ Viewing and Organizing Your Photos
→ Editing Your Photos
→ Recording and Playing Videos
→ Sharing Your Photos and Videos

Shooting and Sharing Photos and Videos

Your Galaxy S6 or S6 Edge has two high-quality cameras built in—one on the back, to shoot pictures of things you're looking at, and one on the front, to shoot pictures of you. These cameras can shoot still photographs or videos, and you can easily share the photos and videos you shoot, via email, text message, and even social media.

Shooting Photos with Your Smartphone's Cameras

Your smartphone's main camera is on the back of the unit, facing away from you. The other, front-facing camera is above the screen, facing toward you.

The main camera on the back of your phone is the best-quality camera of the two, with 16 megapixel (MP) resolution. You use this camera to take pictures of friends and family, events and attractions, landscapes and still lifes.

The front-facing camera takes good pictures, but not quite as good as the main camera, with 5MP resolution. Your phone automatically employs this camera when you make video calls. It's also used for taking selfies—photos of yourself.

Shoot a Photograph

You can shoot photos in portrait mode, with the phone held vertically, or in landscape mode, with the phone held horizontally. Taking a photo is as easy as aiming and then tapping the screen.

(1) On your phone's Home screen, tap the Camera icon to open the Camera app.

(2) Turn the camera 90 degrees left or right to shoot in landscape mode. The onscreen controls rotate with the camera.

(3) Tap the front/rear icon to switch between rear- and front-facing cameras.

(**4**) Aim at the subject and use your phone's display as the camera's viewfinder to compose your shot.

(**5**) Touch the screen with two fingers and spread them apart to zoom into the subject (make the subject appear larger).

(**6**) Pinch two fingers together on the screen to zoom out of the subject (make the subject appear smaller in the frame).

(**7**) Tap an area of your phone's screen to focus on the specific person or thing in that area.

(**8**) Tap the Camera icon to take the picture. The screen flashes slightly and you hear a shutter sound. The new picture is stored in your phone's Gallery.

Volume Keys

You can also take a picture by pressing the up or down Volume keys on the side of your phone.

Shoot a Selfie

Shooting a selfie is just like shooting a regular photo with the rear camera. The difference is that you use the front camera and typically stay in portrait mode, with the phone held vertically in your hand.

1. Open the camera app and tap the front/rear icon to switch to the front-facing camera.

2. When you use the front-facing camera, it automatically deploys Beauty mode, which subtly softens the picture for more of a glamour look. To increase or reduce this Beauty effect, tap the Beauty icon and then adjust the onscreen slider.

3. Smile for the camera and then tap the Camera icon to take the picture.

Select a Shooting Mode

Your Samsung S6 or S6 Edge offers several shooting modes you can employ when taking a picture. You select a shooting mode before you take a picture.

1. From within the Camera app, tap Mode to view the available modes. Which modes are available depends on whether you're using the main or the front-facing camera.

2 Tap the mode you want to use.

3 Depending on which mode you select, additional options or actions might be available. Follow the onscreen instructions to proceed.

4 Tap the Camera icon to take your picture in the selected mode.

Download More Modes
You can download additional shooting modes for your phone's camera from Samsung's Galaxy Apps Store. Just tap the Download icon from the Modes screen.

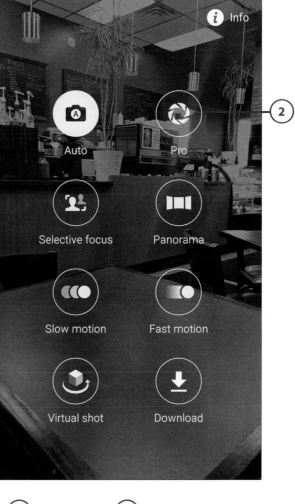

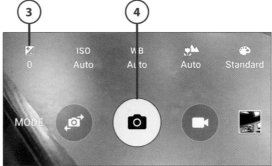

Apply Special Effects

Your phone's camera enables you to apply a variety of special effects when you shoot your photos. Like shooting modes, you apply special effects filters before you shoot a photo.

1. From within the Camera app, tap the Effect icon. You see a screen full of available effects.

2. Each effect thumbnail shows your current photo with that effect applied. Tap the effect you want to use.

3. When you're done using an effect, remember to return to the Effect screen and tap No Effect for future photos.

Download More Special Effects

You can download additional special effects for your phone's camera from Samsung's Galaxy Apps Store. Just tap the Effect icon and then tap Download.

Select Quick Settings

Your Samsung smartphone offers several settings you can configure to best optimize the pictures you take. The most useful of these are available as Quick Settings that appear across the top (in portrait mode) or side (in landscape mode) of your phone's screen/viewfinder. The available settings differ depending on which shooting mode you're in.

(1) Adjust the Beauty Mode effect with the front-facing camera by tapping the Beauty icon and then adjusting the onscreen slider.

(2) Take a time-delayed photo by tapping the Timer icon and then selecting a time, from 2 to 10 seconds.

(3) Turn on the HDR effect by tapping On the HDR icon.

HDR
HDR stands for High Dynamic Range, and it uses multiple shots to create photos with greater contrast and dynamic range than normal.

(4) Employ special photographic effects, as described previously, by tapping the Effect icon and then choosing the effect.

(5) Use the LED flash for the main camera by tapping On the Flash icon. Turn off the flash by tapping Off the Flash icon.

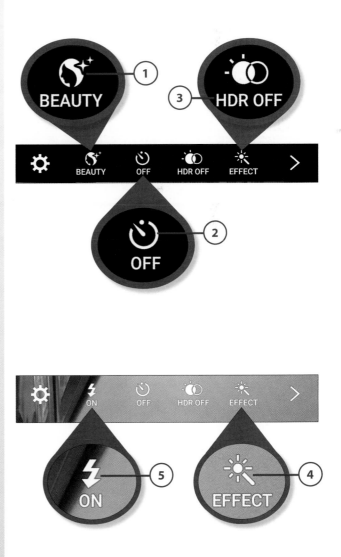

Configure Other Camera Settings

There are several other settings you can configure to personalize the way your phone's camera functions.

1 From within the Camera app, tap Settings to display the Camera Settings screen.

2 Tap Picture Size (Rear) and make a new selection to change the size, resolution, and aspect ratio of the photos you take.

3 Tap Video Size (Rear) and make a new selection to adjust the resolution and aspect ratio of the videos you shoot.

4 Turn on auto-focus tracking, where you tap to select a subject and the camera keeps that subject in focus as it moves, by tapping On Tracking AF.

5 Tap On Video Stabilization to turn on video stabilization, which helps to keep the picture steady when you're shooting videos.

6 Tap On Grid Lines to display grid lines on the camera display to help you compose your pictures.

7 Tap On Location Tags to enable GPS location tagging, where your location is automatically added to the shooting information (called *metadata*) that accompanies each photo.

8 Tap On Review Pictures to have your phone automatically display each picture as you take it.

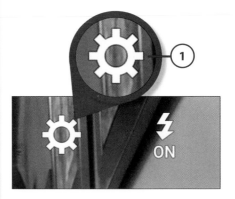

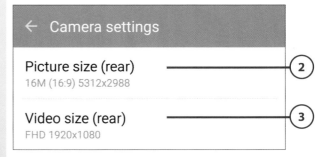

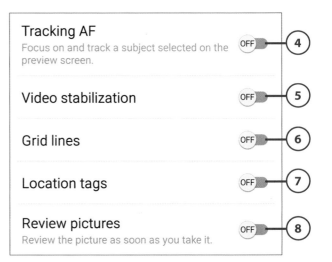

9 Tap On Quick Launch to have your phone open the Camera app when you double-tap the Home key.

10 Tap On Voice Control to be able to operate your phone's camera using voice commands.

11 By default, tapping the up or down Volume keys on the side of your phone takes a picture. To change this function so that tapping the Volume keys either records video or zooms in and out, tap Volume Keys Function and make a selection.

12 Tap Off Shutter Sound to turn off the shutter sound your phone's camera makes when you take a photo.

13 Tap Reset Settings to reset all your phone's setting to the factory defaults.

Quick launch
Open Camera by pressing the Home key twice in quick succession.   OFF   **9**

Voice control   OFF   **10**

Volume keys function
Take pictures   **11**

Shutter sound   ON   **12**

Reset settings

13

Viewing and Organizing Your Photos

The photos you take are automatically saved in your phone's Gallery app. You use the Gallery app to view photos, as well as manage the photos you've taken.

View Pictures in the Gallery

The Gallery app displays your photos either by Time, Albums, Events, or Categories.

1 From your phone's Home screen, tap the Gallery icon to open the Gallery app.

Gallery

1

(2) By default, the Gallery app displays various albums of your photos. To instead display your photos by Time (date and time taken), Events (that you create), or Categories (Pictures, Videos, or People), tap the down-arrow next to Albums and make a new selection.

(3) Tap an album thumbnail to display the photos within that album or category.

(4) If you have more than one album, you see all your albums displayed on the left side of the screen. Tap an album to view that album's photos on the right side of the screen.

(5) Tap a photo to view it fullscreen.

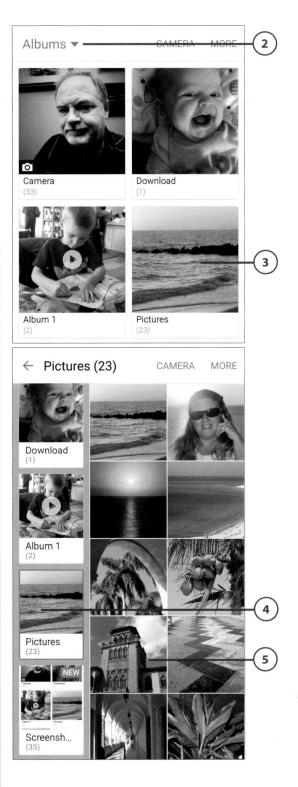

(6) Swipe the screen to the left to move to the next photo in the album.

(7) Swipe the screen to the right to move to the previous photo in the album.

(8) Double-tap on the screen to zoom into the photo (make it larger). Alternatively, pinch the screen to zoom in.

(9) Place two fingers on the screen and spread them apart to zoom out of the photo (make it smaller).

Manage Your Photos

The Gallery app offers various options for viewing and managing your photos.

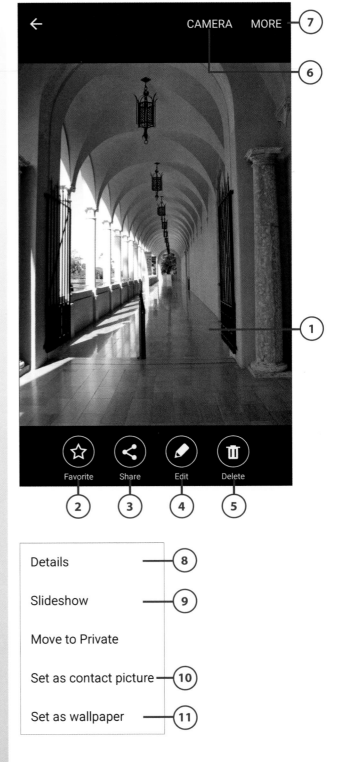

1. When viewing a photo, tap the screen to display the viewing and editing controls.

2. Tap the Favorite (star) icon to make this photo a favorite (which makes it easier to recall in the future).

3. Tap the Share icon to share this photo with others. (More on this in the "Sharing Your Photos and Videos" section, later in this chapter.)

4. Tap the Edit icon to edit the photo. (More on this in the "Editing Your Photos" section, later in this this chapter.)

5. Tap the Delete icon to delete this photo.

6. Tap Camera to switch to the Camera app.

7. Tap More to display more options.

8. Tap Details to view details (what photographers call *metadata*) about this picture.

9. Tap Slideshow to launch a slideshow of photos in this album.

10. Tap Set as Contact Picture to set this photo as your contact (profile) picture.

11. Tap Set as Wallpaper to set this photo as your phone's wallpaper.

12 Select where you want this photo used as wallpaper—on your phone's Home screen, Lock screen, or both.

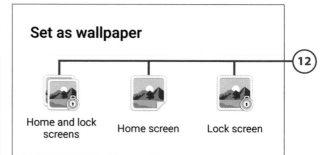

Create a New Album

Within the Gallery app, a photo album is essentially a folder where photos are stored. Photos you shoot are automatically stored in the Camera album. Images you download from the Internet or other sources are stored in the Downloads album. Screenshots you take are stored in the Screenshots album.

You can also create new albums to help you organize your photos.

1 From within the Gallery app, make sure you're viewing in Albums view.

2 Tap More.

3 Tap Create Album to display the Create Album panel.

4 Enter a name for the new album.

5 Tap Create.

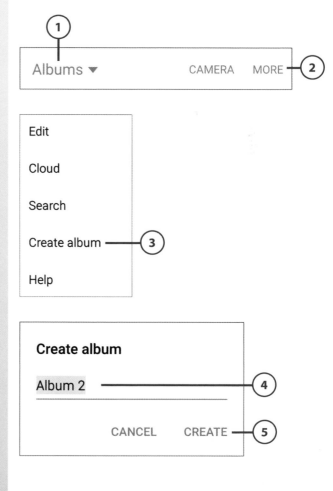

(6) You see the new album displayed on the left of the screen, and your photos are displayed on the right. Tap to select those photos you want to move to the new album.

(7) Tap Done.

(8) Tap Move when you're prompted to copy or move the items. (Unless you want the photos to reside in both the original and new albums, in which case tap Copy.)

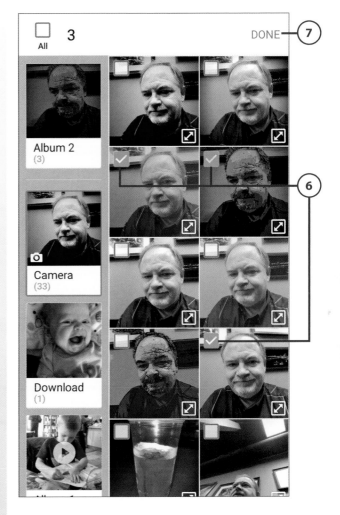

Create album

Copy or move 3 items?

CANCEL   COPY   MOVE

Delete Photos

You can tap the Delete icon to delete any photo you're currently viewing. You can also delete one or more photos from the host album or category.

1. From within the Gallery app, select the album or category you want to view.

2. Tap More.

3. Tap Edit.

Pictures (23)   CAMERA   MORE

Album 1
(2)

Album 2
(3)

Pictures
(23)

Edit

Share

Create album

Slideshow

Help

(4) Tap to select those photos you want to delete. Each selected photo appears with a green check mark.

(5) Tap Delete.

(6) Tap Delete in the confirmation box.

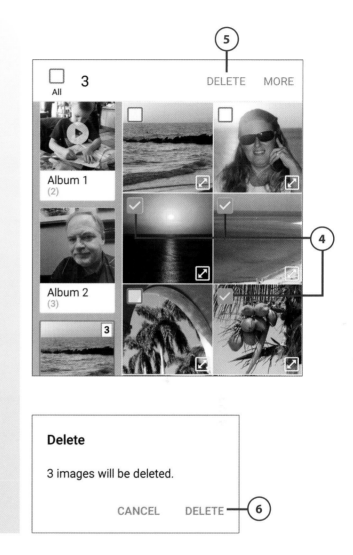

Editing Your Photos

The photos you shoot with the Camera app can be edited in the Gallery app. This way you can touch up your photos without having to use a third-party photo editing app—or transfer them to your computer to edit in Photoshop or a similar software program.

Employ Auto Adjust

Sometimes you take a photo that just looks a little off—the colors aren't quite right, maybe it's a little too light or too dark. For many photos, the Gallery app's Auto Adjust option can make these little changes for you, automatically. (And if you don't like the automatic changes, you can always undo them!)

(**1**) From within the Gallery app, tap to open the picture you want to edit.

(**2**) Tap to display the editing controls.

(**3**) Tap Edit to display the quick editing panel.

(**4**) Tap Auto Adjust. The adjustments are made to the photo; if you don't like the results, tap Off Auto Adjust.

Rotate an Image

Even the smartest smartphone camera sometimes gets confused. You shoot a picture in landscape orientation and it displays rotated, in portrait mode. Fortunately, there's a quick fix for this problem.

(1) Open the picture you want to rotate and then tap the screen to display the editing controls.

(2) Tap Edit to display the quick editing panel.

(3) Tap Rotate and the picture rotates 90 degrees clockwise. Continue tapping this control to rotate the picture further.

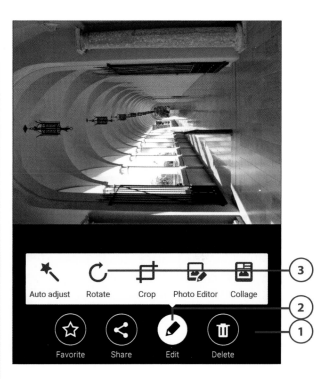

Crop a Photo

It's not uncommon to include more in the picture than what you wanted to focus on. In this instance, you want to crop the picture so that the important subject is larger in the frame, and the unnecessary edges are cropped off.

(1) Open the picture you want to crop then tap the screen to display the editing controls.

(2) Tap Edit to display the quick editing panel.

(3) Tap Crop to display the crop box and grid.

④ Tap and drag any of the crop handles along the edges and corners until only that part of the picture you want to keep is included.

⑤ Tap Save.

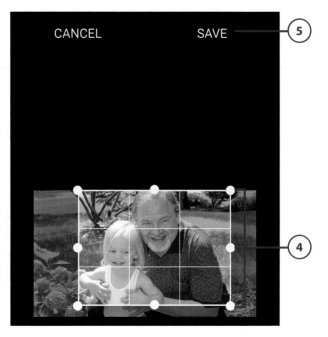

Perform Detailed Adjustments

The Gallery app includes the basic rotate and crop controls, as discussed in the preceding tasks, as well as some more detailed adjustments that enable you to spin and flip the images you shoot.

① Open the picture you want to adjust and then tap the screen to display the editing controls.

② Tap Edit to display the quick editing panel.

③ Tap Photo Editor to display the photo editing controls.

④ Tap Adjustment to display the adjustments screen.

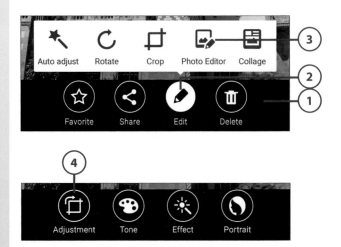

(5) Spin the picture (similar to rotate, but in smaller increments) by tapping and dragging the slider underneath the photo—right for clockwise, and left for counterclockwise.

(6) Tap the horizontal flip icon to flip the picture horizontally (left to right).

(7) Tap the vertical flip icon to flip the picture vertically (top to bottom).

(8) Tap the rotate icon to rotate the picture 90 degrees clockwise.

(9) Crop the picture by tapping and dragging any of the crop handles.

(10) Tap Apply to apply your changes.

Adjust Brightness, Contrast, and Color

The Gallery app also enables you to adjust the brightness, contrast, color, and other tonal settings for your picture.

(1) Open the picture you want to edit then tap the screen to display the editing controls.

(2) Tap Edit to display the quick editing panel.

(3) Tap Photo Editor to display the photo editing controls.

(**4**) Tap Tone to display the adjustments screen.

(**5**) Adjust the brightness by tapping Brightness and then dragging the Brightness slider—left for darker, right for brighter.

(**6**) Adjust the contrast by tapping Contrast and then tapping to drag the Contrast slider.

(**7**) Adjust the color saturation by tapping Saturation and then tapping to drag the Saturation slider—left for less color, right for more color.

(**8**) Adjust the color temperature by tapping Temperature and then tapping to drag the Temperature slider—left for cooler colors, right for warmer.

(**9**) Adjust the color tint by tapping Hue and then tapping to drag the Hue slider.

(**10**) Tap Apply to apply your changes.

Apply Special Effects

Just as you can apply special effects when shooting a photo, you can also add effects during the editing process. In fact, there are more effects available in the Gallery app's Photo Editor than in the Camera app.

1. Open the picture you want to edit and then tap the screen to display the editing controls.

2. Tap Edit to display the quick editing panel.

3. Tap Photo Editor to display the photo editing controls.

4. Tap Effect to display the effects screen.

5. All available special effects are displayed in a row at the bottom of the screen. Swipe this row left or right to access additional effects.

6. Tap to select the effect you want. The picture displays with that effect applied.

7. Adjust the intensity of an effect by tapping and dragging the slider left (for less intensity) or right (for more).

8. Tap Apply to apply the effect.

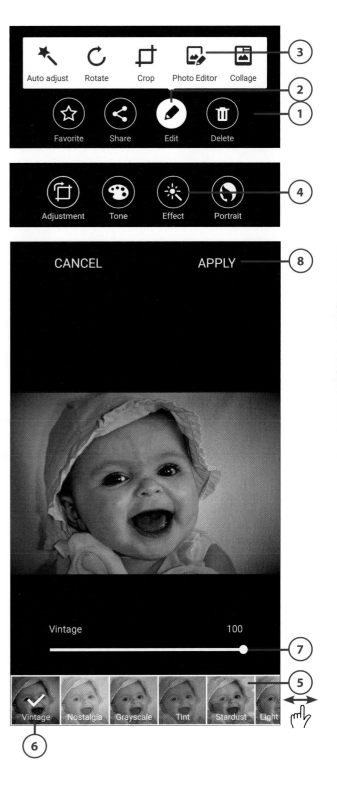

It's Not All Good

Changes Are Permanent

When you're done applying special effects or make other changes to a picture in the Gallery, you must tap Save on the next screen. When you do this, the edited picture overwrites the original version. You can't undo your changes after you've tapped Save. (You can, however, undo your changes before they're saved, by tapping Undo.) So make sure you like the changes before you save them!

Fine-Tune Portraits—and Remove Red Eye

When you're shooting people's faces, you might want to do a little fine-tuning to make them look as glamorous as possible—even if it's just removing that awful red eye effect.

(1) Open the picture you want to edit then tap the screen to display the editing controls.

(2) Tap Edit to display the quick editing panel.

(3) Tap Photo Editor to display the photo editing controls.

(4) Tap Portrait to display the portrait editing screen.

(5) Brighten the subject's face by tapping Brighten Face and then tapping to adjust the Face Brightness slider.

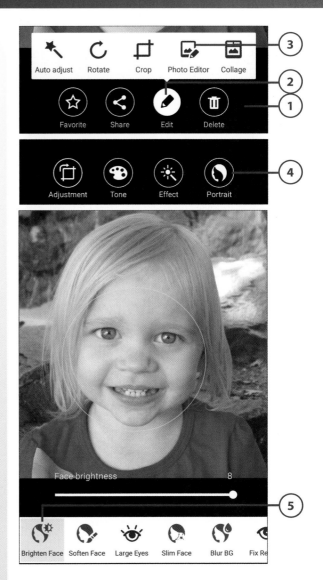

(6) Soften the subject's face (make it less sharp) by tapping Soften Face and then tapping to adjust the Soften Face slider.

(7) Make the subject's eyes subtly larger by tapping Large Eyes and then tapping to adjust the Large Eyes slider.

8 Make the subject's face slightly narrower by tapping Slim Face and then tapping to adjust the Slim Face slider.

9 Blur the background while keeping the subject's face in focus by tapping Blur BG and then tapping to adjust the Blur BG slider.

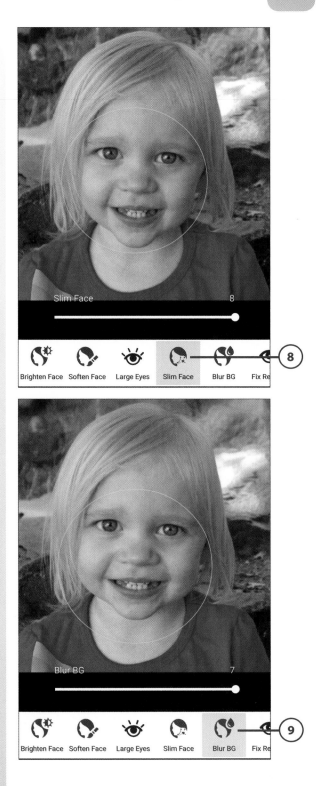

10 Remove the red eye effect by tapping Fix Red Eye and then tapping each of the eyes you want to fix.

11 Tap apply when done.

Create a Photo Collage

If you take several pictures of the same subject, you might want to combine them into a photo collage. The Gallery app enables you to create collages of multiple photos.

1 Open the first picture you want to include the collage.

2 Tap Edit to display the quick editing panel.

3 Tap Collage to display the collage editing controls.

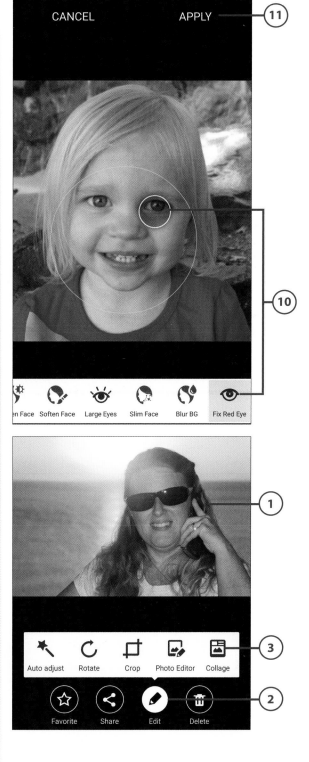

(4) Tap + or Add to display the Gallery to select more photos for this collage.

(5) Tap to select the photo(s) you want to add.

(6) Tap Done and the photos are added to the collage.

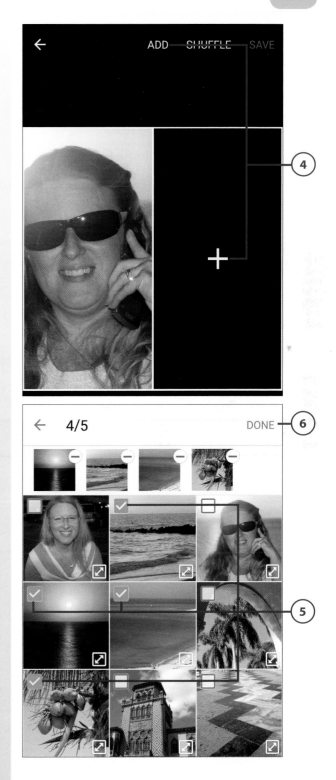

(7) Tap Aspect Ratio to select the aspect ratio of the collage—1:1 or 16:9.

(8) Tap Layout to select the desired layout of the photos.

(9) Tap Border to select a border for the collage. Use the Roundness slider to adjust corner roundness; use the Margin slider to adjust the space between photos in the collage.

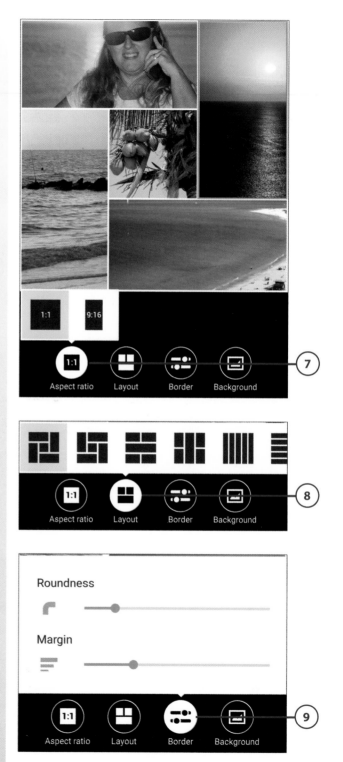

10. Tap Background to select the background behind the pictures in the collage. Choose from available background patterns or tap the rainbow thumbnail to display a color chooser and then pick the solid color background you want.

11. Tap Shuffle to randomly change the order and layout of the pictures in your collage.

12. Tap Save when the collage is to your liking.

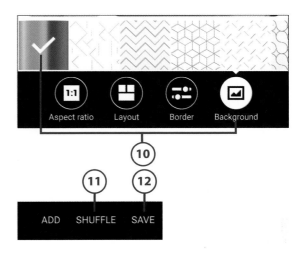

Recording and Playing Videos

You can use either the main or front-facing camera on your Galaxy S6 or S6 Edge to shoot videos as well as still photos. Many of the same controls are available when shooting video as when shooting photos.

Record a Video

You shoot a video much the same way you shoot a still photo, and with the same app—your phone's Camera app. Videos are recorded at the resolution and aspect ratio you've selected in the Camera app's settings, as described earlier in this chapter in the "Configure Other Camera Settings" task.

1. On your phone's Home screen, tap the Camera icon to open the Camera app.

(2) Turn the camera 90-degrees left or right to shoot a widescreen picture. The onscreen controls rotate with the phone.

(3) Tap the front/rear icon to switch between rear- and front-facing cameras.

(4) Aim at the subject and use your phone's display as the camera's viewfinder to compose your shot.

(5) Tap the video camera icon to begin recording. The elapsed time displays at the bottom of the screen, along with a flashing red dot.

It's Not All Good

Widescreen Videos

Most viewers expect to see videos in widescreen format—*not* in portrait or vertical format. This means you do *not* want to hold your phone normally when shooting videos. Instead, rotate the phone 90 degrees left or right so that it's horizontal—and the picture you see onscreen is wider than it is tall.

(6) Touch the screen with two fingers and spread them apart to zoom into the picture.

(7) Pinch two fingers together on the screen to zoom out of the picture.

(8) Tap the Capture icon to capture a still photo while you're recording the video.

(9) When you're done recording, tap the large Stop button. The video is now processed and saved to your phone's Gallery.

It's Not All Good

Slow and Fast Motion

The Galaxy S6 or S6 Edge offers two interesting video shooting modes. You can record at a high frame rate, which enables you to play back parts of the video in slow motion. Similarly, you can record with a slower frame rate, which enables you to play back parts of the video in fast motion.

You enable these effects *before* you start recording. Tap Mode and then tap either Slow Motion or Fast Motion. Record your video as normal.

After you're done recording, tap the thumbnail at the bottom right to review your video. Tap the screen to begin playback; use the controls at the bottom of the screen to indicate when and how long you want the slow motion or fast motion effect to appear.

Play a Video

All the videos you record are stored in the Gallery app. Use this app to access and view your videos.

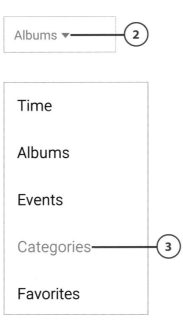

1. From your phone's Home screen, tap the Gallery icon to open the Gallery app.

2. Tap the down arrow at the top of the screen to display the menu of options.

3. Tap Categories.

(4) Tap to open the Videos category.

(5) You now see all the videos you've recorded. Tap to open the video you want.

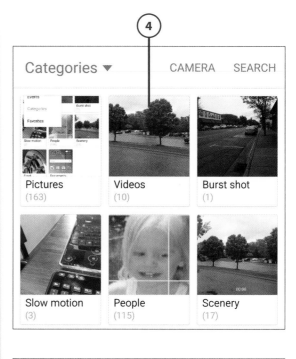

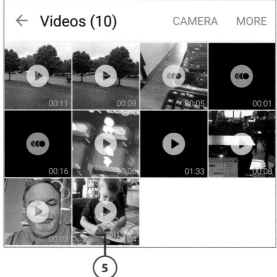

(6) Tap anywhere on the screen to begin playback.

(7) If prompted to choose an app to open this video, tap Video Player and then tap Always.

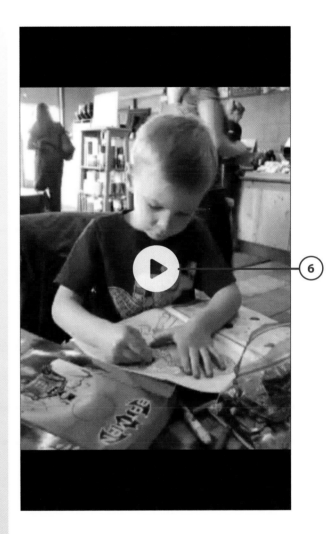

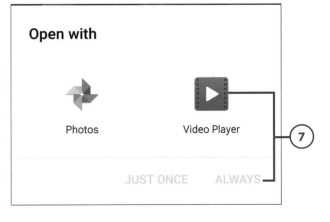

8 The video begins to play. Tap the screen to display the playback controls.

9 Tap the Pause button to pause playback. The button changes to a Play button; tap the Play button to resume playback.

10 Tap and drag the slider (sometimes called a "scrubber") to move to another portion of the video.

11 Tap the previous button to play the previous video.

12 Tap the next button to play the next video.

13 Tap Pop-Up to display the video in a small window at the top of the screen while you work in other apps.

14 Tap More and then tap Delete to delete this video.

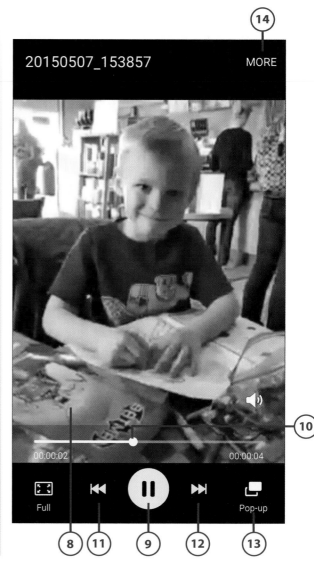

Sharing Your Photos and Videos

You can easily share the photos and videos you take in a number of different ways. You can share them via email, via text messages, and via various social media.

Shoot and Share a Photo

Many times you take a picture and decide there and then that it's worth sharing. Maybe you want to text it to a friend or family member, or you want to post it to Facebook. It's easy to do.

(1) Using the Camera app, shoot the photo.

(2) Tap the thumbnail at the bottom of the screen to display the photo you just shot.

(3) Tap the screen to display the controls at the bottom.

(4) Tap Share to display the Share Via pane.

Favorite   Share   Edit   Delete

(5) Swipe right and left to view other ways to share.

(6) Tap how you want to share this photo. To share via email, tap the Email icon.

(7) If prompted to resize the image, tap a selection. The original size creates large files that may be difficult to handle via email; a smaller size is easier to send but of lower quality. (If you're unsure which size to pick, Large is normally a good compromise.)

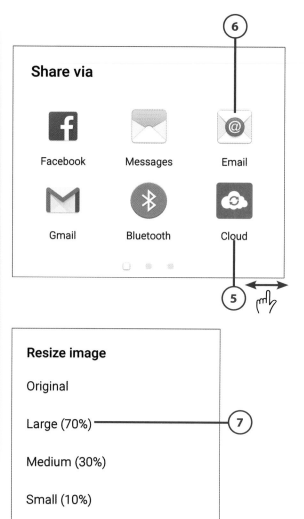

8   Complete the email as normal, entering the recipient into the To box, the subject into the Subject box, and any text message into the main text box.

9   Tap Send to send the email with your photo attached.

10 Tap the Messages icon to share the photo via text message.

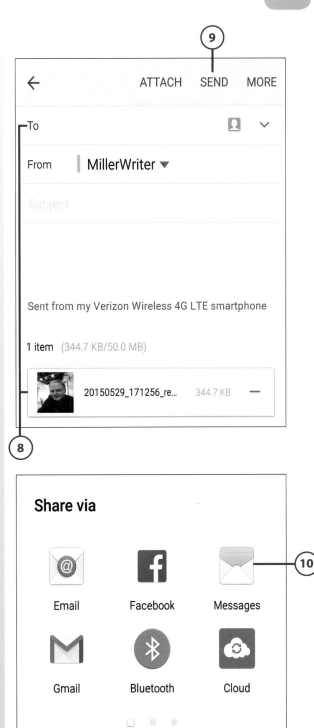

11 The photo is resized and added to a new text message. Complete the message as normal, entering the recipient into the Enter Recipients box and your text message beside the photo.

12 Tap Send to send the text message with your photo attached.

13 Tap the Facebook icon to share via Facebook.

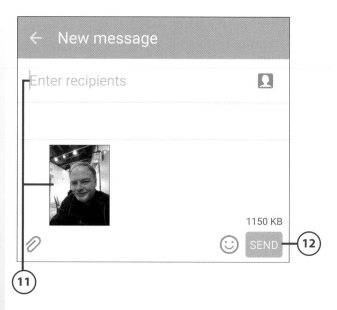

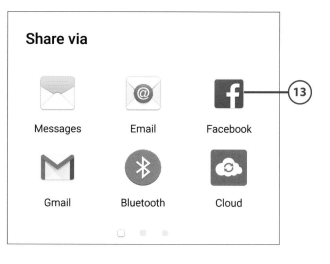

14 You see the photo added to a Facebook post. Complete the post as normal, adding any text message to the Say Something About This Photo box.

15 Tap Post to post the photo to your Facebook feed.

Share Items from the Gallery

You can also share any photo or video you've shot from the Gallery app.

1 From within the Gallery app, open the album or category that contains the photo(s) or video(s) you want to share.

2 Tap More.

(3) Tap Share.

(4) Tap to select the item(s) you want to share.

(5) Tap Share to display the Share Via pane.

(6) Tap the icon for how you want to share these items and then complete the sharing process accordingly.

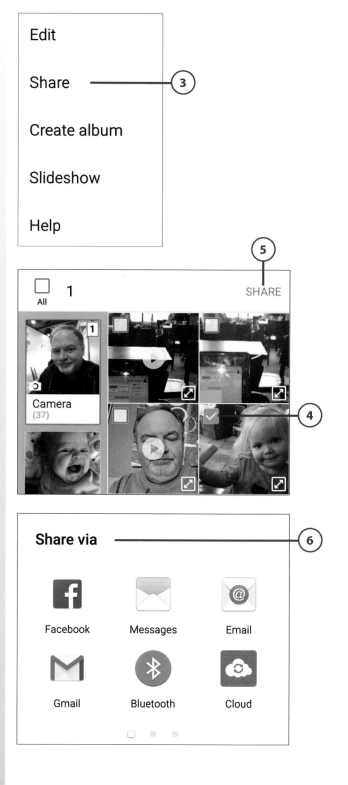

In this chapter, you walk through using your smartphone to listen to your favorite music. Topics include the following:

→ Listening to Streaming Music Services
→ Listening to Music Stored on Your Phone

Listening to Music

Back in the old days, we listened to music on record players in our living rooms. Then things got portable with transistor radios, both AM and FM. Later, Sony brought us the Walkman portable cassette player, and then came compact discs (and Sony's Discman portable CD player). It's been more than a decade since music went digital, thanks to the Apple iPod.

It's hard to believe, but iPods are already passé. Instead, we now listen to music on our smartphones. Your Samsung Galaxy S6 or S6 Edge has enough internal storage to hold a fairly large collection of downloaded digital music, or you can do like all the kids are doing and get your music online via streaming music services. The latter choice is particularly appealing, as you get access to just about any song you want without having to purchase and store anything.

Listening to Streaming Music Services

The music business is changing—again. We've all lived through several seismic changes in how our music is delivered, and now we're in the middle of another one.

Instead of buying music one track or album at a time, either online or in retail stores, more and more people are subscribing to online music services that let you listen to all the songs you want, either for free or a low monthly charge. These services, such as Pandora and Spotify, stream music in real time over the Internet to any connected device, including your smartphone. There's nothing to download, and nothing to store on your device.

Listen to Pandora Radio

Pandora Radio is much like traditional AM or FM radio, in that you listen to the songs Pandora selects for you, along with accompanying commercials. However, it's a little more personalized than traditional radio in that you create your own personalized stations. All you have to do is choose a song or artist; Pandora then creates a station with other songs like the one you picked.

You access Pandora from the Pandora app, available for free from the Google Play Store.

Free Versus Paid

Pandora's basic membership is free, but it's ad-supported. (You have to suffer through commercials as you listen.) To get rid of the commercials, pay for the $4.99/month Pandora One subscription.

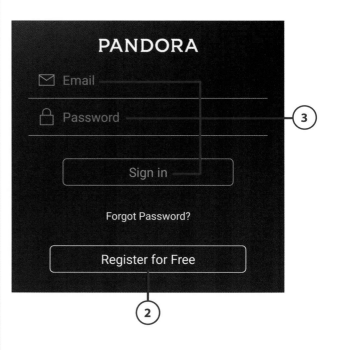

1. From the Home or Apps screen, tap the Pandora icon to open the Pandora app.

2. If you don't yet have a Pandora account (the basic account is free), tap Register for Free and follow the onscreen instructions.

3. If you already have an account, enter your email address and password, then tap Sign In.

4 Tap Create Station to create a new station.

5 Enter the name of a song, genre, artist, or composer into the box at the top of the screen. As you type, Pandora makes suggestions; tap the selection you want, or continue typing. The new station is created and starts to play.

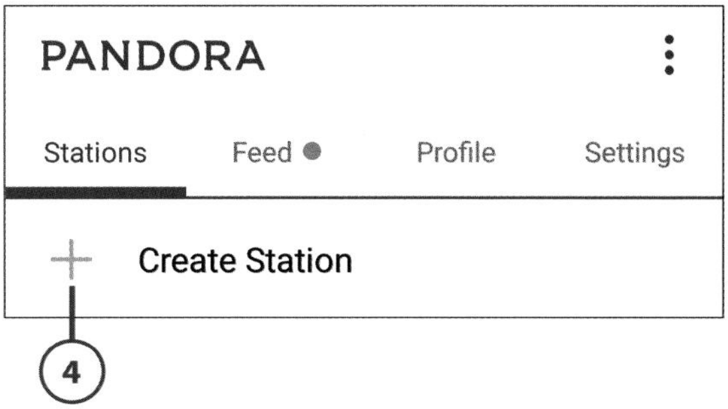

PANDORA   ⋮

Stations   Feed ●   Profile   Settings

＋   **Create Station**

4

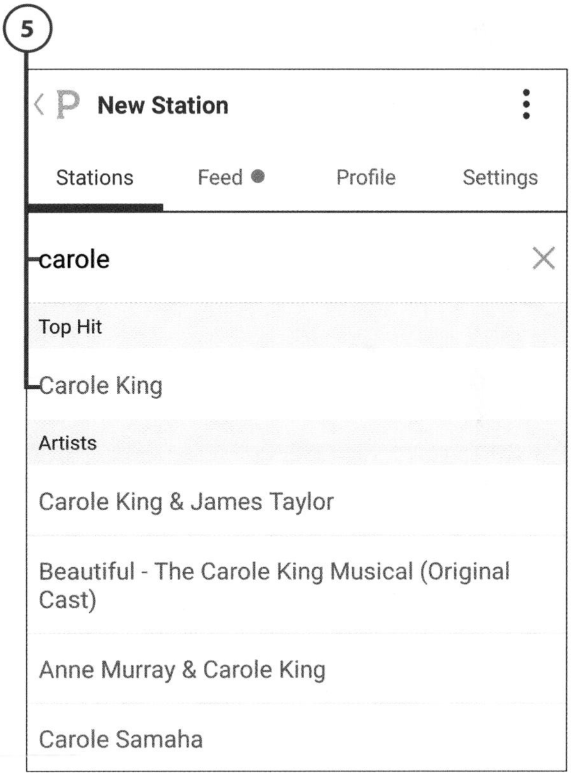

5

❮ P **New Station**   ⋮

Stations   Feed ●   Profile   Settings

carole   ✕

Top Hit

Carole King

Artists

Carole King & James Taylor

Beautiful - The Carole King Musical (Original Cast)

Anne Murray & Carole King

Carole Samaha

6 Tap the Pause button to pause playback. Tap Play to resume playback.

7 Tap the thumbs-up icon to like the current song. Pandora will play more songs like this one.

8 Tap the thumbs-down icon if you don't like the current song. Pandora skips to the next song, doesn't play the current song again, and plays fewer songs like it.

9 Tap the next track button to skip to the next song without disliking it. (You can't repeat songs on Pandora, or return to songs you've just listened to.)

10 Tap the up button above the playback controls to learn more about this song and artist.

11 Tap the back arrow at the top of the screen to return to your station list.

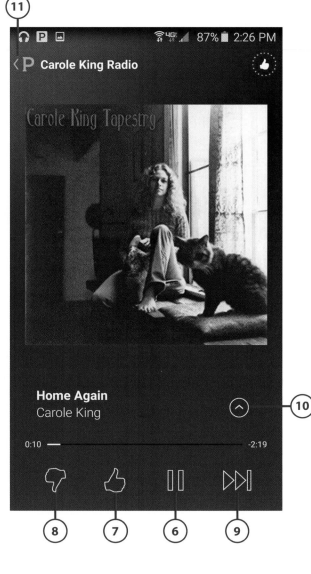

12 Tap another station name to play a different station.

Local Radio Stations Online

If you'd rather listen to your local AM or FM radio station—or to a radio station located in another city —there are apps for that. The iHeartRadio and TuneIn apps offer free access to local radio stations around the world, over the Internet. Both apps can be downloaded for free from the Google Play Store.

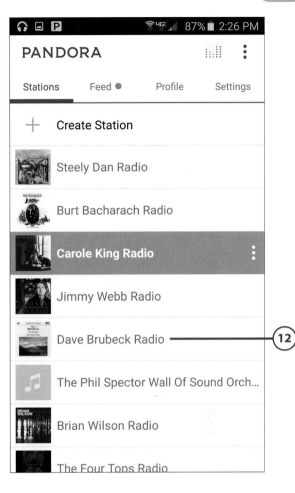

Listen to Spotify Music

The other big streaming music service is Spotify Music. You listen to Spotify Music via the Spotify app, which you can download for free from the Google Play Store.

>>>Go Further
SPOTIFY PREMIUM

Spotify on your smartphone is a little different from Spotify on your computer. The computer version of Spotify lets you select individual songs to listen to. The mobile version, however, only lets you browse by artist or genre, not by song—unless, that is, you pay for a subscription.

Spotify charges $9.99/month for its Premium service. With the Premium service, you get the option of playing specific songs (which you don't have with a free membership). In addition, the Premium service removes ads that play if you have a free membership.

So, it might be worth it to pay for Spotify Premium on your smartphone. It's less valuable if you listen on a computer, but for smartphone listening, it makes the service much more useful.

1. From the Home or Apps screen, tap the Spotify icon to open the Spotify app.

2. If you don't yet have a Spotify account (the basic account is free), tap Sign Up and follow the onscreen instructions.

3. If you already have an account, tap Log In and enter the necessary information.

4 Scroll down to the Genres & Moods section and tap a selection to browse that type of music. You see a variety of curated playlists for that category.

5 Tap a playlist to open it.

6 Scroll down to see all the songs in the playlist.

7 Tap Shuffle Play to begin playback.

8 Tap the control bar at the bottom of the screen to display the player fullscreen.

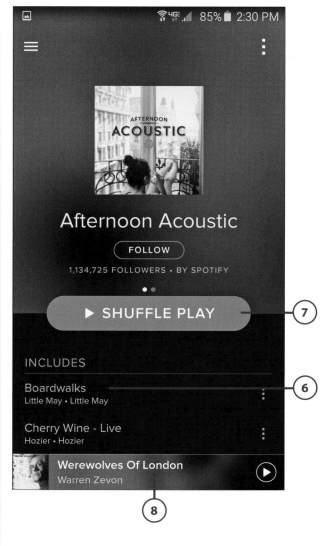

9 Tap the Pause button to pause playback —which then turns into a Play button. Tap the Play button to resume playback.

10 Tap the Next button to skip to the next track.

11 Tap the X at the top left to return to the previous screen while playback continues.

12 Tap the Options button to search for specific artists.

13 Tap Search.

14 Enter the name of the artist into the Search box. As you type, Spotify displays a list of suggestions.

15 Tap the artist you want, or continue typing. You see a playlist of the artist's songs.

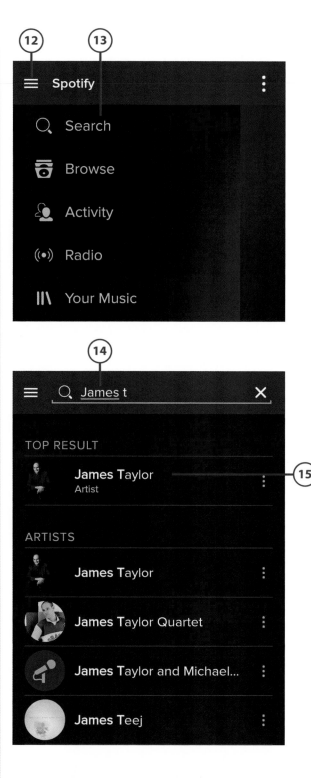

(16) Tap Shuffle Play to begin playback.

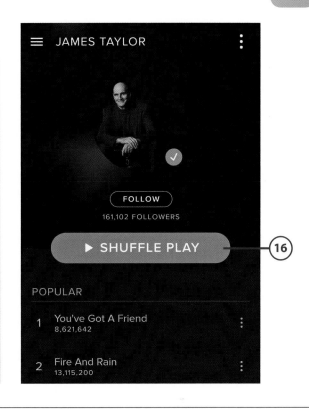

Downloading Music from Online Music Stores

If you prefer to download music rather than stream, there are many online music stores you can choose from, such as Google Play Music and Amazon Digital Music. For access to additional tasks on downloading music, see the online task "Download Music" on the book's website: www.informit.com/title/9870789755445.

>>>Go Further
TRANSFERRING MUSIC FROM YOUR COMPUTER TO YOUR PHONE

You might have already purchased digital music from your computer. You might have also "ripped" music from compact discs to store digitally on your PC. All that music is available to you on your phone, as soon as you copy it from one device to another.

There are many ways to copy digital music from your computer to your smartphone. For example, if you have a Windows PC, you can use the Windows Media Player (WMP) software on your PC to do the transfer. Just connect your phone to your PC with a USB cable, launch the WMP software on your computer, and then click the Sync tab. You can drag any and all tracks from your computer (displayed in the main part of the Windows Media Player window) to the Sync panel, and then click the Start Sync button. The music is copied to your phone—and, in the process, converted to the optimal file format for best storage and playback on your mobile device.

Alternatively, on either a Mac or PC, you can use MobileGo app and software for transferring. MobileGo is an Android file manager app that can transfer all types of files between your computer and your smartphone. Install the software on your computer and the app on your S6 or S6 Edge, and then follow the onscreen directions to find and transfer the files you want on your phone. MobileGo also can transfer any iTunes music you might have stored on your computer. (Learn more about and download MobileGo at www.android-manager.org. There's a free trial version available, but the full software costs $39.95.)

Listening to Music Stored on Your Phone

After you've purchased, downloaded, or copied music to your smartphone, you need an app that plays that music. There are lots of music player apps available from the Google Play Store:

- Fusion Music Player   Free
- Google Play Music   Free
- MediaMonkey Pro $3.49
- Music (Samsung)   Free
- n7player Music Player   Free
- PlayerPro Music Player $3.95
- Poweramp Music Player $3.99 (free version also available)

We'll focus on two of these apps, which are likely preinstalled on your phone—Samsung's Music app and Google Play Music.

Play Music with the Music App

Samsung's Music app is included with all Galaxy S6 and S6 Edge smartphones. It's a good basic music player, with the ability to create and playback playlists, as well as songs, albums, artists, and genres.

1. From the Home or Apps screen, tap the Music icon to open the Music app.

2. Tap the down arrow at the top-left corner to display the menu of options.

3. Tap what you want to play— Playlists, Tracks (individual songs), Albums, Artists, Genres, Folders, or Composers.

Playlists

Tracks

Albums

Artists

Genres

Folders

Composers

(4) View all the songs in a genre, on an album, or by an artist by tapping that genre, album, or artist.

(5) Tap Shuffle Tracks to shuffle all tracks within that album or genre.

(6) Tap a track to play that individual track. Playback controls display at the bottom of the screen, along with the current track's name.

(7) Tap the Pause button to pause playback, which then changes to a Play button. Tap the Play button to resume playback.

(8) Tap the Next button to play the next track.

(9) Tap the Previous button to play the previous track.

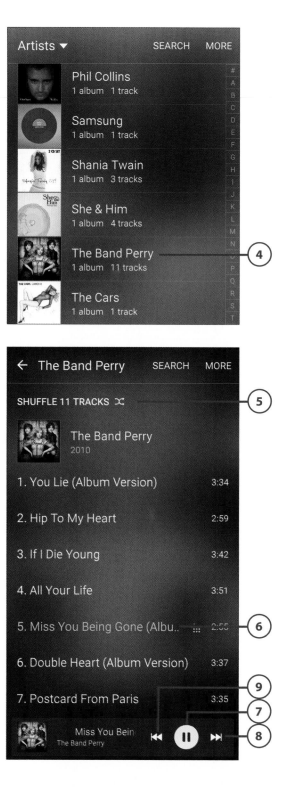

10 Create a playlist of your favorite tracks by tapping the down arrow at the top left and then tapping Playlists.

11 Tap to open and play any existing playlist.

12 Tap Create Playlist to open the Create Playlist panel.

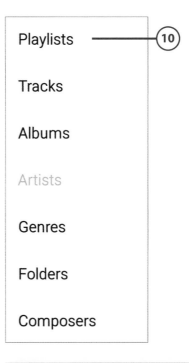

Playlists

Tracks

Albums

Artists

Genres

Folders

Composers

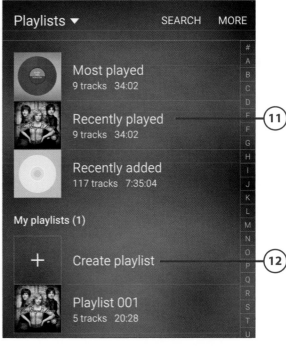

Playlists ▼   SEARCH   MORE

Most played
9 tracks   34:02

Recently played
9 tracks   34:02

Recently added
117 tracks   7:35:04

My playlists (1)

+   Create playlist

Playlist 001
5 tracks   20:28

13 Enter a name for this playlist.

14 Tap Create. You see a listing of all the tracks stored on your phone.

15 Tap to select those tracks you want in this playlist.

16 Tap Done.

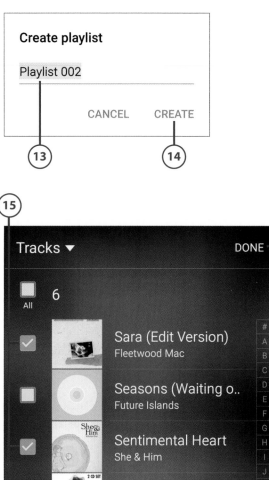

17 Tap Shuffle Tracks to play this new playlist.

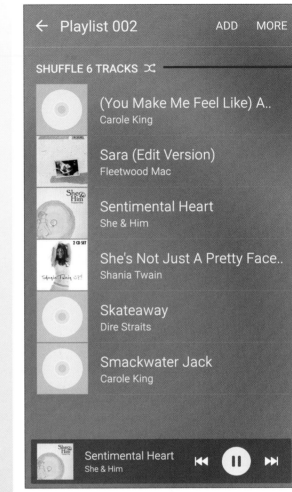

Play Music with the Google Play Music App

Another good—and free!—music player is Google Play Music. We've already used this app to download music from the Google Play Store; you can also use this app to play the music you purchase, as well as any other music stored on your phone.

1 From the Home or Apps screen, tap the Play Music icon to open the app.

2 Tap the Options button at the top-left corner to display the menu of options.

(3) Tap My Library to view the music stored on your phone.

(4) Tap the Genres tab to view your music by genre.

(5) Tap the Artists tab to view your music by artist.

(6) Tap the Albums tab to view your music by album.

(7) Tap the Songs tab to view your music by individual song.

(8) From within a given tab, tap the genre, artist, or album you want to listen to.

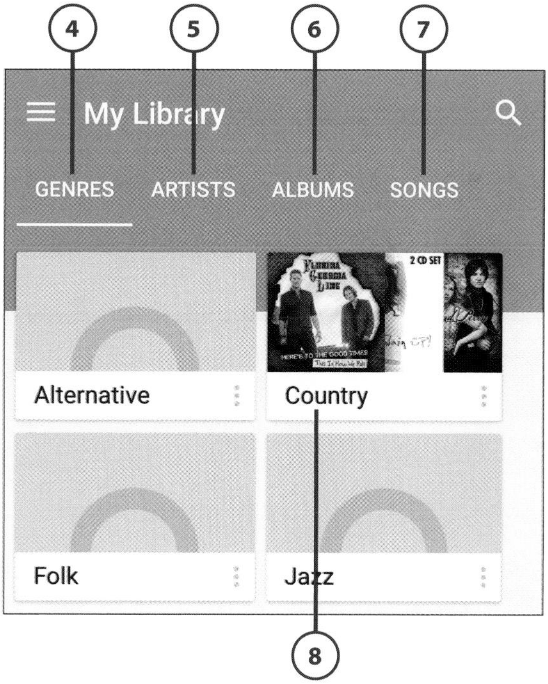

🎧 Listen Now

🎵 **My Library** ———————————— (3)

☰ **Playlists**

((•)) **Instant Mixes**

🛍 **Shop**

(4)   (5)   (6)   (7)

☰ **My Library**   🔍

GENRES   ARTISTS   ALBUMS   SONGS

Alternative ⋮   Country ⋮

Folk ⋮   Jazz ⋮

(8)

9 From within a genre or artist screen, tap an individual album to view all the songs in that album.

10 Tap the big orange Play button to play all the songs on that album.

11 Tap an individual song to play that song.

12 Tap the Pause button to pause playback. The Pause button turns into a Play button. Tap the Play button to resume playback.

13 Swipe up from the bottom of the screen to view more playback controls.

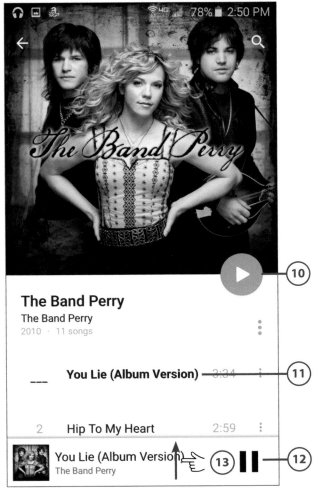

(14) Tap the Repeat button once to repeat all the songs in this album. Tap this button twice to repeat the current song.

(15) Tap the Pause button to pause playback. The Pause button turns into a Play button. Tap the Play button to resume playback.

(16) Tap the Next button to play the next song.

(17) Tap the Previous button to play the previous song.

(18) Tap the Shuffle button to shuffle the order of playback.

(19) Tap the Back key on your phone to return to the My Library screen.

(20) Create a new playlist by finding a song you want in that playlist and then tapping that song's Menu button.

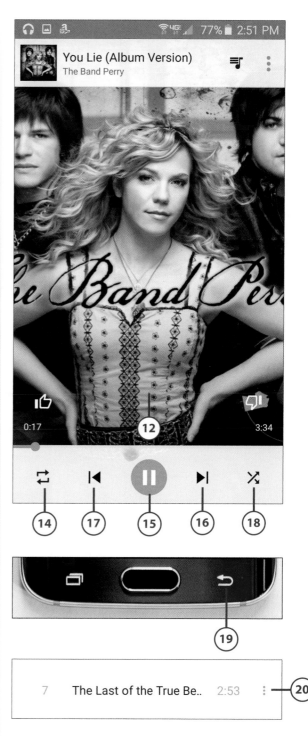

21 Tap Add to Playlist to display the Add to Playlist panel.

22 Tap the name of a playlist to add this song to an existing playlist.

23 Tap New Playlist to display the New Playlist panel and create a new playlist.

Start instant mix

Play next

Add to queue

Add to playlist ———**21**

Go to artist

Delete

Shop this artist

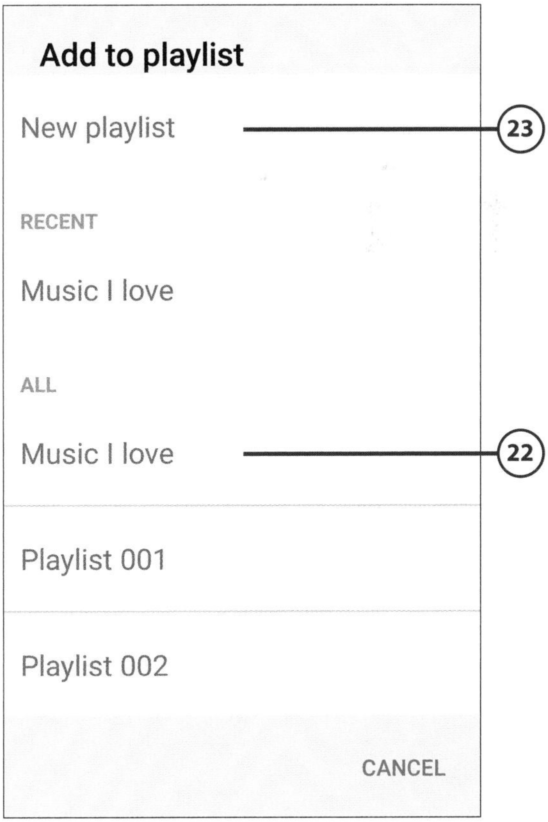

Add to playlist

New playlist ——————**23**

RECENT

Music I love

ALL

Music I love ——————**22**

Playlist 001

Playlist 002

CANCEL

(24) Enter a name for this playlist into the Name box.

(25) Enter an optional description of this playlist into the Description box.

(26) Tap Create Playlist. The song is added to the playlist. Repeat steps 21 and 22 to add other songs to this playlist.

(27) To play a playlist, return to the My Library screen, tap the Options button, and then tap Playlists.

(28) Scroll down the screen and tap the playlist you want to play.

New playlist

Name ———— **(24)**

Description ———— **(25)**

Public
Anyone can see and listen

CANCEL   CREATE PLAYLIST —— **(26)**

Listen Now

My Library

Playlists ———————— **(27)**

Instant Mixes

Shop

☰ Playlists   🔍

Recent Playlists

—— **(28)**

My Folk   ⋮   Music I love   ⋮

29 Tap the Play button to begin playback.

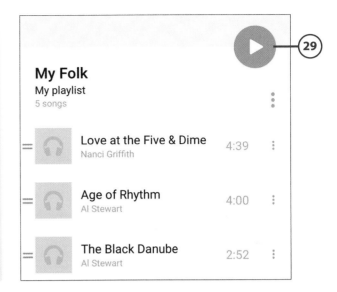

>>>Go Further
LISTENING TO SMARTPHONE MUSIC IN YOUR CAR

Many newer cars let you play music from your smartphone over the car's audio system. How this is done depends on the car.

Some cars let you connect your phone via USB. To do this, connect your phone's charger cable to the USB connector in your car and then switch your audio system to the auxiliary input. You might be able to control your phone's playback via your car's audio system, or you might have to start playback on your phone.

Other cars let you connect your phone via Bluetooth to the car's audio system. Follow your car's instructions to make the connection; you then should be able to use your car's audio system to control playback.

SAMSUNG
70% 4:13 PM
Chopped Collection
2012 TV-G 1 Season
It's all about skill, speed, and ingenuity in this cooking-competition show where up-and-coming chefs turn everyday items into an extraordinary meal.
Starring: Ted Allen
Creators: Food Network, Michael Krupat
RECOMMEND
+ MY LIST
Season 2
1. Viewers' Choice Baskets
Fans on Pinterest, Facebook and Twitter suggest the ingredients for this Viewers' Choice competition, resulting in possibly the cruelest baskets ever.

In this chapter, you learn how you can watch movies, TV shows, and other videos on your Samsung S6 or S6 Edge. Topics include the following:

→ Watching TV Shows and Movies on Netflix
→ Watching TV Shows on Hulu
→ Watching Videos on YouTube

Watching TV Shows, Movies, and Other Videos

Watching TV in your living room is fine, but what if you want to entertain yourself when you're not in your living room? You can use your Samsung smartphone to watch a variety of TV shows and movies over the Internet, whatever room you're in—and even when you're in your car or away from home. It's all a matter of picking the right app and subscribing to the best video streaming service—Netflix, Hulu, or something different.

Watching TV Shows and Movies on Netflix

For a low $8.99/month subscription, you can watch all the movies and TV shows you want on Netflix—and there's a lot available. Netflix offers a mix of both classic and newer movies, as well as a surprising number of classic and newer television programs. There's something there to please just about everyone.

To watch Netflix, you need to download and install the Netflix app on your smartphone, which you can do (for free) from the Google Play

Store. You also need a Netflix subscription; you can sign up from either the Netflix app or website (www.netflix.com).

First Time Use

The first time you open the Netflix app, you're prompted to either create a new Netflix account or log into an existing one. Each subsequent time you open the app, it automatically logs in to this account and displays the appropriate content tailored exclusively to your viewing habits.

Watch a Movie or TV Show on Netflix

Netflix offers a variety of new and older movies for your viewing pleasure, as well as all manner of current and classic television programming. The selection varies from month to month, so keep looking for what's new!

1. From your phone's Home or Apps screen, tap the Netflix icon to open the app.

2. The first thing you see in the Netflix app is any videos you haven't yet finished watching (Continue Watching). Scroll down to view other sections—My List, Popular on Netflix, Trending Now, Top Picks, and so forth.

3. Swipe left or right through any section to view more programming of that type.

4. Tap the Options button to view the different genres.

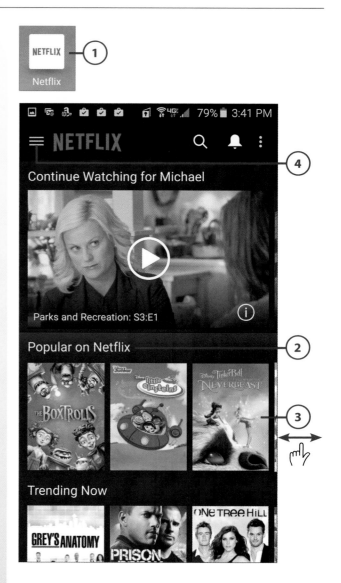

5 Tap the type of programming you want to watch—TV, Action, Comedies, and so forth.

6 Search for a specific movie or show by tapping the Search (magnifying glass) icon to display the search panel.

7 Use the onscreen keyboard to type the name of the movie or show into the Search box.

8 As you type, Netflix displays matching suggestions. Tap one of these suggestions, or finish entering your search.

(9) If you choose to watch a TV show, you typically can choose from different episodes in different seasons. Tap the Season down arrow to select a season; you see all the episodes from that season.

(10) Tap an episode to begin watching it.

(11) If you choose to watch a movie, tap the Play button at the top of the screen.

Playback Controls

When watching a video on Netflix, tap the screen to display the playback controls, which you can use to pause and otherwise control video playback.

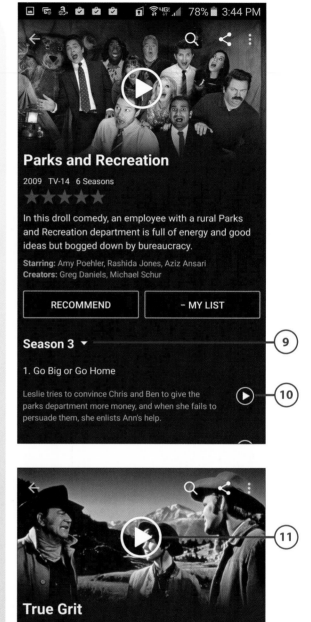

It's Not All Good

Too Much Data

Watching streaming video on Netflix, Hulu, and similar sites requires a lot of bandwidth; movie and TV shows contain a lot of data. So, you probably don't want to watch these apps when you're on a cellular connection, as it will quickly max out your data plan.

Instead, wait until you're connected to a solid Wi-Fi network or hotspot. Watching video over Wi-Fi won't affect your data plan at all.

Watching TV Shows on Hulu

If you want to watch current episodes of network TV shows, then Hulu is the app for you. Although Hulu does offer some movies and older TV programs, its real forte is newer programming.

The web version of Hulu, which you can watch on your computer, is free but limited. To watch Hulu on your smartphone, you need to subscribe to Hulu Plus. Whereas the Hulu app is free (and downloadable from the Google Plus Store), the Hulu Plus subscription runs you $7.99/month. You can sign up either from the Hulu app or website (www.hulu.com).

First Time Use

The first time you open the Hulu app, you're prompted to either create a new account or log into an existing one. Each subsequent time you open the app, it automatically logs in to this account.

(1) From your phone's Home or Apps screen, tap the Hulu icon to open the app.

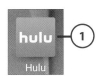

(2) The Hulu app's home screen displays a variety of recommended programming. Scroll down to view more.

(3) Swipe right or left in any section to view more options.

(4) Tap the Options button on the top left to browse for programs.

(5) Tap the type of programming you want to watch.

(6) Search for a specific program by tapping the Search icon to display the search panel.

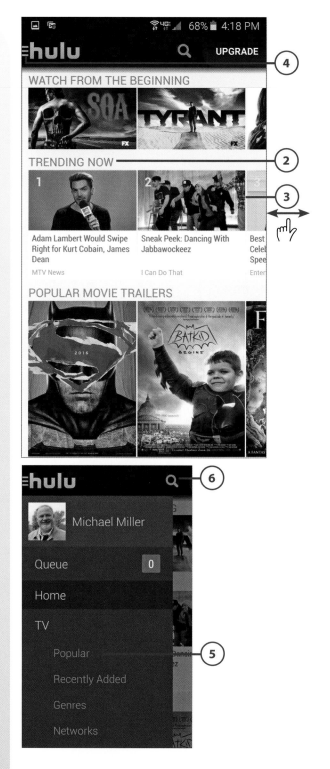

7 Enter the name of what you want to watch. As you type, Hulu displays suggested programs.

8 Tap a program to view its screen.

9 Tap an episode to view more details.

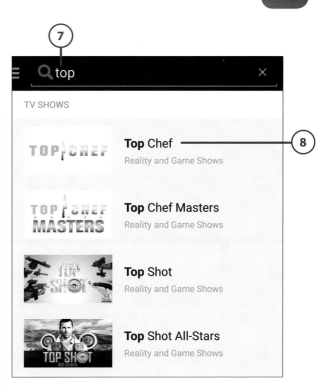

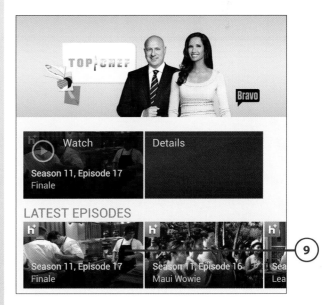

10 Tap Play Video to begin watching this program.

Playback Controls

When watching a video on Hulu, tap the screen to display the playback controls, which you can use to pause and otherwise control video playback.

Watching Videos on YouTube

Then there's YouTube. If you haven't checked out YouTube yet, you're missing a lot. YouTube is a website (and accompanying app) that lets people upload their own videos, then shares those videos with other users. (It also has a lot of commercial videos available, including a ton of music videos both new and classic.)

YouTube is the place to find the latest "viral" videos—those videos that get super-popular when people share them with all their friends. Cat videos, baby videos, blooper videos, you name it, it's on YouTube.

How-To Videos

YouTube is also a great place to find advice and instruction. Whether you need to replace a garbage disposal or improve your golf swing, YouTube has instructional videos online to help you!

Watch YouTube

You watch YouTube videos from the YouTube app. You might have this app already installed on your Galaxy S6 or S6 Edge; if not, you can download it (for free!) from the Google Play Store.

First Time Use

The first time you open the YouTube app, you might be prompted to sign in with your Google Account; if so, do so. (It's also possible that the app will automatically pick up your Google credentials from elsewhere on your phone.) After this, the app should automatically sign into your account whenever you launch it.

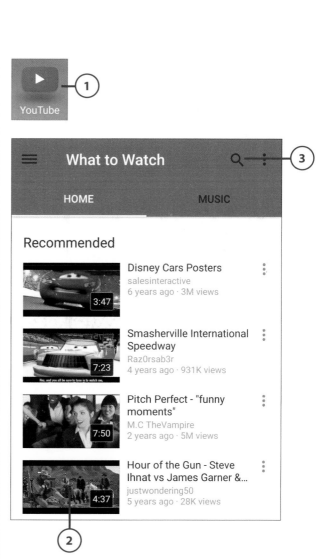

1. From your phone's Home or Apps screen, tap the YouTube icon to open the app.

2. The YouTube app's home screen displays a variety of recommended programming. Scroll down to view more.

3. Search for a video by tapping the Search button at the top of the screen; this opens a new Search YouTube panel.

(4) Enter the name of what you want to search for. As you type, YouTube displays suggested searches.

(5) Tap an item to view videos of that type.

(6) Tap the video you want to watch.

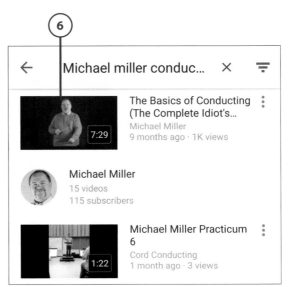

7 Playback begins in a small window at the top of the screen. To view the video full-screen, turn your phone sideways.

8 Tap the screen to view playback controls.

9 Tap the large Pause icon in the middle of the screen to pause playback. The icon now changes to a Play icon; tap this to resume playback.

10 Tap and drag the scrub (slider) control to move directly to another part of the video.

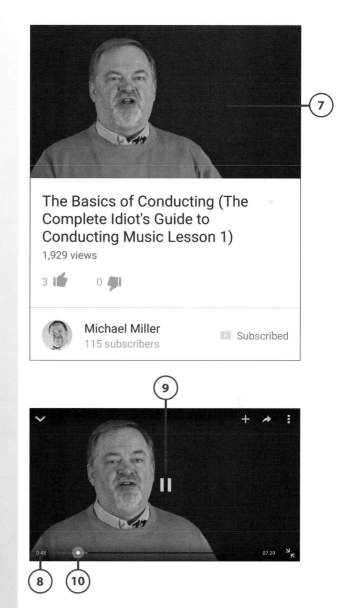

In this chapter, you get started with using social media apps on your smartphone. Topics include the following:

→ Using Facebook
→ Using Pinterest

20

Using Facebook, Pinterest, and Other Social Media

A social network is an online community that enables users to connect with and share their thoughts and activities with one another. Think of it as an online network of friends and family, including former schoolmates, co-workers, neighbors, and other people who share your interests

The big social media networks—Facebook, Pinterest, Twitter, and LinkedIn—all have mobile apps that run on your Samsung Galaxy S6 or S6 Edge. Connecting to one of these social networks is as easy as installing the app (they're all free and available in the Google Play Store), creating or signing into your account, and then starting to post. You can stay connected wherever you happen to be!

Twitter, LinkedIn, and Instagram

For bonus tasks covering these three apps, see the online task "Other Social Networks" on the book's website: www.informit.com/title/9870789755445.

Using Facebook

The largest and most popular social network today is Facebook, with more than 1 billion active users worldwide. Although Facebook started life as a social network for college students, it has since expanded its membership to people of all ages. In fact, the fastest growing segment of Facebook users are those aged 45 and older.

People use Facebook to connect with current family members and reconnect with friends from the past. If you want to know what your friends from high school or the old neighborhood have been up to over the past several decades, chances are you can find them on Facebook.

In addition, Facebook helps you keep your friends informed about what you're doing. Write one post and it's seen by hundreds of your online "friends." It's the easiest way I know to connect with almost everyone you know.

Like all the social networks discussed in this chapter, Facebook is completely free to use. You access Facebook from its mobile app.

Navigate the Facebook App

You can download the Facebook app, for free, from the Google Play Store. The first time you launch the app, you're prompted to either sign into an existing account (if you have one) or create a new account. Follow the onscreen instructions to proceed from there.

1 From your phone's Home or Apps screen, tap the Facebook icon to launch the Facebook app. You now see Facebook's News Feed screen.

Facebook

(**2**) The News Feed is where you read posts made by your Facebook friends, newest first. Scroll down the screen to view older posts.

(**3**) Refresh the News Feed by pulling down from the top of the screen and then releasing.

(**4**) Tap the News Feed icon to return to the News Feed at any time.

(**5**) When a person you know sees you on Facebook, she might send you a friend request. You have to be friends with someone on Facebook to see their posts in the News Feed. To view your friend requests, tap the Friend Requests icon or swipe to the left from the News Feed screen.

(**6**) Tap the Notifications icon or swipe from the left from the previous screen to view notifications from Facebook.

(**7**) Tap the Menu icon to view your favorite pages and groups.

Pages and Groups

In addition to posts from individuals, Facebook also offers official "pages" from companies and celebrities, as well as topic-specific groups. You can "like" a public page to receive posts from that page, or join a group to post and receive messages from other members of that group.

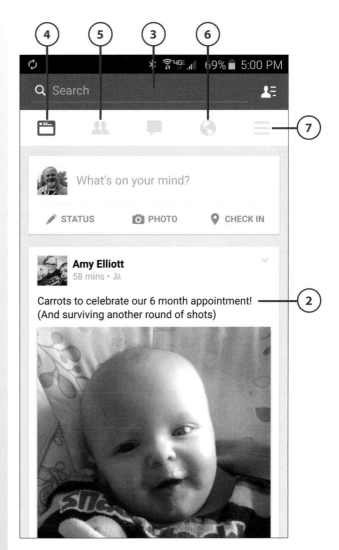

Read and Respond to Posts

The messages people post to Facebook are called status updates or just posts. You read and respond to posts from your friends on the News Feed screen.

(1) From the News Feed screen, tap the Like icon to like a post.

(2) Tap the Comment icon to comment on a post.

(3) Tap the Share icon to share a post.

(4) Tap the poster's name to view that person's Timeline page. (The Timeline page serves as a person's home base, displaying his personal profile, posts he's made, and photos he's uploaded.)

(5) If the post includes a photo, tap the photo to view it full screen.

(6) If the post includes a video, tap the video thumbnail to begin playback on a new screen.

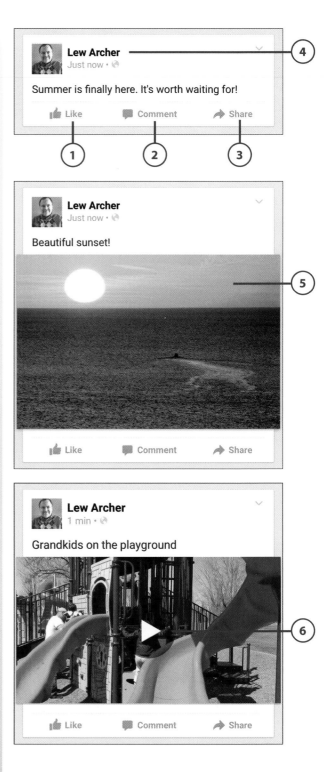

7 If the post includes a link to another web page, tap the link or thumbnail to view that page on a new screen.

Lew Archer
Just now •

I like this guy's page. www.millerwriter.com

Home - Michael Miller
Michael Miller is a successful writer and...
millerwriter.com

👍 Like   💬 Comment

Post a Status Update

You create new status updates from the app's News Feed screen. The status updates you post are displayed on your friends' News Feeds.

1 In the What's On Your Mind? box, tap the Status icon to display the Write Post screen.

2 Type the text of your message into the What's on Your Mind? area.

3 Tap the Camera icon to include a photo or video with your post.

4 Tap the Tag Friends icon to tag another person in your post.

5 Tap the What Are You Doing? icon to tell others what you're doing.

6 Tap the Add Location icon to include your location in the post.

7 Change who can see the post by tapping the Privacy icon in the To: section.

8 Tap Post to post the status update.

More About Facebook

Learn more about Facebook in my companion book, *My Facebook for Seniors*, available online and in bookstores everywhere.

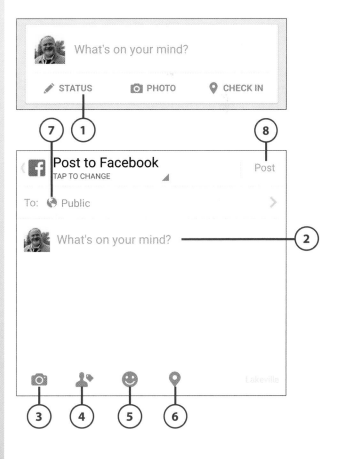

What's on your mind?

✏️ STATUS   📷 PHOTO   📍 CHECK IN

Post to Facebook
TAP TO CHANGE

To: 🌐 Public

What's on your mind?

Lakeville

Using Pinterest

Facebook isn't the only social network that may interest you. Pinterest is a newer social network with particular appeal to middle-aged and older women—although there are a growing number of male users, too.

Unlike Facebook, which lets you post text-based status updates, Pinterest is all about images. The site consists of a collection of virtual online boards that people use to share pictures they find interesting. Users "pin" photos and other images to their personal message boards, and then they share their pins with online friends.

You can pin images of anything—clothing, furniture, recipes, do-it-yourself projects, and the like. Your Pinterest friends can then "repin" your images to their boards—and on and on.

Like Facebook, Pinterest is totally free to use. You access Pinterest from the Pinterest app.

View and Repin Pins

You can download the Pinterest app, for free, from the Google Play Store. The first time you launch the app, you're prompted to either sign into an existing account (if you have one) or create a new account. Follow the onscreen instructions to proceed from there.

1. From your phone's Home or Apps screen, tap the Pinterest icon to launch the Pinterest app. You see a variety of pins.

2. The pins in your feed include items you've personally pinned, items pinned by people you follow, and recommended pins from Pinterest. Tap a pin to view it full-screen.

3. Tap the Pin It button to repin this item to one of your boards.

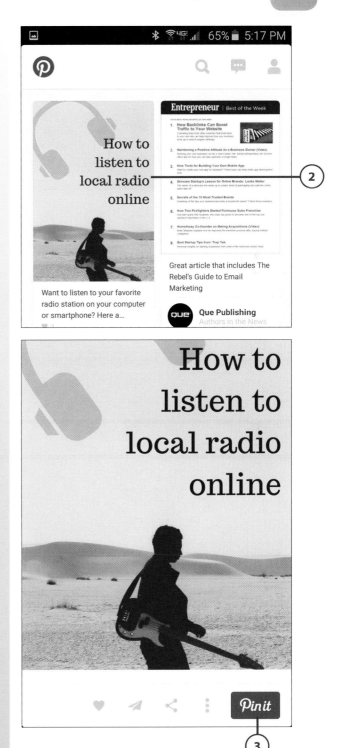

4 Accept or edit the current description of the item.

5 Scroll down and select which board you want to pin this to. The item is pinned to that board.

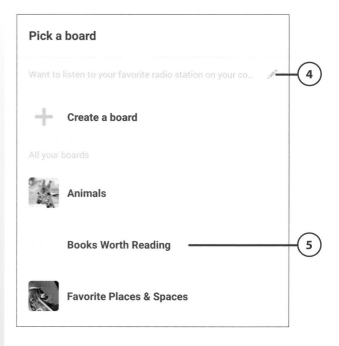

Pin from a Website

Many Pinterest users find images outside of Pinterest to pin to their boards. When you see an image on a website, you can easily pin it to a Pinterest board.

1 From the Chrome web browser, navigate to the web page that contains the image you want to pin.

2 Tap the Menu button in the browser.

3 Tap Share to display the Share Via panel.

4 Tap Add a Pin. You see thumb-nails of all the images on that web page.

5 Tap the thumbnail you want to pin.

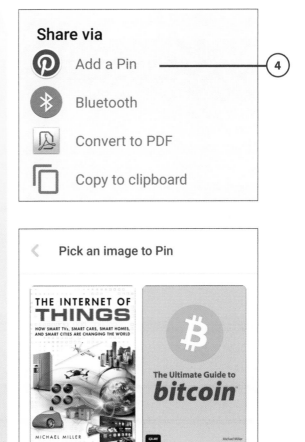

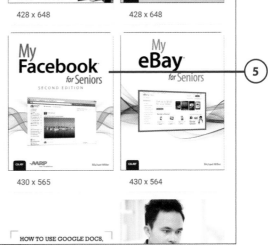

6. Enter a description for this pin.

7. Tap the boards button and select the board you want to pin to.

8. Tap the Pin It button. The selected image is pinned to that board on Pinterest.

More About Pinterest

Learn more about Pinterest in my companion book, *My Pinterest*, available online and in bookstores everywhere.

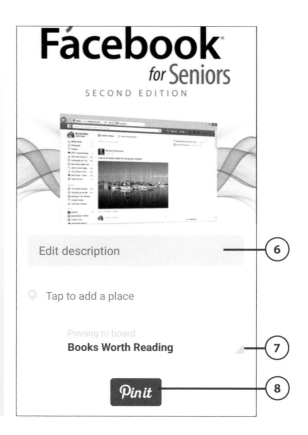

>>>*Go Further*

PRIVACY ON SOCIAL NETWORKS

It's important, when using any other social network, to be aware of your privacy. It's easy to think of Facebook or Pinterest as a personal diary, but they're not. These social networks are extremely public; when you post a message or photo, it could be viewed by millions of people you don't even know.

If you value your privacy, you want to configure your settings on each network so that what you post is seen only by select people. Ideally, you want only your friends to see what you post; that means changing the posting privacy options from public to another more private setting. In addition, some networks (such as Facebook) let you adjust your privacy on a post-by-post basis. This way you could post something that you want your family members to see but don't want to show to co-workers or other friends.

How you adjust a network's privacy settings differs from network to network. In the Facebook app, for example, tap the Menu button at the top-right corner and then scroll down the next screen and tap Privacy Shortcuts; everything you need to configure, privacy-wise, is listed there.

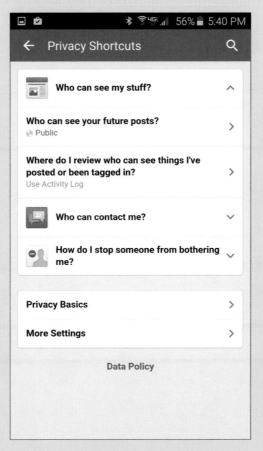

Of course, the best way to keep some things private on a social network is to not post them at all. You're old enough to know when to be discreet; resist the urge to post private information, private thoughts, and photos that ought to stay private. If you don't post 'em, nobody'll see 'em.

Finally, never, ever post your private contact information on a social network—or anywhere, online, for that matter. If you don't want strangers calling you up or showing up at your door, don't share your phone number or street address with them. In addition, never post about going out of town (or even out on the town); it's not unheard of for burglars to troll the social networks so they'll know when a house is empty and ripe for the looting.

Bottom line: Be careful out there!

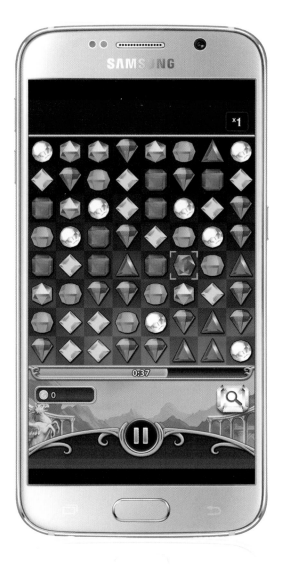

In this chapter, you are introduced to some of the many mobile games you can play on your new Samsung smartphone. Topics include the following:

→ Downloading Games from the Google Play Store

Playing Games

Let's face it. When you have some free time on your hands, you like to play games. Word games, puzzle games, card games, you name it. Games are fun to play and help you pass the time.

As you may have already discovered, your new Galaxy S6 or S6 Edge smartphone is actually a pretty neat little game system. Because you always have your phone with you, it's easy to pull it out, fire up your favorite game, and spend a few minutes (or more) playing solitaire or Words with Friends or whatever your favorite game is. There are tons of games you can download and play on your phone, so there's something for everybody.

Downloading Games from the Google Play Store

As you know, your Samsung smartphone runs Google's Android operating system, so most Android games should play on your device. (You can't run iOS games, however—they're for Apple's iPhones.) You can find a wide selection of Android games in the Google Play Store—many for free!

Download a Game

Finding and downloading games is pretty much the same process as downloading apps from the Google Play Store. Browse or search for the game you want and then tap to download and install on your phone.

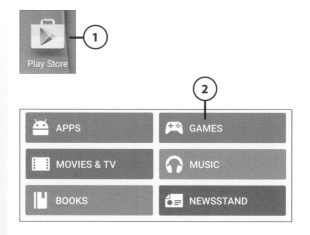

(**1**) From your phone's Home screen, tap the Play Store icon to open the Google Play Store.

(**2**) Tap Games to display available games.

(**3**) Tap in the Search box and enter the name or type of game you're looking for.

(**4**) Browse for games by category by tapping the Categories tab.

(**5**) Tap the category you're interested in to display games of that type.

Game Recommendations

For a list of games you might enjoy, see the bonus online task "Discover Games" on the book's website: www.informit.com/title/9870789755445.

6 Tap a tab at the top of the screen to narrow your results—Top Paid, Top Free, Top Grossing, Top New Paid, Top New Free, or Trending.

7 Tap the game you're interested in.

8 Tap the Install button to download a free game.

9 Tap Accept in the permissions panel. The game is downloaded to and installed on your phone.

10 Tap the price button to purchase a paid game.

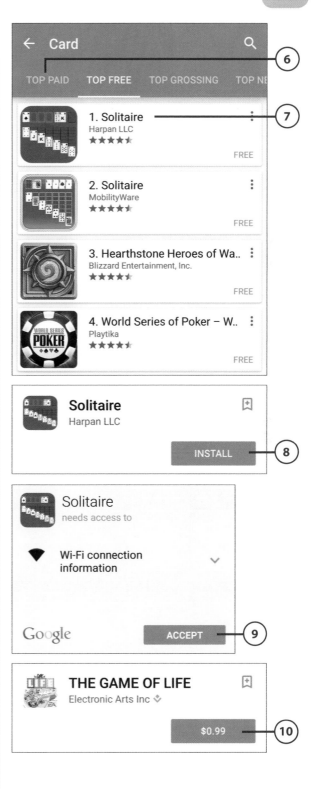

11) Tap Accept in the permissions panel. The purchase panel opens.

12) Tap the payment area to enlarge the panel and then tap Payment Methods.

13) From the Payment Methods panel, select how you want to pay.

14) If you have not yet set up a payment method, tap either Add Credit or Debit Card or Add PayPal; then follow the onscreen instructions to add your payment information.

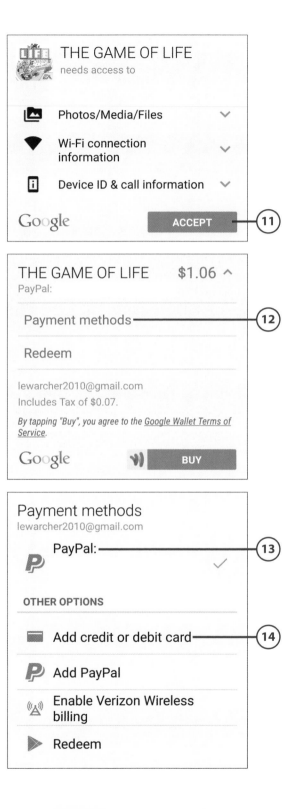

15 Tap the Buy button to complete the transaction and download the app.

THE GAME OF LIFE $1.06 ⌄

PayPal:

By tapping "Buy", you agree to the Google Wallet Terms of Service.

Google   ⠺)   **BUY** ── **15**

It's Not All Good

In-Game Purchases

Given the huge number of free games in the Google Play Store, how do these companies make any money? There are actually two ways.

First, many game companies sell ads within their games. These ads take up valuable screen space, but the hope is that people will be interested enough to tap through and actually buy something. Because in-game ads are so annoying, many companies sell ad-free versions of their games in addition to the free ad-supported versions. You might find it worthwhile to pay a few bucks to get rid of the ads in your favorite games.

Other game companies make money by trying to sell you things within the game. That is, they encourage (or even require) in-app purchases for things like extra in-game currency, more lives, and even access to higher levels. In some games, you can't proceed past a certain point without making an in-app purchase. I hate games that require this sort of pay-to-play, especially when my eight year-old grandson runs into a brick wall that only grandpa's money can fix.

These in-app purchases can also be a little deceiving, especially if you're new to the game. You might think you're just getting more information or moving on naturally, but then later find you've been billed $5 or $10 or more for an in-app purchase. For this reason, be very careful what you tap when you're playing your mobile games—you don't want to spend more money than you want to!

In this chapter, you find out how to use your smartphone for word processing, spreadsheets, and presentations. Topics include the following:

→ Using Google Docs Apps

22

Doing Office Work on Your Phone

The previous chapter covers how to play games on your new smartphone. Life isn't all fun and games, however; when you need to do some real productivity work, you can use your phone for that, too.

Using Google Docs Apps

Several full-featured productivity apps are available for your Galaxy S6 or S6 Edge smartphone. Google offers its Google Docs apps, and Microsoft offers Android versions of its Office apps.

Now, trying to do full-fledged number crunching or desktop publishing on your phone is going to be a little frustrating. The screen is only so big, and doing heavy-duty typing with the onscreen keyboard isn't the most comfortable thing around. Still, if you want to dash off a quick letter, do some simple budget work, or even give a presentation you previously created on your PC, it's easy enough to do on your smartphone screen.

We'll start by examining Google Docs. There are three of them:

- Google Docs word processor
- Google Sheets spreadsheets
- Google Slides presentations

Google Docs: Suite and App

Google Docs is the name of the entire office suite (Docs, Sheets, and Slides) and the word processing app. Yes, it's confusing. Complain to Google.

These apps are all cloud-based applications, which means you don't store the documents on your phone or computer. Instead, all the files you work on are stored online, in what techies call the *cloud*. You use your phone (or your computer) to access and work on your documents. The work you do is then saved online, for access again another day.

All of the Google Docs apps are available free from the Google Play Store. (They may even be preinstalled by your carrier on some phones.) The apps are all free, and work great together—and with Google's other Android apps.

Google Drive

All the files created with Google Docs, Sheets, and Slides are stored in Google Drive, Google's cloud-based storage service. Learn more about Google Drive in Chapter 23, "Copying Files To and From Your Phone—And Backing Up Your Important Data."

Work with Google Docs Documents

You can use the mobile version of Google Docs to view, edit, and create word processing documents. Docs automatically saves files online (in Google Drive) in its own proprietary file format; it can also read and write Microsoft Word's .doc and .docx file formats.

1. From your phone's Home or Apps screen, tap the Docs icon to open the Google Docs app.

2. The Docs home screen displays documents you've previously created or edited. Tap to open an existing document *or…*

3. Create a new document by tapping the blue + icon at the bottom right.

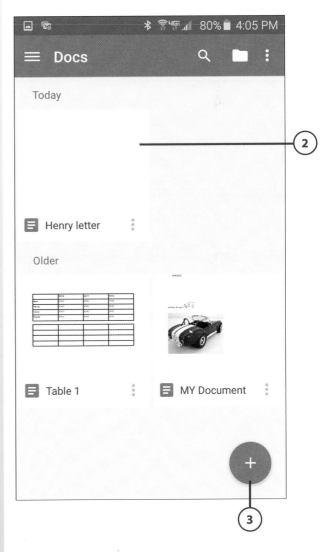

4 Use the onscreen keyboard to enter text at the cursor.

5 Format the text you enter by tapping the Format button at the top of the screen.

6 Format text attributes, such as font, size, bold, italic, and so forth, by tapping the Text tab and making a selection.

7 Format paragraph attributes, such as alignment, line spacing, and so forth, by tapping the Paragraph tab and making a selection.

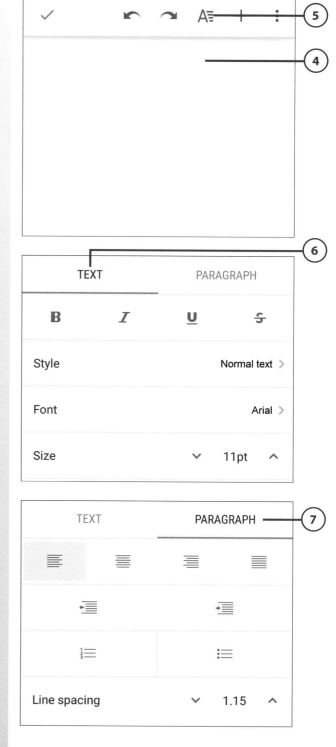

8 Insert an image, table, web link, or comments by tapping the + icon at the top of the screen and then making a selection.

9 Name or rename this document by tapping the Menu button at the top right.

10 Tap Details to display more information about this document.

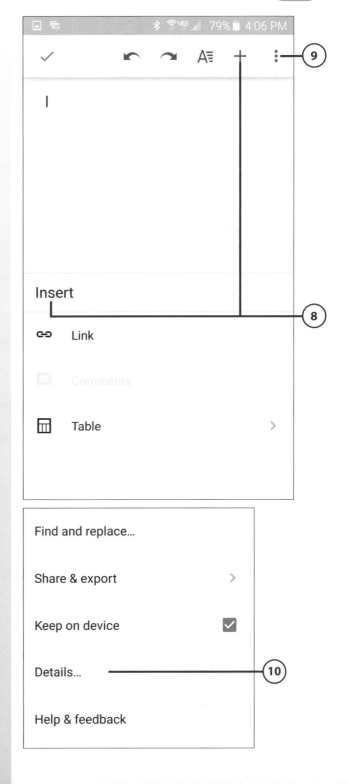

(11) Tap Rename to display the Rename Document panel.

(12) Type a new name for this document.

(13) Tap OK.

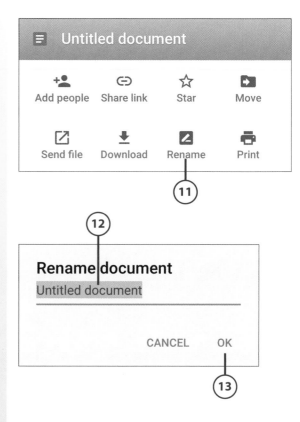

Work with Google Sheets Spreadsheets

Working with Google Sheets is much like working with Google Docs, except a lot more numbers are involved. Google Sheets is similar to Microsoft Excel in that you can use formulas and functions to create complex numerical comparisons.

(1) From your phone's Home or Apps screen, tap the Sheets icon to open the Google Sheets app.

2. The Sheets home screen displays spreadsheets you've previously created or edited. Tap to open an existing spreadsheet *or…*

3. Create a new spreadsheet by tapping the green + icon at the bottom right.

4. Within the spreadsheet, tap to select a cell into which you want to enter data.

5. Tap the Function box at the bottom of the screen to display the onscreen keyboard and then enter the numbers, words, or formula you want.

6. Insert a function by tapping the Function (fx) button to display a list of functions by category; tap to select the function.

7. Tap the check mark to enter this data into the selected cell.

(**8**) Name or rename this spreadsheet by tapping the Menu button at the top right.

(**9**) Tap Details to display more information about this spreadsheet.

(**10**) Tap Rename to display the Rename Spreadsheet panel.

(**11**) Type a new name for this spreadsheet.

(**12**) Tap OK.

Find and replace...

Share & export   >

Keep on device   ☑

Details...   ──── (**9**)

➕ **Untitled spreadsheet**

+👤 Add people	🔗 Share link	☆ Star	➡ Move
↗ Send file	⬇ Download	✎ Rename	🖨 Print

(**11**)   (**10**)

Rename document

Untitled document
_____

CANCEL   OK

(**12**)

It's Not All Good

Limited Functionality

All of the Google Docs mobile apps are limited in functionality when compared to their computer versions. For example, Docs lacks sophisticated document formatting. Sheets lacks the ability to display or work on charts. And Slides doesn't offer transition and animation effects. Use these mobile apps on your phone to do quick and necessary work; when you need the full functionality, use the full-featured apps available on your desktop or notebook computer.

Work with Google Slides Presentations

Google Slides is Google's version of Microsoft PowerPoint. The mobile version of Slides isn't that great for creating presentations (it's too limited in functionality), but it is fine for doing some last-minute edits and then giving live presentations—from your smartphone. (You need to connect your smartphone to a larger screen or projector, of course.)

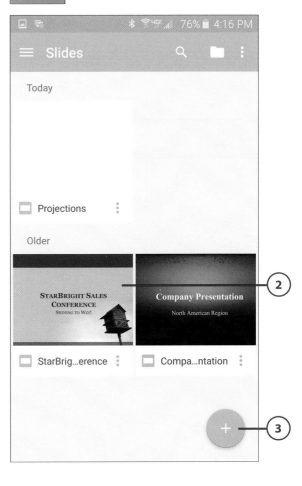

(1) From your phone's Home or Apps screen, tap the Slides icon to open the Google Slides app.

(2) The Slides home screen displays presentations you've previously created or edited. Tap to open an existing presentation *or...*

(3) Create a new presentation by tapping the yellow + icon at the bottom right.

4 The slides in your presentation are displayed at the bottom of the screen. Tap to select a specific slide.

5 Tap the New Slide button on the lower right to add a new slide to the presentation.

6 Tap the type of slide you want to add.

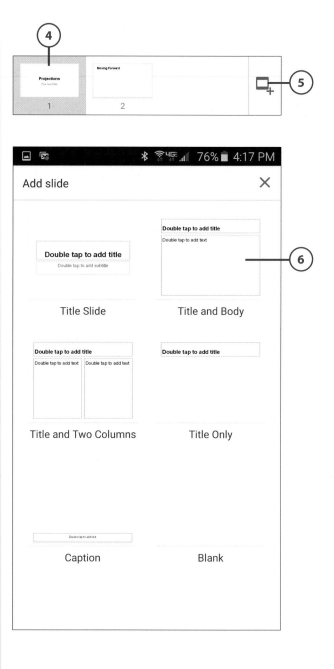

7 Double-tap a text placeholder on the slide to display the onscreen keyboard and enter or edit text.

8 Name or rename this presentation by tapping the Menu button at the top right.

9 Tap Details to display more information about this presentation.

10 Tap Rename to display the Rename Presentation panel.

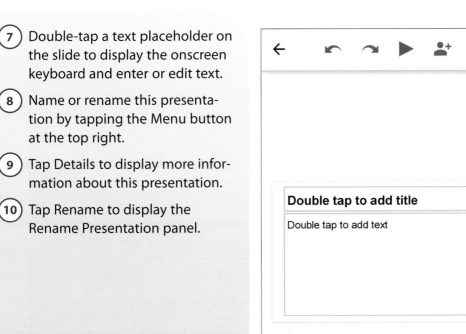

Double tap to add title

Double tap to add text

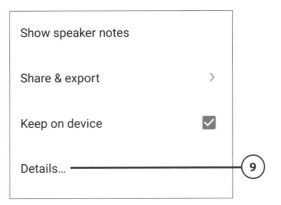

Show speaker notes

Share & export   >

Keep on device   ☑

Details...

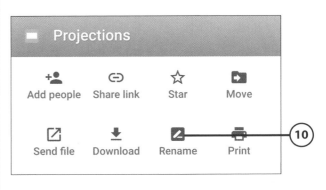

■ Projections

| Add people | Share link | Star | Move |

| Send file | Download | Rename | Print |

11 Type a new name for this presentation.

12 Tap OK.

13 Tap the Play button at the top of the screen to begin the presentation—after connecting your phone to a larger display or projector, of course.

14 The presentation now appears full screen. Tap the screen or swipe from right to left to advance to the next slide.

15 Swipe the screen from left to right to return to a previous slide.

16 Tap the Back key on your phone to end the presentation.

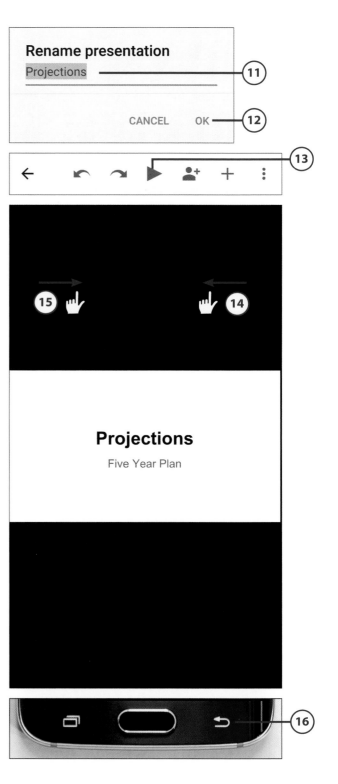

>>>*Go Further*

USING THE MICROSOFT OFFICE MOBILE APP

Many people like to use Google Docs for their productivity work. Others are more wedded to the tried-and-true Microsoft Office, which is used in a vast number of companies and organizations.

Microsoft has recently released mobile versions of its Office apps—Word, Excel, and PowerPoint—for Android phones and tablets. You can find these apps in the Google Play Store. Like the Google Docs apps, the Microsoft Office Mobile apps are free.

Also like Google Docs, Microsoft Office Mobile apps store all their files in the cloud—in this instance, in Microsoft's OneDrive. (OneDrive is very much like Google Drive, but from Microsoft.) You can use the Office Mobile apps to work on the same Office files you use at work or home.

Bonus Tasks

For access to additional tasks on using the Microsoft Word, Excel, and PowerPoint mobile apps, see the online task "Office Mobile App" on the book's website: www.informit.com/title/9870789755445.

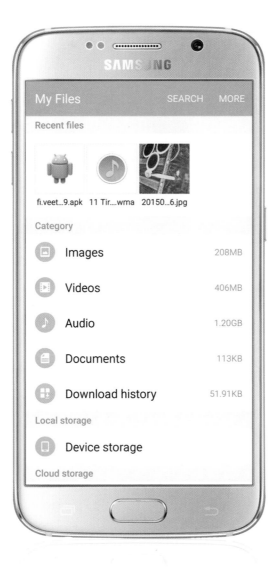

In this chapter, you learn about the files stored on your phone and how to manage them. Topics include the following:

→ Using the My Files App
→ Storing Files on Google Drive
→ Transferring Files Between Devices
→ Backing Up Your Data

Copying Files To and From Your Phone—And Backing Up Your Important Data

Your Samsung Galaxy S6 or S6 Edge is like a miniature computer that fits in the palm of your hand. Yes, it makes phone calls, but it also does just about everything a notebook or desktop computer does—including store important data in a collection of digital files.

All sorts of files are stored on your smartphone. Picture files, music files, video files, contact files, maybe even word processing and spreadsheet files. Plus all the system files necessary for your phone to run.

How, exactly, do you manage all these files? How do you copy files from your computer to your phone, and vice versa? And is there a better way to store these files than on your phone?

Read on to learn the answers to these questions—and more.

Using the My Files App

You manage your phone's files with the My Files app, which is preinstalled on all Samsung smartphones. This app lets you view and manage the files you have stored on your phone, as well as those in the cloud via Google Drive.

View and Manage Your Files

The My Files app is stored in the Samsung folder on the Apps screen. By default, it displays files by category—Images, Videos, Audio, and Documents.

1. From your phone's Home screen, tap the Apps icon to display the Apps screen.

2. Tap to open the Tools folder.

3. Tap the My Files icon to open the My Files app.

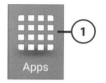

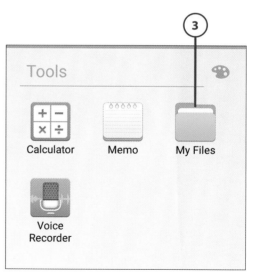

4 Tap the type of files you want to view—Images, Videos, Audio, or Documents.

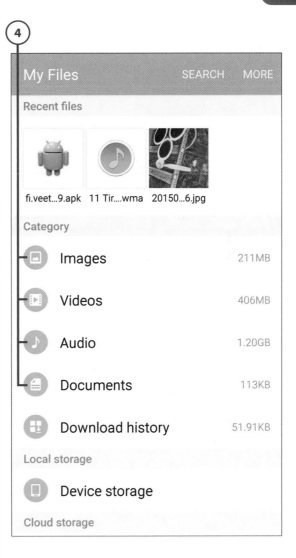

Change the File Display

By default, My Files displays the selected files in a list, with a thumbnail image for each file. You can choose to view more or fewer details about these files.

1 From within the My Files app, tap to select the type of file you want to view.

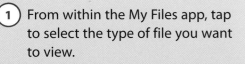

(2) Tap More.

(3) Tap View As to display the View
As pane.

(4) Tap Detailed List to view details
(size and date) of each file.

(5) Tap Grid to view only file thumb-
nails, in a grid layout.

HOME   SEARCH   MORE —(2)

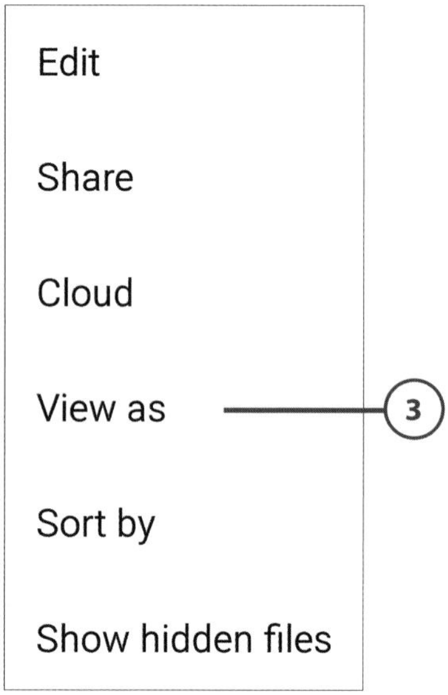

Edit

Share

Cloud

View as ———(3)

Sort by

Show hidden files

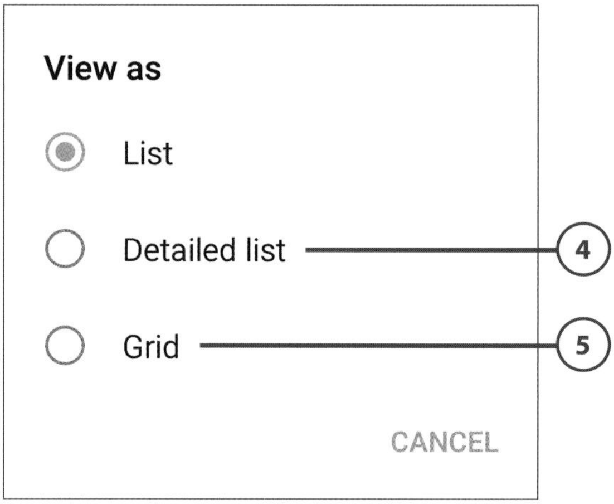

View as

◉ List

◯ Detailed list ———(4)

◯ Grid ———(5)

CANCEL

Change the Sort Order

By default, files are sorted in reverse chronological order, newest first. You can opt to sort your files by type, name, or size instead.

1. From within the My Files app, tap to select the type of file you want to view.

2. Tap More.

3. Tap Sort By to display the Sort By pane.

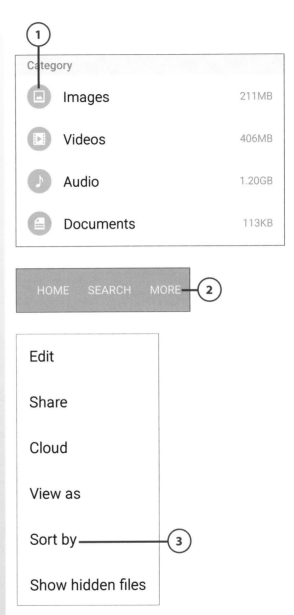

④ Select how you want the files sorted—by Time, Type, Name, or Size.

⑤ To change the sort from descending order to ascending order, tap Ascending.

⑥ Tap Done.

Sort by ──────────── ④

⦿ Time

◯ Type

◯ Name

◯ Size

Order

◯ Ascending ────────── ⑤

⦿ Descending

CANCEL   DONE ── ⑥

View Downloaded Files

The My Files app keeps separate track of files you download from the Web. Although these downloaded files are listed in their respective category (Images, Videos, Audio, or Documents), they're also listed on the Download History screen.

① From within the My Files app, tap Download History.

② You see your downloaded files, with the most recent listed first.

Category

🖼 Images   213MB

▶ Videos   406MB

♪ Audio   1.20GB

📄 Documents   113KB

⊞ Download history   51.91KB ── ①

← 　　　　　　 HOME   SEARCH   MORE

Download history

 Lael smiling.jpg ────────── ②

View Files by Location

The Images, Videos, Audio, and Documents screens simply filter files by type. In actuality, files on your phone are stored in individual *folders*. These are just like the folders on your computer, a convenient way to orga-nize your files.

1. From within the My Files app, tap Device Storage to display a list of the folders on your phone.

2. Tap a folder to see the files stored within.

Google Drive

The My Files app can also manage your files stored online in Google Drive. Read more about Google Drive later in this chapter in the "Storing Files on Google Drive" section.

Open a File

You can open image, video, audio, and document files directly from the My Files app. When you open a file, it opens in the appropriate app. (For example, when you open an image file, it opens in the Gallery app for viewing.)

1. From within the My Files app, navigate to and tap the file you want to open.

Local storage

📱 Device storage ———————(1)

←   HOME   SEARCH   MORE

Device storage

📁 Playlists

📁 Download

📁 Pictures ————————————(2)

📁 Music

📁 DCIM

📁 Albums

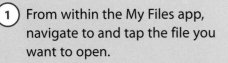

←   HOME   SEARCH   MORE

Images

Easter 08 Alethia.jpg

DVDs 103.jpg

Collin-3 half by 5.jpg ———(1)

08-June-grad-party.jpg

(2) For certain types of files, you might be prompted as to which app you want to use to open the file. Tap the desired app.

(3) Tap Always to always open this type of file with this app.

(4) Tap Just Once to open only this particular file with this app.

Add a File Shortcut to the Home Screen

If you have a file that you need to access on a frequent basis, it might be more convenient to place a shortcut icon for that file on your phone's Home screen. Then you can open the file just by tapping its icon.

(1) From within the My Files app, navigate to the file you want to create a shortcut for.

(2) Tap More.

(3) Tap Edit.

(4) Tap to select the file you want.

(5) Tap More.

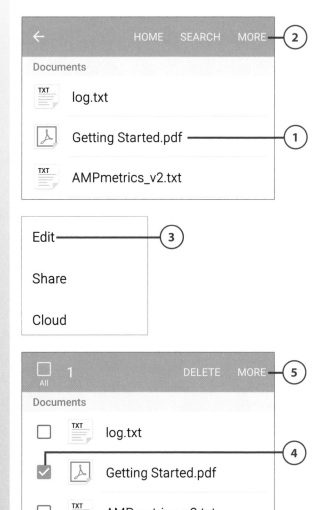

(6) Tap Add Shortcut on Home Screen. The shortcut is now created.

Move

Copy

Rename

Add shortcut on Home screen —(6)

Move to Private

Details

View Your Storage Usage

You can also use the My Files app to keep track of how much storage space you've used and have left on your phone.

(1) From within the My Files app, tap the Storage Usage button.

(2) You see the Storage Usage panel, with different types of files displayed in different colors. Tap OK when done.

STORAGE USAGE —(1)

Storage usage
Device storage: 6.89GB / 23.96GB

■ Images
■ Videos
■ Music
▨ Documents
▨ Others

OK —(2)

Delete Files

If you start to run low on storage space, you can use the My Files app to delete unused or unwanted files.

(1) From within the My Files app, navigate to the location that hosts the file(s) you want to delete.

(2) Tap More.

←   HOME   SEARCH   MORE —(2)

Audio —(1)

 09 Tumbling Dice.mp3

07 Poor, Poor Pitiful Me.mp3

05 Let It Bleed.mp3

01 Gimme Shelter.mp3

(**3**) Tap Edit.

(**4**) Tap to select the file(s) you want to delete.

(**5**) Tap Delete.

(**6**) Tap Delete in the confirmation box. The file is now deleted.

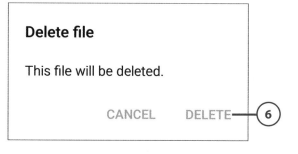

Edit ——————————— (**3**)

Share

Cloud

View as

Sort by

Show hidden files

(**4**)   (**5**)

☐ 1   DELETE   MORE
All

Audio

☑ 09 Tumbling Dice.mp3

☐ 07 Poor, Poo...tiful Me.mp3

☐ 05 Let It Bleed.mp3

Delete file

This file will be deleted.

CANCEL   DELETE —— (**6**)

Storing Files on Google Drive

Your Samsung smartphone has a lot of available storage inside; how much you have depends on the model of phone you have. Still, even with the relatively large amount of storage available, it's probably not enough to hold all the files you might use. For example, if you have a lot of videos or photos, they take up a lot of storage space. Same thing if you want your phone to host a large music collection. Over time, your phone's storage space will fill up.

The solution to this issue is to store at least some of your files somewhere else— somewhere not physically on your phone but still accessible from your phone. That somewhere is in what we call the *cloud*, which is a part of the Internet. Several cloud storage services are available, but the one that's best integrated into Samsung and other Android phones is Google Drive.

Use Google Drive from the My Files App

You can access Google Drive either from its own app or from the My Files app. It's the My Files integration that makes Google Drive especially useful for most users.

1. From within the My Files app, scroll to the Cloud Storage section and tap Google Drive.

2. You see all the files and folders you've previously uploaded. Tap a folder to view its contents.

3. Tap a filename to open that file.

Cloud storage

Google Drive ———————————— 1

HOME   SEARCH   MORE

Google Drive

Google Buzz

My First Subfolder ———————— 2

Lael smiling.jpg ———————— 3

Staten Island

Signing In

The first time you access Google Drive, you are prompted to either sign into your Google Account or create a new account. If you do not yet have a Google Account, tap Add Account and follow the onscreen instructions. If you have a Google Account but are not yet signed into Google Drive, tap your Google Account name.

Use the Google Drive App

As practical as it is to access your Google Drive files from within the My Files app, you'll need to use the Google Drive app to perform more advanced operations, such as uploading and downloading files.

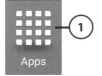
Apps

(1) From your phone's Home screen, tap the Apps icon to display the Apps screen.

Google

(2) Tap to open the Google folder.

(3) Tap the Drive icon to open the Google Drive app.

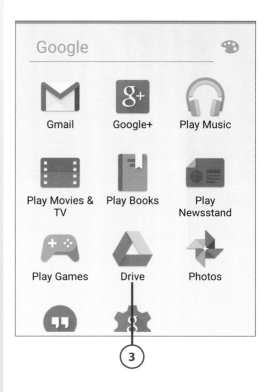

(4) You see all of the files and folders you've previously uploaded to Google Drive. Tap a folder to view the contents of that folder.

(5) Tap a filename to open that file.

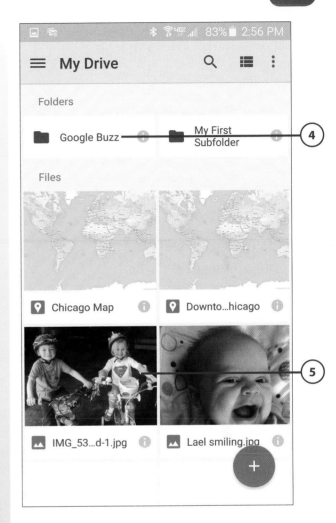

Download a File from Google Drive

You can download to your phone any file stored on Google Drive so that you can use the file even if you don't have a connection to the Internet. You have to download one file at a time.

(1) From within the Google Drive app, tap the Menu button.

(2) Tap Select.

(3) Tap to select the file you want to download. You see a new panel at the bottom of the screen.

(4) Tap the Menu button on this new panel.

(5) Tap Download Copy. The file is downloaded to your phone into the Download folder.

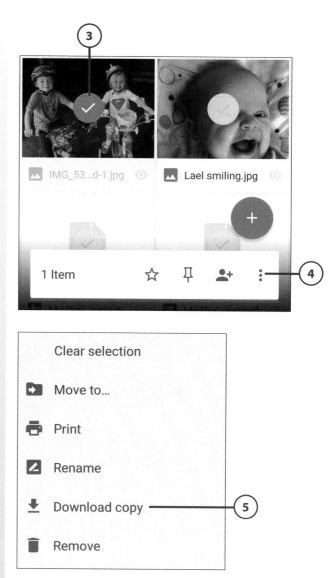

Upload a File to Google Drive

If you have a photo or other file on your phone that you want to access from your computer, or share with other users, you can upload that file from your phone to Google Drive.

(1) From within the Google Drive app, tap the red + button to display the New panel.

(2) Tap Upload.

(3) Tap the Options button at the top-left corner to display the Open From panel.

(4) Tap to select where the file is located—Images, Videos, Audio, or Downloads.

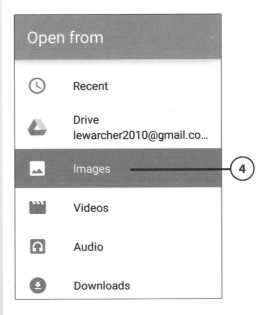

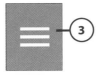

(5) Tap to select the file(s) you want to upload. The file is now uploaded to Google Drive.

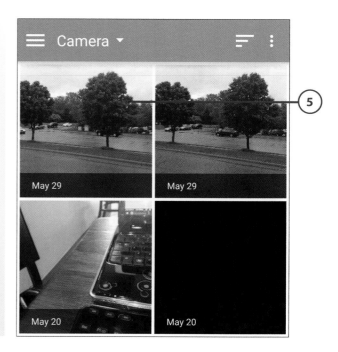

>>>*Go Further*

MICROSOFT ONEDRIVE

Another popular cloud storage service is Microsoft's OneDrive. In fact, some carriers include the OneDrive app (and 100MB of free storage) on their versions of the Galaxy S6 and S6 Edge.

In terms of what it offers, OneDrive is very similar to Google Drive. You get massive amounts of storage online for your photos, videos, music, and documents. You can use OneDrive to store your original files or to make backup copies of files you store on your phone. You can access files stored on OneDrive from any device (smartphone, tablet, or computer) after you've signed into your Microsoft account.

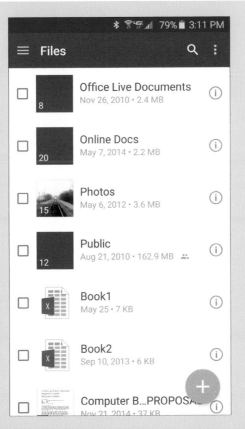

If you don't have the OneDrive app on your phone, you can download it (for free) from the Google Play Store. Open the app, sign into your Microsoft account (or create a new one if you don't have one yet), and then follow the onscreen instructions to get going.

Here's one specific use of OneDrive—to automatically back up all the photos on your phone. Open the OneDrive app, tap Settings, and then tap Camera Backup. Toggle On the backup option, configure the other settings as you wish, and all your photos will be backed up to OneDrive.

Transferring Files Between Devices

Sometimes you have some photos or music or whatever on your computer that you'd like to have on your phone. Other times you might have taken some pictures or videos on your phone that you'd like to transfer to your computer. How do you get those files from one device to another?

Connect Your Phone to Your Computer

The solution to the file transfer conundrum is to use the data cable that came with your phone and connect it to your PC.

1. Connect the microUSB connector on one end of the data cable to the USB/charger jack on the bottom of the phone.

2. Connect the USB connector on the other end of the cable to an open USB port on your computer.

3. Swipe down from the top of your phone's screen to display the Notification panel.

4. Tap the Connected As notification to display the USB Computer Connection screen.

5. If not yet selected, tap to select Media Device (MTP). Your two devices are now connected.

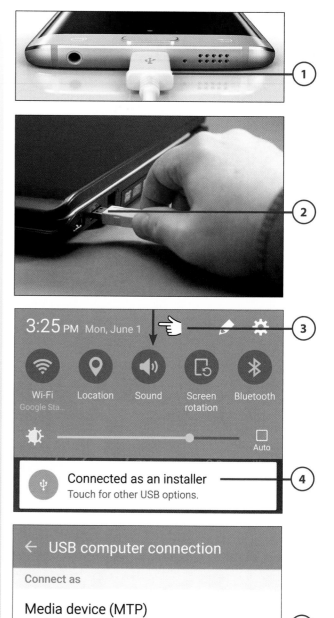

Copy Files from One Device to Another

After your phone is connected to your computer, you can use Windows Explorer or the Mac Finder to access and manage the files on your phone.

1. On your computer, open Windows Explorer or the Mac Finder.

2. In the navigation pane, click to open the Computer or This PC section.

3. Click to select your phone, typically listed as "SAMSUNG-SM-xxxx" or something similar.

4. In the content pane, double-click Phone. This displays all the folders on your phone.

5. Double-click to open the desired folder. Photos are typically stored in the DCIM and Pictures folders; music is typically stored in the Music folder; and videos are typically stored in the Movies folder.

6. Copy a file from your phone by navigating to and right-clicking the file, and then selecting Copy. Then navigate to the desired location on your computer, right-click, and select Paste.

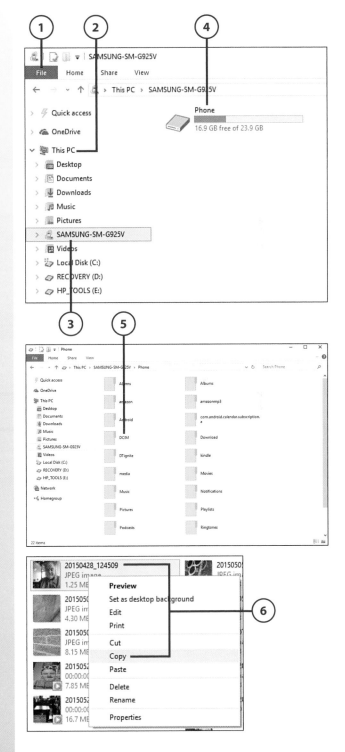

7 Copy a file from your computer to your phone by navigating to and right-clicking the file on your computer, and then selecting Copy. Then navigate to the desired location on your phone, right-click, and select Paste.

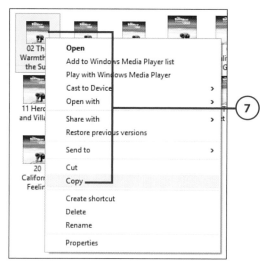

Backing Up Your Data

It's important to create backup copies of the data stored on your phone, in case your data is damaged or your phone is lost. In that contingency, you can restore the backed up data and be up and running again in no time.

Configure Data Backup

Your Samsung smartphone can be configured to automatically back up important data and settings to your Google Drive. All you have to do is enable this functionality.

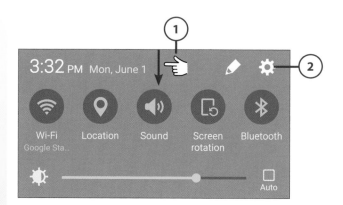

1 Swipe down from the top of your phone's screen to display the Notification panel.

2 Tap Settings to display the Settings screen.

3 Scroll to the Personal section and tap Backup and Reset.

4 Tap On the Back Up My Data switch.

5 Tap Backup Account to display the Set Backup Account panel.

6 Tap the Google Account you want to use, or click + Add Account to add a new account. Your data and settings are automatically backed up to Google's servers using your Google Drive account.

← **Backup and reset**

Google account

Backup account
lewarcher2010@gmail.com — **5**

Back up my data
Back up application data, Wi-Fi passwords, and other settings to Google servers.   `ON` — **4**

Automatic restore
When reinstalling an application, backed up settings and data will be restored.   `ON`

Set backup account

 lewarcher2010@gmail .com — **6**

+ Add account

Making Your Phone More Secure

How safe is your new phone—and everything stored on it? If someone were to steal your phone, how easy would it be for that person to access your important data?

If security worries you, don't fret—you can make your phone and your data more secure. It's a matter of making it more difficult for strangers to unlock your phone and access what's there.

Creating a Safer Lock Screen

The easiest and most effective way to make your phone more secure is to add some sort of protection to the Lock screen. That is, instead of simply swiping to the right to unlock, require some other action that keeps out unwanted visitors.

Add a PIN

The easiest and most common security option is to require a personal information number, or PIN, to unlock your phone. When you power up your phone or awaken the screen, you see a number pad; tap your PIN, and the phone unlocks. If someone tries to enter a different series of numbers, the phone remains locked and unusable.

1. Swipe down from the top of the screen to display the Notification panel.

2. Tap Settings to display the Settings screen.

3. Scroll to the Personal section and tap Lock Screen and Security.

4. Tap Screen Lock Type in the Lock Screen section.

5. Tap PIN to display the Set PIN screen.

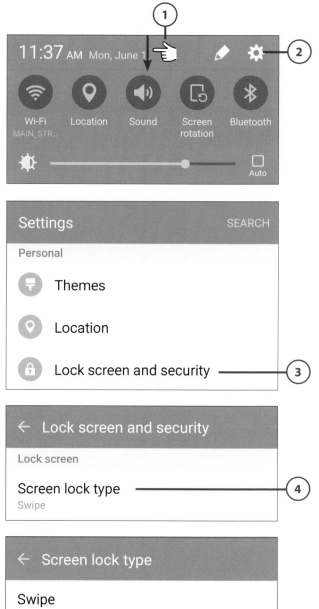

6 Enter the numbers of your PIN. Your PIN must contain at least four numbers; the longer your PIN, the more secure it is.

7 Tap Continue.

8 Re-enter your PIN.

9 Tap OK to display the Notifications on Lock Screen screen.

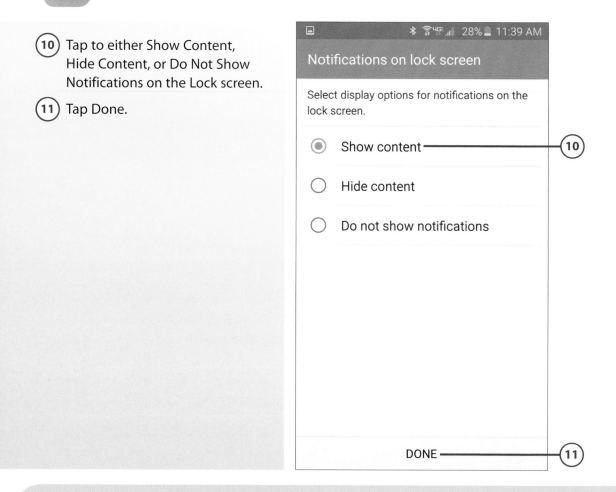

10 Tap to either Show Content, Hide Content, or Do Not Show Notifications on the Lock screen.

11 Tap Done.

>>>Go Further
TOO LONG TO REMEMBER?

There's always a tradeoff between security and usability. The easiest way to unlock your phone is to swipe the Lock screen, but that's also the least secure method. Using a PIN is more secure than a swipe, but now you have to remember four or more numbers. A password is even more secure, but even harder to remember. And if you can't remember your PIN or password, you're locked out of your own phone!

The key is to select a method that offers the best compromise between security and ease of use. Pick a PIN or password that you're likely not to forget. And go ahead and write it down—as long as you keep it separate from your phone, in a secure place. Never, *never* tape your PIN or password to the back of your phone. That defeats the purpose of having one!

Unlock with a Password

Using a PIN to secure your Lock screen provides a good, but not great, level of security. For increased security, use a longer alphanumeric password instead of a relatively short numeric PIN.

(1) Open the Settings screen, scroll to the Personal section, and tap Lock Screen and Security.

(2) Tap Screen Lock Type in the Lock Screen section.

(3) Tap Password to display the Set Password screen.

Re-Enter

If you've previously selected an unlock method (such as a PIN or gesture) and want to change this method, you're asked to enter your PIN or password or gesture or whatever before you can select a new method.

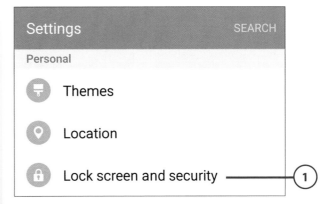

Settings   SEARCH

Personal

🖌 Themes

📍 Location

🔒 Lock screen and security ——— (1)

✱ 📶 28% 🔋 11:37 AM

← Lock screen and security

Lock screen

Screen lock type ——— (2)
Swipe

Swipe
No security

Pattern
Medium security

PIN
Medium to high security

Password ——— (3)
High security

Enter the desired password. Your password must contain at least four characters, including at least one letter. The longer and more complex your password, the more secure it is.

5 Tap Continue.

More Secure

Make your password something only you know, and others can't guess. For this reason, don't use public information (such as your mother's maiden name, children's names, birthdate, and such) as a password. Aim for something complex and obscure enough that it can't be easily guessed.

6 Re-enter your password.

7 Tap OK to display the Notifications on Lock Screen screen.

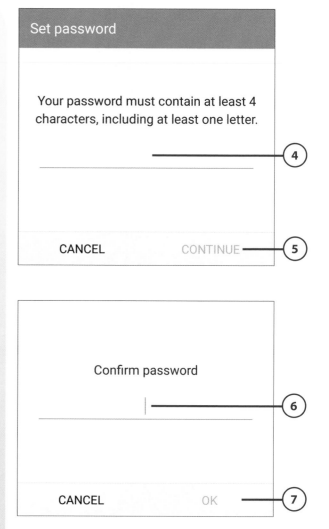

8 Tap to either Show Content,
   Hide Content, or Do Not Show
   Notifications on the Lock screen.

9 Tap Done.

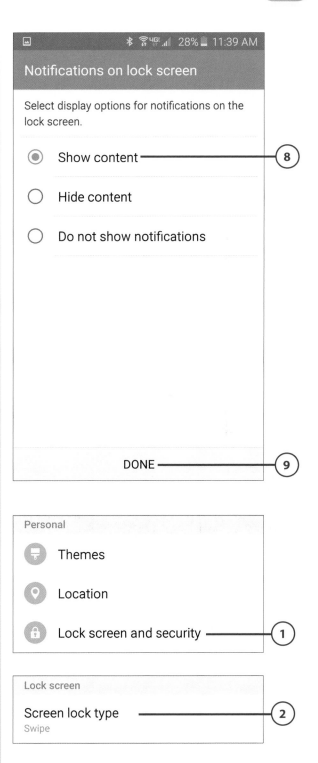

Unlock with a Gesture

You can also opt to unlock your phone
with a gesture across the screen. This
method is easier for you to use on a
day-to-day basis, but unfortunately
it's also less secure than using a PIN or
password.

1 Open the Settings screen, scroll
   to the Personal section, and tap
   Lock Screen and Security.

2 Tap Screen Lock Type in the Lock
   Screen section.

3 Tap Pattern to display the Draw Pattern to Unlock screen.

4 This screen features a grid of nine dots. Use your finger to trace a unique pattern from one dot to another. Make the pattern as simple or as complex as you're comfortable with; a simpler pattern is easier to duplicate, of course, but a more complex one might be more difficult to enter consistently.

5 Tap Continue.

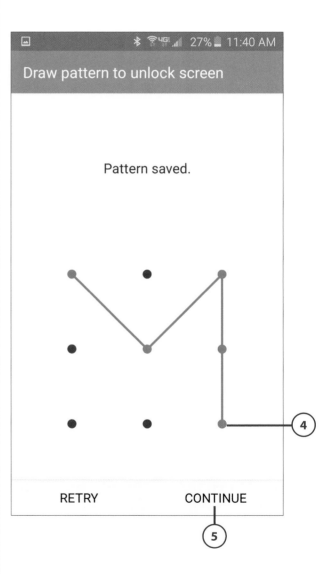

6 Redraw the pattern to confirm it.

7 Tap Confirm.

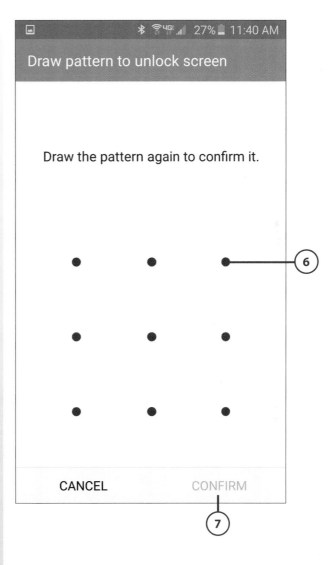

Draw pattern to unlock screen

Draw the pattern again to confirm it.

CANCEL   CONFIRM

8. You are now asked to enter a PIN to use in case you forget or can't draw the pattern. Enter four or more numbers.

9. Tap Continue.

10. Re-enter the PIN.

11. Tap OK to display the Notifications on Lock Screen screen.

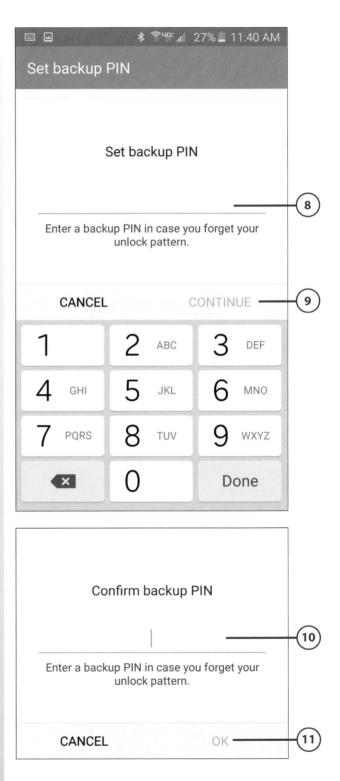

12 Tap to either Show Content, Hide Content, or Do Not Show Notifications on the Lock screen.

13 Tap Done.

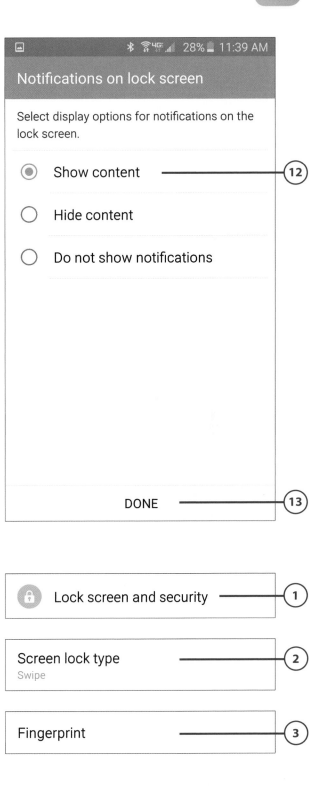

Use Fingerprint Recognition

Your Samsung S6 or S6 Edge offers a newer, high-tech way to secure and unlock your phone—fingerprint recognition. And because no two fingerprints are alike, this approach might be the best security method of all.

After you've configured your phone for fingerprint recognition, you unlock it by placing your thumb or finger (whichever you registered) on your phone's Home key. Your phone "reads" your fingerprint, matches it to the one stored, and—assuming it matches—unlocks your phone. It's extremely easy and extremely effective.

1 Open the Settings screen, scroll to the Personal section, and tap Lock Screen and Security.

2 Tap Screen Lock Type in the Lock Screen section.

3 Tap Fingerprint.

4 Place your thumb or index finger on your phone's Home key and then lift it off.

5 Your progress is noted onscreen. Repeat step 4 while moving your finger slightly until the entire fingerprint is registered. This process takes several attempts.

(6) After your fingerprint is registered, enter a backup password.
This must contain at least six
characters, including at least one
letter and one number.

(7) Tap Continue.

(8) Re-enter your backup password.

(9) Tap OK to display the
Notifications on Lock Screen
screen.

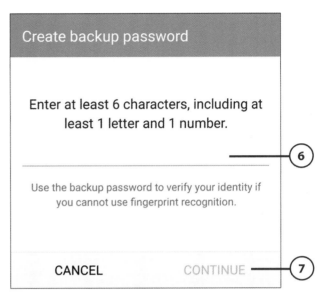

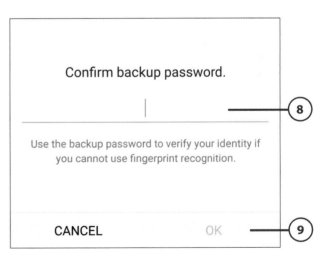

10 Tap to either Show Content, Hide Content, or Do Not Show Notifications on the Lock screen.

11 Tap Done.

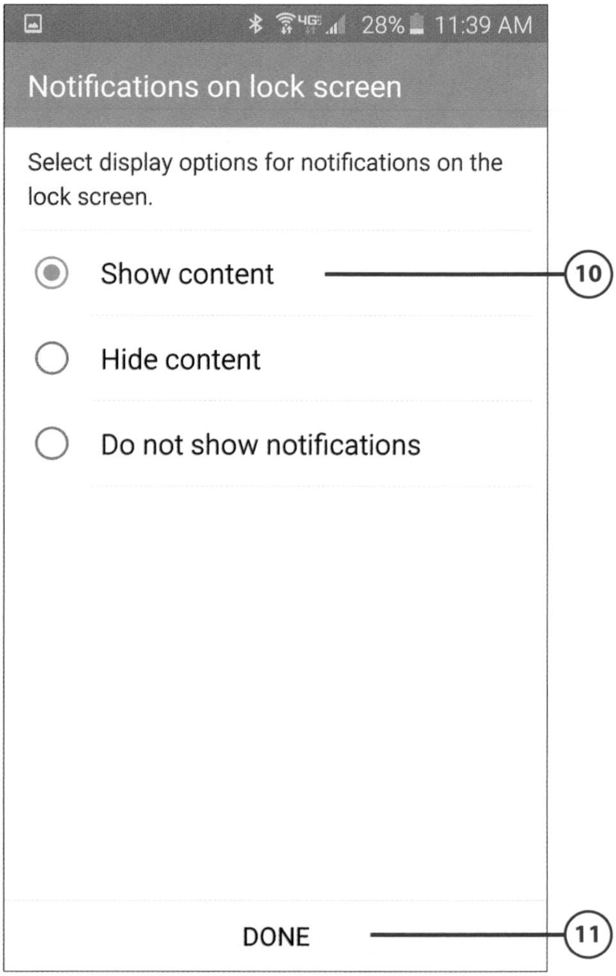

🖼	❄ 📶 28% 🔋 11:39 AM

Notifications on lock screen

Select display options for notifications on the lock screen.

◉ Show content ————————— **10**

◯ Hide content

◯ Do not show notifications

DONE ————————— **11**

Locating a Lost or Stolen Phone

What do you do if you lose your phone, or have it stolen? All is not lost; Samsung's Find My Mobile service lets you lock a lost or stolen phone so that no one else can access your data. You can even track a lost or stolen phone (using your phone's location services) and delete your data remotely.

Enable Find My Mobile

To use the Find My Mobile service, you must have a Samsung account. (If you don't yet have one, you can sign up during the activation process—it's free.) You also must have Location services enabled on your phone for it to be tracked.

(1) Open the Settings screen, scroll to the Personal section, and tap Lock Screen and Security.

(2) Tap Find My Mobile.

(3) If you have a Samsung account, enter your password then tap Confirm. If you don't yet have a Samsung account, tap Add Account and follow the onscreen instructions.

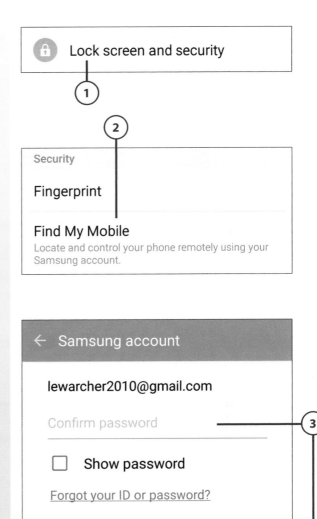

(4) Toggle On Remote Controls.

(5) Toggle On Google Location Service.

(6) Toggle On Reactivation Lock.

(7) Tap SIM Change Alert.

(8) On the next screen, toggle On the switch at the top of the screen.

(9) Enter a message that recipients will receive if someone tries to change or reactivate a stolen SIM card.

(10) Enter the phone number of the person you want to receive this alert. (You can tap Contacts to choose someone from your contacts list.)

(11) Tap Save.

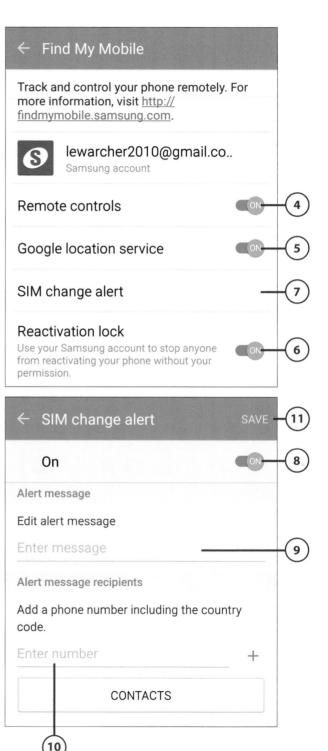

← Find My Mobile

Track and control your phone remotely. For more information, visit http://findmymobile.samsung.com.

S lewarcher2010@gmail.co..
Samsung account

Remote controls   ON —(4)

Google location service   ON —(5)

SIM change alert   —(7)

Reactivation lock
Use your Samsung account to stop anyone   ON —(6)
from reactivating your phone without your
permission.

← SIM change alert   SAVE —(11)

On   ON —(8)

Alert message

Edit alert message

Enter message   —(9)

Alert message recipients

Add a phone number including the country code.

Enter number   +

CONTACTS

(10)

Access Your Phone Remotely

If your phone is lost or stolen, and you have Find My Mobile activated, you can go online from any computer or Internet-connected device to find it.

(1) From any web browser, go to http://findmymobile.samsung.com.

(2) Enter your email address and password for your Samsung account.

(3) Click Sign In to access your account.

(4) Find your device by selecting Locate My Device in the left column and then clicking the Locate My Device button. You see a map with your device pinpointed.

(5) Make your phone ring (so you can find it if it's lost nearby) by clicking Ring My Device in the left column and then clicking Ring.

(6) Put your lost/stolen phone into Ultra Power Saving Mode, to better conserve power until you find it, by clicking Ultra Power Saving Mode in the left column and then clicking I Agree.

Emergency Mode

The Emergency Mode setting on the Find My Mobile website is not for your phone, but for any phone for which you've been listed as an emergency contact. When you click Emergency Mode, you can then put that person's phone into Emergency Mode. Learn more about Emergency Mode in Chapter 1, "Getting Started with Your Samsung Galaxy S6."

(7) Lock your lost or stolen phone by clicking Lock My Screen in the left column. Enter a message to display on the screen if someone finds it. Enter a phone number that anyone who finds the phone can call. Enter a new PIN that can unlock the phone. Then click the Lock button.

(8) Keep anyone who finds the phone from reactivating it by clicking Reactivation Lock in the left column. Enter your Samsung account password and then click the Lock button.

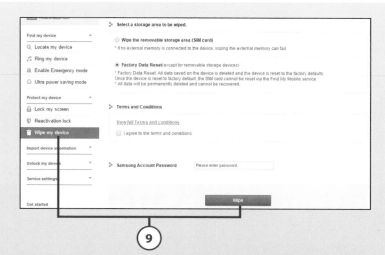

9 Delete the data stored on your phone, as a preemptive measure, by clicking Wipe My Device in the left column. Select Factory Data Reset, agree to the terms and conditions, enter your Samsung account password, and then click Wipe.

It's Not All Good

Wiping as the Last Resort

Wiping your device of all data should only be done as a last resort when all other options have been exhausted, and you fear that a thief might try to access your data without your permission. This option deletes all the data on your phone, so it won't be available to you should you later recover the phone.

>>>Go Further

OTHER WAYS TO MAKE YOUR PHONE MORE SECURE

If you have sensitive data on your phone, you might want to make it even more secure from unauthorized access. You can employ a number of higher-security restrictions. For bonus security information, see the online task "Phone Security" on the book's website: www.informit.com/title/9870789755445.

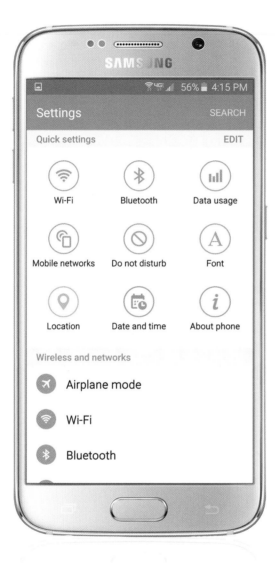

In this chapter, you learn about your phone's various configuration settings. Topics include the following:

→ Configuring Quick Settings
→ Examining Available Settings

Configuring Your Phone's Settings

You can configure a lot of things on your new Galaxy S6 or S6 Edge. There are settings that affect your phone's connections, display, applications, security, accessibility, and more. In this chapter, you walk through all the available settings and find out how to configure them for your own needs.

Configuring Quick Settings

Before we get to the main Settings screen, we need to talk about Samsung's Quick Settings. This phrase actually refers to two separate things.

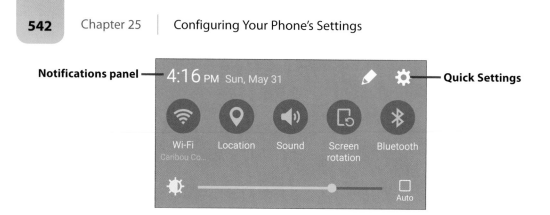

Notifications panel

Quick Settings

The first Quick Settings are those icons you see when you swipe down from the top of the screen to display the Notifications panel. Five settings icons are first visible; swipe to the left on the Notifications panel to view another five.

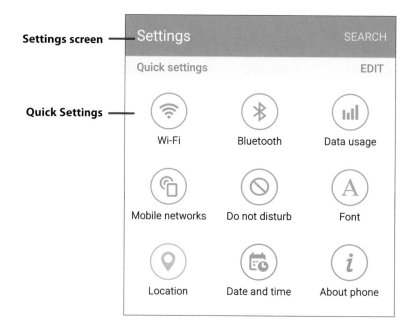

Settings screen

Quick Settings

The second Quick Settings are those you see at the top of the Settings page. This lets you get to your most-used settings without having to scroll down the page to find them.

Both Quick Settings areas can be fully customized. Pick those settings you use most frequently and put them where you can get to them quickly.

Customize Notification Area Quick Settings

By default, Samsung (or your mobile carrier) selects which Quick Settings you see in the Notifications panel. You can change these selections, however, to best suit how you use your phone.

(1) Swipe down from the top of any screen to display the Notifications panel.

(2) Tap the Edit (pencil) icon to display the available Quick Settings.

(3) The top two rows are those icons displayed in the Quick Settings area. (In the first row are those icons you immediately see; in the second row are the icons you see after you swipe to the left on the Notifications panel.) Tap and drag any icon to a new position in the top two rows.

(4) Tap Done to create the new Quick Settings area.

Flashlight

One of my favorite Quick Settings isn't actually a setting. The Flashlight icon turns your phone into a powerful flashlight, using the LED light on the back of the unit. I like to have the flashlight available at the tap of an icon, right in the Quick Settings area.

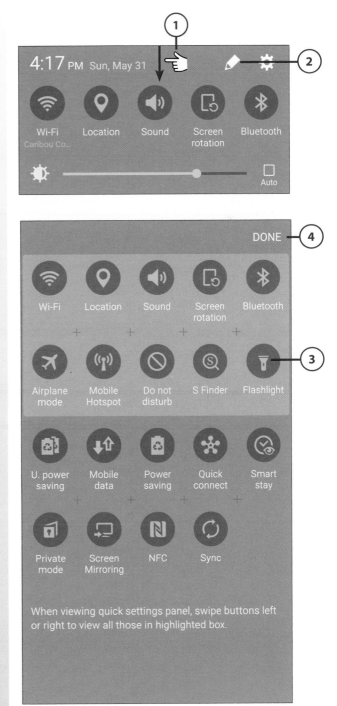

Customize Settings Screen Quick Settings

You have to select which items display in the Quick Settings area of the Settings screen. You can select up to nine settings to display.

1. Swipe down from the top of any screen to display the Notifications panel.

2. Tap Settings to display the Settings screen.

3. Tap + Tap Here to Edit Quick Settings. The Edit Quick Settings screen opens.

4. Tap to select those settings you want to display on the Quick Settings screen.

5. Tap the back arrow to return to the Settings screen.

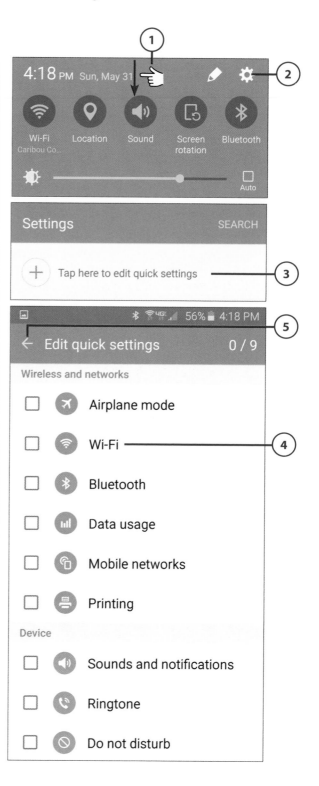

Examining Available Settings

All of your phone's myriad settings are accessed from the Settings screen. This screen is divided into four main areas (plus the Quick Settings area at the top): Wireless and Networks, Device, Personal, and System.

Search

If you can't easily find a specific setting, tap Search at the top of the Settings screen and enter what it is you're looking for.

Access the Settings Screen

The easiest way to access the Settings screen is from the Notification panel. You can also open this screen by tapping the Settings icon on the Apps screen.

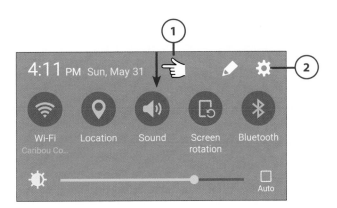

(**1**) Swipe down from the top of any screen to display the Notification panel.

(**2**) Tap the Settings icon to display the Settings screen.

Wireless and Networks Settings

This section and those that follow cover the settings in each category, starting with the Wireless and Networks settings.

- **Airplane Mode:** Switches phone into self-contained mode without Wi-Fi or phone connection, for use on airplanes

- **Wi-Fi:** Switches Wi-Fi on or off, and lets you select a Wi-Fi network

- **Bluetooth:** Switches Bluetooth wireless on and off, and enables pairing with other Bluetooth devices

- **Data Usage:** Displays your phone's data usage and enables you to set data usage alerts

- **Mobile Networks:** Enables you to activate global data roaming access and manage various mobile network settings

- **Advanced Calling:** Available with select carriers, enables upgrade to HD voice and video calling

- **More:** Configure mobile hotspot, data tethering, printing, MirrorLink, and other similar settings

Device Settings

Samsung's Device settings have to do with how your phone looks and works.

- **Sounds and Notifications:** Configure your phone's ringtones and sounds, vibrations, and notifications.

- **Display and Wallpaper:** Change your phone's wallpaper, font, screen time-out, brightness, and similar settings.

- **Edge Screen:** (S6 Edge only) Configure various Edge screen features, including Edge Lighting, People Edge, and Information Stream.

- **Motions and Gestures:** Enable gestures for various phone operations, including direct call, smart alert, and mute.

- **Storage:** Display used storage for various types of data, as well as storage space remaining.

- **Battery:** Display battery usage, as well as enable Power Saving Mode and Ultra Power Saving Mode.

- **Applications:** Access settings for applications installed on your phone. Also access Application Manager and configure your phone's default applications.

- **NFC and Payment:** Enable NFC and Tap and Pay capabilities.

Personal Settings

The settings in the Personal section let you personalize your phone, manage privacy and security, and back up your important data.

- **Themes:** Install new visual themes on your phone.
- **Location:** Enable location services and view location requests from apps.
- **Lock Screen and Security:** Configure screen locking and the Lock screen, enable Find My Mobile, and configure other security settings.
- **Privacy and Safety:** Enable Private Mode and Emergency Mode, as well as send SOS messages.
- **Easy Mode:** Enable Easy mode and select Easy application.
- **Accounts:** Manage and add new accounts to your phone.
- **Language and Input:** Configure default language and keyboard, as well as speech and mouse/trackpad options.
- **Backup and Reset:** Back up and restore your phone's data, as well as reset your phone to factory settings.

System Settings

Finally, your phone's System settings let you configure key details about the underlying system.

- **Date and Time:** Set date, time, time zone, and time/date formats.
- **Accessibility:** Enable and configure various accessibility settings, including vision, hearing, and dexterity and interaction settings.
- **Help:** Access information about how to use your Samsung smartphone.
- **About Phone:** Display key information about your phone—name, model number, Android version, and so forth.
- **System Updates:** Check for and install the latest updates to your phone's operating system.

In this chapter, you discover how to keep your phone running in tip-top condition, and troubleshoot problems if they occur. Topics include the following:

→ Keeping Your Phone Up and Running
→ Troubleshooting Minor Issues
→ Rebooting and Resetting Your Phone

Fixing Common Problems

Your Samsung Galaxy S6 or S6 Edge is a marvelous piece of technology—when it's working right. If you find your phone having trouble connecting to the Internet, or running slower than normal, or running out of battery charge, or even freezing up on you, then you probably think a lot less of that technological marvel in your hand.

What do you do if your phone is operating less than optimally? Read on to learn how to get the most out of your phone—and fix any issues that come up.

Keeping Your Phone Up and Running

Before we get into the problem-and-troubleshooting thing, let's look at what you can do to avoid problems, and keep your phone running in tip-top condition.

Maximizing Battery Life

The one complaint that just about every smartphone user has is that the battery doesn't last long enough. That's a valid complaint; depending on how you use your phone, you might find the battery drifting toward 0% charge by the end of any given day. Fortunately, there are things you can do to maximize how much time you get on a charge.

- **Recharge your battery every night.** Don't let your battery get drained. Plug it in when you go to sleep at night so it'll be full and fresh when you turn it on the next morning.

- **Fast charge your phone when the battery is low.** You can top off your battery quite quickly, thanks to the Galaxy S6's fast charging feature. Plug in for just 10 minutes and you add up to 4 hours of battery life. (You have to use the quick charger that came with your phone, however; other charging units might not charge as rapidly.)

- **Examine battery usage.** Want to know how much power your phone is using—and which apps are draining your battery the fastest? Then open the Settings screen and tap Battery and you can view detailed power usage statistics.

- **Decrease screen brightness.** One thing that drains your battery the most is your phone's screen. A brighter screen drains your battery more than a dimmer one, so adjust the screen brightness accordingly.

- **Turn off location services.** Your phone's GPS and location services can also be a big battery drain. That's because, when enabled, some apps (such as weather apps, I've found) constantly ping for the current location. All this location pinging drains your phone's battery, so disable location services to extend battery life.

- **Turn off Wi-Fi.** Wi-Fi is pretty much a necessity, but if you don't need it (when you're on a long automobile trip, for example), turn it off and you'll save a surprising amount of battery life.

- **Turn off Bluetooth.** Like Wi-Fi, Bluetooth uses a lot of power. If you're not connected to a Bluetooth device, turn off Bluetooth on your phone.

- **Turn off NFC.** Near field communications (NFC) is a great way to pay, but when you're not shopping, it still draws power. Unless you're shopping and ready to pay, turn off NFC to conserve battery life.

- **Close apps when you're done with them.** This is a big one. The apps on your phone theoretically are paused when you're not using them, but even a paused app can still draw some amount of power. That's especially true when the app keeps checking for updated information or your current location. When you're done using an app, tap the Recents key and close it out.

- **Avoid apps that use too much power.** Some apps just use more power than others. I've found that mapping apps, like Google Maps, are particular offenders, but other apps can also drain your battery faster than you'd think. Access the Battery screen (from the Settings screen) to see which apps use the most power, and then use them less frequently.

- **Disable or uninstall apps you don't use.** Some preinstalled apps use power even when you don't run them. Disable these apps or, if you can, uninstall them. Less stuff on your phone makes your battery last longer.

- **Use Power Saving Mode when you're running low on juice.** When your battery dips toward the 25% range, it's time to take action. If you can plug in and recharge, great. If not, enter Power Saving Mode to turn off the color in the display and reduce other nonessential usage. It just might get you through to when you can recharge.

By the way, your battery will become less efficient over time. If you started out getting 20 hours on a charge, a year later you may be down to 15 hours (or less!). That's normal; batteries lose charge the more you use them. When available battery life becomes unusably low, it's time to take your phone in and have its battery replaced.

Using a Performance-Enhancing App

Several companies offer apps specifically designed to free up unused memory and storage space on your phone, and thus increase your phone's performance. Run one of these apps to clear out any "junk" that take up space in your phone's memory and potentially slow down operation.

The following table details some of the most popular (and reputable) performance-enhancing apps.

Performance-Enhancing Apps

App	Cost
CCleaner	Free
Clean Master	Free
DU Speed Booster	Free
The Cleaner—Boost and Clean	Free

Clean Master

I use Clean Master on my Samsung phone. It does a very good job of getting rid of the junk, both speeding up my phone and reducing the phone's operating temperature.

Freeing Up Space by Deleting Unused Apps

As noted previously, disabling or uninstalling apps frees up some amount of memory and reduces power usage. Deleting unused apps also frees up storage space on your phone. When you need more space to install new apps or store more photos or music, you can find that space by deleting apps you don't use anymore. It's that simple.

Troubleshooting Minor Issues

Even if you take all the preventive steps recommended earlier in this chapter, it's still possible for your phone to act up every now and then. Fortunately, most issues you're likely to encounter are minor ones with relatively easy fixes.

You're Locked Out

Here's a common one. You go to enter the PIN or password to unlock your phone, and you get it wrong. And again. And again. And before you know it, your phone won't let you unlock it at all.

Your phone locks itself solid when you enter the wrong PIN or password more than three times in a row. At this point, you're likely to see an onscreen message that tells you the PIN is locked and you need to enter a PUK (phone unlock key). What do you do now?

A PUK is an 8-digit number linked to your phone's SIM card. (You may also need a PUK if you've enabled SIM card locking and forgotten that PIN.) Entering the PUK unlocks your phone and lets you set a new PIN.

Where do you find your phone's PUK? You need to contact your mobile carrier or log onto your account page on your carrier's website. After you obtain the PUK, enter it from your phone's Lock screen then, when prompted, create a new PIN. You should be good to go from there.

An Individual App Freezes

What do you do when you're using an app and it freezes? Close it! Tap the Recents button to display the stack of recent apps and then swipe away the frozen one. You should be able to restart the app from the Home or Apps screen and (hopefully) have it run properly.

Your Phone Freezes

What about if your entire phone freezes? Well, if your screen is frozen, you need to reboot it. Rebooting is covered later in this chapter in the "Rebooting and Resetting Your Phone," so turn there for details.

Your Phone Won't Turn On

If your phone won't turn on at all, the first thing to suspect is a discharged battery. Connect your phone to a power supply and try turning it on again. (You might need to wait a few minutes for the phone to receive a minimal charge.)

Remember, the proper way to turn on your phone is to press and hold the Power key on the right side of the unit. Just tapping the Home key on the front won't turn on a phone that's been powered off.

If your phone works when connected to a power outlet but not when it's running on battery, then you have a dead battery. You need to replace it.

Your Phone Is Running Slow

If your phone is running slow, you probably have too many apps open. Tap the Recents key and close some of the apps you're not currently using.

If your phone continues to run slow, reboot it. This frees up any trapped memory and starts things off fresh.

Finally, if slow running is a constant problem, consider installing and using one of the performance-enhancing apps discussed previously in this chapter. They help you identify where your problems lie and help you clean up some of the junk you don't need.

Your Mobile Signal Is Weak

Your smartphone is still a phone, and mobile phones sometimes run into reception problems. When you have trouble connecting or staying connected to phone calls, the problem is probably your mobile carrier, not your phone.

Check the number of bars you have on the Home screen's status bar. If you only have one or two bars (or even none!) then you're not getting a strong enough signal. Try moving to another part of the room or to another room in your house. If that doesn't help, try moving to a totally different location. (For what it's worth, I've found I can improve my reception by moving from one end of my living room couch to the other!)

Cell signals are notoriously fickle, and some carriers have better coverage than others. If you continually have issues with weak signals in your home, consider changing carriers. You might find that Verizon has better coverage than AT&T in your area, or vice versa.

You Have Trouble Connecting to Wi-Fi

These days you'll spend a lot of time with your phone connected to a home or public Wi-Fi network. What do you do if your Wi-Fi signal cuts out unexpectedly—or if you can't connect at all?

First, make sure you're connected to the right network. In many locations you'll have multiple Wi-Fi networks or hotspots available. This may even be the case in your home, where you might see your own Wi-Fi network and those of your next-door neighbors. Make sure you're not connected to the wrong or weaker network.

If you have a consistently weak connection at home, try moving your Wi-Fi router. A router buried in one corner of your house will have trouble sending a signal to devices at the opposite end (or different floor) of the building. Put the router in a more central location—or, conversely, move your phone closer to the router.

If you have an unstable Wi-Fi connection, one that constantly drops due to poor signal strength, turn on your phone's Smart Network Switch. This will automatically switch you from a weak Wi-Fi signal to a stronger mobile data connection and let you stay connected to the Internet. Open the Notifications panel, tap Wi-Fi, tap More, and then tap Smart Network Switch. When prompted tap On the switch.

Finally, if you're having connection problems with a particular Wi-Fi network, try rebooting your phone. Rebooting sometimes fixes connection problems like this, for whatever reason.

Rebooting and Resetting Your Phone

Some problems are so severe that they require you to reboot your phone—that is, turn it off and turn it back on. Other problems are even more serious, and might require you to reset your phone to its original factory condition. If you need to reboot or reset, here's how to do it.

Reboot Your Phone

In the grand scheme of things, rebooting your phone isn't a big deal. It sounds more serious than it is; all it really means is that you power down your phone and then power it back up. It's quite easy.

(1) Press and hold the Power key on the right side of your phone to display the options panel.

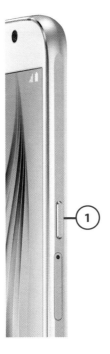

(2) Tap Restart.

(3) Tap Restart again. The phone powers down and then immediately powers back up, displaying the Lock screen.

⏻ Power off

✈ Airplane mode
Turned off

⟳ Restart ———————— (2)

🚫 Emergency mode
Turned off

CANCEL

Restart

The device will restart.

CANCEL   RESTART ——— (3)

Reboot a Frozen Phone

If your phone is frozen or otherwise unresponsive, you can't reboot normally. In this instance, you have to perform what is called a *hard boot*. To do this, press and hold the Power key and the Volume down key simultaneously, for more than 7 seconds. The phone should now power off and then power back on.

Reset Your Phone's Settings

Sometimes it's the settings you've set that are causing your problems. You may be able to fix things by resetting all your settings to their default conditions.

Resetting your settings does *not* delete any data stored on your phones. It merely returns your phone to its factory default settings.

1. Swipe down from the top of any screen to display the Notifications panel.

2. Tap Settings to display the Settings screen.

3. Scroll to the Personal section and tap Backup and Reset.

4. Tap Reset Settings.

5. Tap the Reset Settings button.

6. Tap OK in the Warning box. Your phone's settings are now reset to factory defaults, and all your data and other files remain intact.

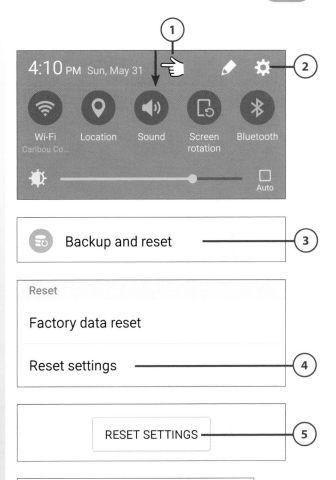

4:10 PM Sun, May 31

Wi-Fi   Location   Sound   Screen   Bluetooth
Caribou Co...   rotation

Auto

Backup and reset ———— 3

Reset

Factory data reset

Reset settings ———— 4

RESET SETTINGS ———— 5

Warning

Selecting OK will cause changes to some of the customizations you have made such as the ringtone you have selected, the brightness of the screen, and the behavior of the keyboard. Reset system settings? You can't reverse this action.

CANCEL   OK—— 6

Reset Your Phone to Factory Condition

When your phone experiences recurring severe problems, there's a more extreme solution you can employ. The Factory Data Reset option not only resets all your phone's settings, it also deletes all your data—pictures, music, you name it. By deleting everything, your phone is returned to factory fresh condition.

That said, this is an extreme measure, to be taken only under extreme conditions. And, before you do it, you want to back up all your data and settings. We talked about backing up your data in Chapter 23, "Copying Files To and From Your Phone—And Backing Up Your Important Data," so turn there for instructions.

After your data is backed up, you can reset your phone.

It's Not All Good

Everything Is Deleted!

Performing a Factory Data Reset permanently erases *all* data from your phone. This includes your phone's settings, of course, but also your Google and Samsung account settings, email accounts and messages, photos, videos, music, and other documents and files. You should reset your phone only if all other measures are unsuccessful, and after you've backed up your data and settings.

(1) Swipe down from the top of any screen to display the Notifications panel.

(2) Tap Settings to display the Settings screen.

(3) Scroll to the Personal section and tap Backup and Reset.

4 Tap Factory Data Reset.

5 Read the requisite warnings and then scroll down to the bottom of the screen and tap the Reset Phone button.

6 When prompted for your password or fingerprint, provide it and follow the remaining instructions to reset the phone.

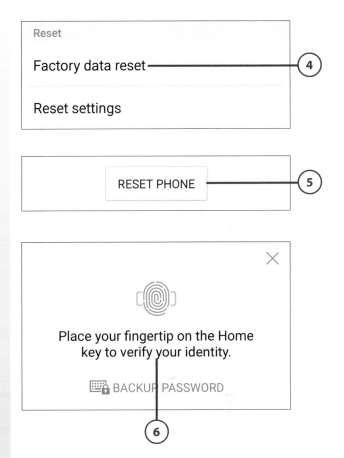

Reset

Factory data reset ⸺ **4**

Reset settings

RESET PHONE ⸺ **5**

Place your fingertip on the Home key to verify your identity.

BACKUP PASSWORD

6

Index

More Best-Selling **My** Books!

Learning to use your smartphone, tablet, camera, game, or software has never been easier with the full-color My Series. You'll find simple, step-by-step instructions from our team of experienced authors. The organized, task-based format allows you to quickly and easily find exactly what you want to achieve.

Visit quepublishing.com/mybooks to learn more.

REGISTER THIS PRODUCT
SAVE 35%*
ON YOUR NEXT PURCHASE!

How to Register Your Product

- Go to quepublishing.com/register
- Sign in or create an account
- Enter the 10- or 13-digit ISBN that appears on the back cover of your product

Benefits of Registering

- Ability to download product updates
- Access to bonus chapters and workshop files
- A 35% coupon to be used on your next purchase – valid for 30 days
  - To obtain your coupon, click on "Manage Codes" in the right column of your Account page
- Receive special offers on new editions and related Que products

Please note that the benefits for registering may vary by product. Benefits will be listed on your Account page under Registered Products.

We value and respect your privacy. Your email address will not be sold to any third party company.

* 35% discount code presented after product registration is valid on most print books, eBooks, and full-course videos sold on QuePublishing.com. Discount may not be combined with any other offer and is not redeemable for cash. Discount code expires after 30 days from the time of product registration. Offer subject to change.

quepublishing.com